Themes in modern
European history
1830–90

THEMES IN MODERN EUROPEAN HISTORY

General editor: Michael Biddiss, University of Reading

Already published

Themes in Modern European History 1780–1830
edited by Pamela M. Pilbeam

Themes in Modern European History 1890–1945
edited by Paul Hayes

Themes in modern European history 1830–90

edited by

BRUCE WALLER

 Routledge
Taylor & Francis Group

LONDON AND NEW YORK

First published 1990 by Unwin Hyman Ltd

Reprinted 1992, 1995, 2002 by
Routledge
2 Park Square, Milton Park, Abingdon, Oxon, OX14 4RN
270 Madison Avenue, New York, NY 10016

Transferred to Digital Printing 2003

Routledge is an imprint of the Taylor & Francis Group

Digitally printed in Great Britain by
Butler and Tanner, Frome, Somerset

British Library Cataloguing in Publication Data

Themes in modern European history 1830–1890.
1. Europe, 1815–1918
I. Waller, Bruce
940.28

Library of Congress Cataloging in Publication Data

Themes in modern European history, 1830–1890/edited by Bruce
Waller.
p. cm.
Includes bibliographical references.
1. Europe—History—19th century. I. Waller, Bruce.
D359.T47 1990   90–30433
940.2′8—dc20

ISBN 0–415–09075–X

Contents

Introduction

What was the nineteenth century? A simple question perhaps. Was it just a hundred-year cycle, or was it a period with some identifiable unity? If the latter, where do we find a guide? Do we look to politics, economics, art, or somewhere else? Or do we seek a combination of characteristics which make a meaningful configuration? There are indeed several nineteenth centuries. The hundred-year stretch from 1800 onwards makes more sense than many historians think, for it began with Napoleon's *coup d'état* on 18 Brumaire 1799, when drums began to roll all over Europe, and lasted till the advent of *Weltpolitik* at the century's close, as grey German ships slipped into the sea. In each case the military challenge burnt out, but left amongst the ash enduring strife, vast political change and accelerating innovation. Napoleon Bonaparte and William II failed to establish lasting dominion, but the first, by spreading the residue of the French Revolution, helped to unify and strengthen Europe, and the Kaiser's technology helped to forge one world out of several continents. So the statistician's century (1800–1900) is a unit, begun and terminated by epochal events. But there are two other nineteenth centuries. One began in 1789 and ended in 1918, for the onset of revolution in France introduced an element of hope and a dynamic force connected with it that Europe had never hitherto seen on such a scale. This optimism was sustained in various forms until 1918, when it collapsed in a cataclysm of defeat and sickness, leaving a desert of lasting despair and uncertainty, for even the victors were prostrate. The hope born of desperation placed in Woodrow Wilson soon vanished. This is the 'long century', one with several distinct phases but nevertheless a period with clearly visible contours. There is also a 'short century', the subject of this book. It stretches from 1830 to 1890 – that period which is quintessentially the nineteenth century. It has faint traces of the old regime and few hints of what was to come in our day.

With the death of Goethe in 1832 the classicism of the Enlightenment was interred. Romanticism was in full bloom but it already began to look less to the past and the eternal, and increasingly to the present and its problems. The trend was towards greater realism. By mid-century numerous artists and authors were thoroughly realistic. This was partly the result of optimism, which turned minds to improvement in this, rather than the next, world. It derived also, oddly perhaps, partly from disappointed hope. Many had expected great things from the 1848 Revolution and they were troubled by the apparently meagre permanent advance. As diminished hope was accompanied by strengthening frustration, the realistic cast of mind hardened, leading to what we call 'naturalism', realism without illusion, the concern not only with the here and now, but with life in the raw. The Romantics had looked to the past and to heaven, the realists to the field and street, the naturalists to the alley and cellar. As they gradually stripped life of idealism, the barriers to brutality fell too. Nastiness was not only unveiled, it was frequently endorsed. In 1890 Nietzsche was arguing for a complete reversal of morals and values. In the sciences – physics and electricity, for instance – much was changing. In 1890 many past certainties were challenged; reality appeared more fluid than it had seemed. Psychoanalysis was just emerging; it drew heavily on the scientific and artistic trends of the day and so combined both. It demonstrated the infinite complexity yet basic simplicity of the human mind. It also suggested a new morality.

Optimism, realism and science were the signs of the nineteenth century. Their heyday lasted from 1830 to 1890. That which was most typical of the last century ran its course in sixty years. The same trends can be seen in many aspects of life. In politics the 1830s opened with two ideological groups facing each other: the Holy Alliance in the East and the *entente cordiale* between France and Britain in the West. The force of ideals quickly faded and was replaced by tough realism and, finally, in the 1880s by something which looked very much like naturalism – power politics. In domestic affairs there was generally talk of high-minded issues during the 1830s; fifty years later it was about interest groups. In the economy, post-Napoleonic pessimism wore away gradually, yielding after 1848 to twenty-five years of increasing optimism, which in turn receded with the onset of depression in 1873 while pessimism again made headway, especially in the 1880s. As the Industrial Revolution spread eastwards and southwards through the continent, it brought the promise of material and moral improvement. Railway construction actually enabled the conquest of large-scale starvation. Europe was finally freed from the tyranny of nature. But by the 1880s the growth of cartels seemed to point in the direction of a new subjugation. The labour movement had been moderate and romantic in the 1830s – both the French socialists and the British Owenites; it became apparently vigorous and scientific after mid-century. By the late 1880s it looked as if masses of workers were gathering for a cataclysmic showdown against the strengthening ranks of business.

From 1830 to 1890 great strides were made in technology, medicine, health and education. Before 1830 such development had seemed unlikely. By 1890 the bulk of the European population was better off and more educated. A rising population had not, broadly speaking, led to impoverishment. But another fear was becoming apparent by 1890; it was the worry about the instability of volatile and semi-educated masses who were for the first time in history sufficiently sophisticated not only to influence politics but also to cause trouble on an enormous scale. So although life for most Europeans of all classes in those areas which had undergone extensive modernization was much healthier, comfortable and generally more pleasant in 1890 than in 1830, and although the man in the street still looked to the horizon with hope, the optimistic faith in a future without problems was fading fast amongst intellectuals. It was replaced by the growing conviction that civilization existed on the slopes of a volcano.

Historians are accustomed to reading the nineteenth century – of whatever length – as punctuated only by the apparently unsuccessful revolution of 1848. If we regard the short century as embodying all that was characteristic of the period, we can more easily see that the century has four turning points: 1830, 1848, 1867–70 and 1890, each of approximately equal importance. The century appears to have a certain generation-long rhythm.

After the defeat of Napoleon, the treaties of Paris and Vienna were aimed at a settlement, embodying a compromise between the old regime and the new developments of nationalism and liberal-constitutional rule. That much of the establishment strove with some success for a return to pre-revolutionary Europe we can see illustrated in the history of France. If Charles X and his circle had succeeded, there can be little doubt that others would have followed. But the revolution of 1830 not only stopped this, it also reversed the trend to restoration. The constitutional liberalization in France resulting from the events in July 1830 was significant enough in itself. It was far more important that the wheel of reaction, already in motion, was stopped and reversed. The rest of Europe was suddenly faced with a liberalizing France instead of an increasingly reactionary one, and, however reluctantly, it fell in behind. The revolutionaries in 1848 had unjustifiably high hopes for rapid advance. The easy initial success turned hope to expectation. The eventual seeming-collapse was therefore devastating. Had the liberals considered the disappointment and nervousness of the re-established regimes they might have appreciated the extent of their victory. Governments in the 1850s were sufficiently uneasy to enact a series of modernizing reforms. In central Europe serfdom disappeared and most states came to possess parliaments as well as constitutions. Austria was apparently completely restored, but the insurrectionary turmoil in that state had given the forces of change powerful backing. After the accession of Alexander II in 1855 even Russia began to bestir itself. To the West, traditional monarchy disappeared in France and was replaced by a modern (albeit 'imperial') dictatorship which needed popular backing.

A further revolution occurred between 1867 and 1870. This time the cause was war, but the effect was as profound as if it had stemmed from popular action. The Habsburg Empire became Austria-Hungary, a constitutional land with powerful parliaments and based partly on the principle of nationality. Germany and Italy became united and constitutional states. France turned republican through defeat in war and not as a result of barricade fighting. The lesson of the years from 1867 to 1870 was that the indirect impact of war can be as devastating as battle in the streets. The inevitable divisiveness of the latter can be counterproductive.

The silent revolution of 1890, or thereabouts, is easily overlooked but was equally grave. It was a revolution wrought by artists, scholars, scientists, authors, businessmen and labour leaders. The challenge to earlier morality, values and sense of artistic propriety, the demise of hope amongst Europe's luminaries, the collapse of the previous scientific framework and its substitution with a maze of uncertainty, the rise of cartelized big business and banking and the challenge of unionized labour partly disunited, but also partly united under crusading Marxism, and finally the very rapid expansion of the common man's influence in public affairs – all this brought decisive change. We can see then that the nineteenth-century revolutions were of four different kinds. First of all there was the localized and apparently insignificant Paris uprising of 1830 which reversed the trend of European history. There were the widespread and mainly political revolutions of 1848. Then there were the wars which precipitated the great national, liberal and (in France) democratic revolutions from 1867 to 1870. Finally, revolution in morals, thought and the economy began in about 1890.

Historians have a special interest in the short nineteenth century for two reasons. First, it saw the maturing of historical method. Not surprisingly, this was a slow process. But one man, Leopold von Ranke, perhaps the greatest historian ever, made the crucial contribution. Within a generation the study of history was completely reformed. By arguing that every age was 'immediate to God' he gave the past enhanced standing and made it seem worthy of study. In his first book, published in 1824, he proposed to see history 'as it had actually happened' – *wie es eigentlich gewesen* (the most famous remark on the historian's task). Previously historians had moralized in the Christian tradition, taught lessons, as during the Enlightenment, or simply fantasized, as the Romantics did. Ranke sought to relate factual history based on documentary evidence recorded during the period he studied. He was the first historian to do it systematically and to produce convincing and attractive results. Once he had shown that this could be done, others followed, and so scholarly history was born. This may well be the most enduring contribution inspired by Romanticism's fascination with the past, and yet the critical method led well beyond it. Ranke was a conservative Prussian convert, and as such not quite as dispassionate as he thought. But this matters little compared with the effort at even-handed history he made and the example he provided for subsequent historians. With little exaggeration we may attribute to him a Copernican revolution in history writing.

The second reason that historians study the sixty years following 1830 is the especially favourable availability of sources. The growth of literate state bureaucracies and the rule of law had produced the need and desire to record everything important. By

1830 official records were so complete that historians could discover what the major decisions were, and also to some extent how they had been reached. But records were not so tediously detailed that a diligent researcher became submerged in trivia. By 1890 the official records in most states were becoming elephantine. The quality of handwriting and paper were also in decline. The methods of preserving documents had steadily improved till about this date, but they as well began to deteriorate. Paradoxically, the introduction of the typewriter (invented in 1867) was a mixed blessing. Readability was improved and since several copies of the finished product could readily be made, drafts began to disappear. So it was sometimes more difficult to trace the origins of a given policy. The telegraph, which first appeared in our period, and spread everywhere, was in one respect a boon because it forced concision, but it also induced over-simplification. The proliferation of committee meetings was of dubious merit as well. It furnished added material, but multiplied confusion. The telephone, however, which was being installed in the 1880s, created real problems for the historian because it enabled important tracks to be covered much more easily than before.

Prior to 1830, newspapers, magazines and books were numerous enough to provide information on a wide range of topics and reflect various points of view. By 1890 this information was extraordinarily detailed and the span of different views was becoming unmanageably extensive. Public opinion, if we mean by this the views of those who are interested in and can influence public affairs, was in 1830 confined to a small group of patricians and middle-class people. Sixty years later it extended to very much wider groups everywhere in Europe west of Russia. Whether periodical publications reflected it very carefully is impossible to say. But it was becoming apparent that public opinion, whether confined to a small group or spread among the masses, is neither easy to gauge nor very stable.

Apart from the archives and the press there were also government publications which sought to acquaint the interested public with wider issues. These publications took many forms, such as handbooks, collections of statistics, and reports. The best known were the 'blue books', or coloured books. They are called 'blue books' after the official British publications which were bound in blue paper. Other governments had different colours, for instance,

France – yellow, and Austria – red. As a rule, wherever a strong Parliament existed there were many 'blue books'; otherwise there were few. Britain produced the most by far. The publications were so numerous and detailed that readers felt they were getting the whole story, although they were not. Much of the material was accurate and frank, but no government willingly printed damaging documents. When it came to foreign policy, they had to be especially careful not to upset other governments which had been consulted about matters affecting them. When compromising reports slipped through, British foreign secretaries were taken to task. Foreigners were so concerned, that communications were sometimes only made on condition that no trace would ever find its way into 'blue books'. If one knows the views of any given government and what the ticklish problems at the time were, one can profit from reading 'blue books', otherwise not.

The nineteenth century was renowned for letter-writing. Postal delivery became cheap, efficient and fast; in much of Europe during the 1880s it was as good as it is today. In some places it was better. Letters were written with care, and correspondence was meticulously preserved. Many leading statesmen employed private secretaries to transcribe outgoing letters and file incoming ones. Frequently they were lovingly bound in morocco. Probably most of them are available to scholars. One must not expect to find billets-doux gathered in pink ribbon, but otherwise these collections are remarkably complete. They add another dimension to the official documents, which usually are kept bland. The raciest tit-bits were kept for the smoking-room and so left no trace. Nineteenth-century politicians and businessmen were a good deal more discreet than our own are today.

Retiring cabinet ministers seldom rushed into print, but the prominent figures did occasionally leave memoirs, written afterwards, mainly to settle accounts. Ollivier, Bismarck and Beust are excellent examples of this. Diarists were generally not the key men, for such people lacked the time and inclination for this sort of thing. But, especially in Britain, families of deceased statesmen often asked a friend to compile an appropriate 'Life and Letters'. These were nearly always favourable, but they do help to bring the men to life.

Niepce and Daguerre invented photography at the start of our short nineteenth century. By the Crimean War it was already widely and adroitly used. It is not true that the photograph is pitilessly honest; that it can on the contrary be very misleading was quickly discovered, and this knowledge was put to artistic and political effect. But the new art does give us a comparatively reliable record of how people and things appeared. It offered artists a standard with which to measure their skill and later one against which to rebel. In the late 1870s Edison showed the way to sound recording. By 1890 relatively accurate and increasingly cheap light and sound registration gave the historian additional information and his craft a new dimension.

By and large the nineteenth century is an ideal era for historians to study. Their art matured and the sources were fuller and more varied than ever before, yet not so detailed, trivial or slapdash as to inhibit a general view.

The focus of this book is chronologically on those sixty years which epitomize the century. Its geographical concentration is equally clear. The five most important areas are studied in some depth while regions of lesser importance are omitted. In harmony with this spirit, the more directly thematic chapters are carefully aimed at salient features only. The purpose is therefore not encyclopaedic coverage but rather a discussion of essential themes. Each of the six authors has his own individual slant. Since the historian's craft is more bedevilled and ennobled by differences of opinion than many, it was thought useful to illustrate this within the confines of one book. It is appropriately introduced by a comparative study of revolution; this is followed by a section on France, the mother of revolution, which shows that country to be also in many respects profoundly conservative. Next there are two chapters on central Europe – Germany and Italy – which discuss the achievement and failings of the movement for simultaneous unification and liberalization. We see in the essay on Austria how it started first by fending off liberalism and nationalism and ended by attempting to turn sanitized versions of each to its own good. The last of the geographical chapters is on Russia. In the first half of the period covered in this book it was proudly immune from any modern contagion. In the second half its resistance was rapidly worn away, so that by 1890 the country was ready for swift change and vulnerable to internal attack.

The rest of the book is devoted to more clearly thematic studies.

They are introduced by a chapter on cultural history illuminating certain aspects of the idea of progress. The next one discusses the three most important political movements of the day – liberalism, nationalism and socialism. Then there is a section on material change, where the impact of industrialization and the revolution in warfare are studied. The two final chapters discuss inter-state affairs and imperialism. Relations between states fit well into the general nineteenth-century flow from Romanticism through realism to naturalism. The Crimean War is seen as crucial for its influence both on international relations and on the approach to politics in general. Finally the paradoxical relations of Europe with the outside world – a mixture of generosity and viciousness – during the whole period are discussed. The authors realize that their coverage of themes had to be selective. They hope, however, that by concentrating on essentials, they can contribute in a modest way to a deeper understanding of the century preceding our own when for a time Europe held the world's compass.

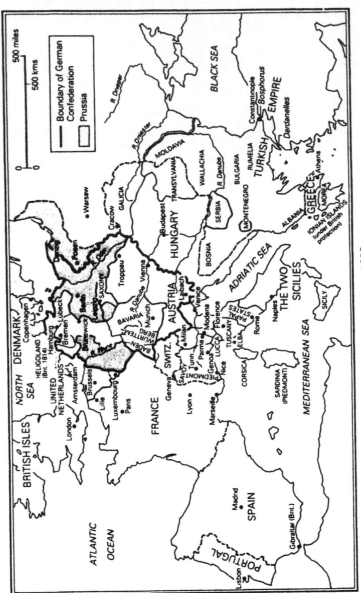

Europe: January 1830

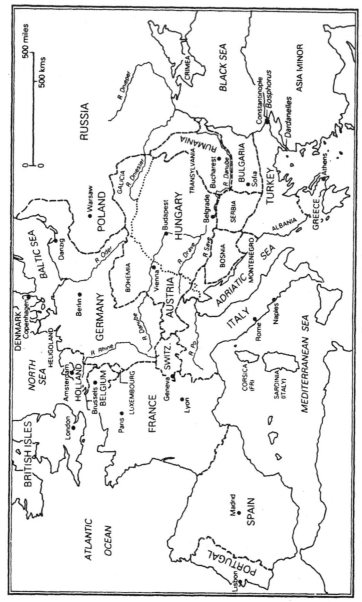

Europe: 1890

1

Revolutionary movements in nineteenth-century Europe

ROGER PRICE

Introduction

This essay seeks to explain the incidence of revolution in nineteenth-century Europe. The necessary reference point has to be the French Revolution of 1789 and the assault upon monarchy, the nobility and the church, and the long wars between 1792 and 1815. This experience promoted a polarization of opinion between conservative social and political élites and those groups, largely excluded from power, wanting political liberalism and social reform. Conservative fears and repression would greatly aggravate the hostility between these. Repression alone could never be totally effective, given the inherent weakness of the bureaucratic machines (particularly in comparison with twentieth-century models). Moreover, in addition to fear, it frequently inspired contempt and so served to stimulate opposition. Thus the conservative and governmental determination to crush liberal, democratic and national aspirations maintained a high degree of political and social tension. The situation was greatly exacerbated by a complex of factors including a continued suspicion of France. This reflected doubts about the stability of its internal political system and the sincerity of the French commitment to the 1815 territorial settlement. There was also a growing awareness of the unrest caused by population growth, which in many areas threatened to outstrip resources, and by the disruptive effects of industrial development, urbanization and the commercialization of agriculture.

Two major waves of revolution occurred in the first half of the century and threatened the internal and international order agreed on by the powers at Vienna in 1815. The first came in 1830–2, most notably in France and the Netherlands. As a result in France the Bourbon monarchy, closely associated with aristocratic political predominance, was replaced by a regime which extended political rights to wider groups of property owners and increased the authority of Parliament; in the Low Countries the independence of Belgium was recognized. Elsewhere, and especially in Britain and some German states, varying degrees of political liberalization were conceded. Events in one country clearly influenced those in others by stimulating hopes and fears. The search for common patterns should not be pursued too far, however, given differences in political traditions and social situations. 1848 saw revolution on a much greater scale – both geographically and in terms of the demands made for political and social reform. Encouraged by the partial success of 1830, reacting against the way in which governments had turned to repression subsequently, liberals and democrats were all the more determined, after the unexpected collapse of the French, Austrian and Prussian governments, to achieve far-reaching reforms. The hysterical fear of revolution which this promoted amongst conservatives was to lead to brutally repressive measures in the short term, and in the longer term to efforts to ensure social stability through reforms from above. These would have a decisive impact upon the development of social systems and on the political evolution of the various European states.

What was it about the late eighteenth and first half of the nineteenth centuries that made these periods particularly susceptible to revolution? The obvious place to begin is with the causes of revolution. These must include discontent with existing political and/or social systems, and in relation to this such factors as the scale and location (social and geographic) of discontent. Thus, where mass unrest due to material deprivation coincided with the articulate and organized expression of grievances amongst the upper and middle classes the political situation was obviously more unstable than where the property-owning classes remained fundamentally united in support of a government believed to be committed to their vital interests. Discontent in a capital city was always more threatening than disorders in the provinces. Another major factor was governmental response to discontent. Timely concessions might reduce the likelihood of disorder; they were made in Britain in 1832 by means of the Parliamentary Reform Law and in 1846 through the repeal of the Corn Laws, and in many of the minor German states in both 1830 and 1848. On the other hand where such concessions gave the appearance of weakness they might encourage further demands. In contrast, the refusal to compromise might persuade opponents that the way to reform through legal, institutionalized channels was closed and that recourse to force was unavoidable. However, governments obviously determined to defend their position through the use of repressive violence might well succeed in persuading opponents that the likely cost of protest was too high to be risked. In this situation political demobilization could result, and this was one amongst a complex of reasons for the absence of revolution in many European states in both 1830 and 1848. The answers to the question posed above are thus likely to be both structural and political: structural in terms of the discontent caused by economic change and population growth, and political given the inability or unwillingness of some ruling groups to accept the diminution in their power that would result from the incorporation of aspiring interest groups into the political system.

Acceptable generalizations are not easy to make, given the great variety of economic, social and political systems to be found in nineteenth-century Europe, embracing Britain – the symbol of advanced industrialization, with its constitutional monarchy, and those other west European states evolving towards a capitalistic society; the monarchies of central and eastern Europe, progressively more absolute the further east one looks; the agrarian societies of the Mediterranean, plagued as in the case of Spain, Portugal and Greece by bitter, and often armed, conflict between conservatives and liberals; the Italian states, subject to various forms of absolutist government; and the Balkans, slowly throwing off Ottoman rule. Throughout the first half of the nineteenth century, with the exception of Britain and Belgium, and to a lesser degree France and parts of Western Germany, pre-industrial economic and social structures remained largely intact, preserved by poor communications and geographical fragmentation. In certain other crucial respects too the *ancien régime* survived well into the nineteenth century. Even in France, where constitutional monarchy had been established in 1815, the monarchy retained the substantial authority believed by élites to be essential for the preservation of order. Further east, absolute monarchy survived with little more than the force of custom, local privilege, and practical realities (small bureaucracies, limited tax revenues, poor communications, etc.) to enforce restraint. Furthermore landowners retained positions of social and political predominance, even in Britain and France where wealth, and the adoption of the appropriate life-style had allowed successful members of the professional and business class to accede to positions of influence. The further east one looked the more complete was aristocratic dominance, reinforced by the surviving institutions of serfdom and protected by absolute monarchy. The wealthy controlled access to scarce resources (particularly the land), to employment, and to charity, and, because of their virtual monopoly of key positions in representative assemblies, the bureaucracy and the army, dominated the process of law-making, controlled the means of coercion, and possessed multi-faceted means of exercising power. In spite of our present perception of accelerating economic and social change, it is important to stress continuity with the eighteenth century.

The causes of revolution

In an influential article published in 1948 the French historian Labrousse insisted on the importance of economic crisis as a cause of social unrest, and additionally on the fact that not all such crises led on to revolution. Discontent not only needed to be politicized, and governmental responses to the crisis judged to be inadequate, but conflict situations had to develop – in 1830 and 1848 in France by accident, rather than from a widespread desire for revolution.[1]

Differing levels of economic development between countries, and regional variations within them, render hazardous generalizations about the impact of economic difficulties. Nevertheless the revolutions of 1830 and 1848 (and indeed that of 1789) were all preceded by major crises. In many respects, and in spite of rising agricultural productivity, these were typical pre-industrial crises, caused by two or three successive poor harvests in most regions between 1827 and 1829, and then again in 1845 and 1846. These greatly intensified the social problems caused by population growth, and by the transition to capitalistic production in both agriculture and industry. Harvest shortfalls resulted in a sharp rise in food prices and in a reduction of the income of most small farmers. Consumers were forced to spend increasing portions of their incomes on basic foodstuffs and correspondingly less on manufactured goods. As a result, the crisis spread to industry, causing widespread unemployment and short-term working. As their incomes declined, many workers were faced with increases of the order of 50 per cent in the price of such essentials as bread and potatoes. Such situations, together with the disorders caused by protests about high prices, led to a general loss of confidence throughout society; this further reduced demand for industrial products and services and resulted in a generalized economic and social crisis. The export of bullion to finance food imports had a further deflationary impact on the whole economy.

These situations were fundamentally similar to that which had prevailed before 1789, but in the late 1820s and especially 1840s there were also signs of change in the character of economic crises due to the accelerating development of international financial markets and a commercial and industrial economy. In this state of transition from pre-industrial structures, many regions suffered from the impact of both a pre-industrial crisis caused by poor harvests and a modern crisis which was due to loss of confidence in major financial markets together with industrial over-production/under-consumption and commercial glut. Significantly both the most advanced economy (Britain) and some of the more backward, that is, those least integrated into inter-regional trade, were less severely affected by crisis than those undergoing structural change. These areas for this and other reasons did not experience revolution.

Where revolution occurred, it appears that economic and political crises coincided. To a degree the two were obviously interrelated, and governments were blamed for the misery and anxiety which affected most of the population. This situation also reinforced demands for constitutional reform, reawakening the liberal and democratic aspirations created in the aftermath of 1789 in favour of parliamentary institutions or an extension of the franchise. By the beginning of the nineteenth century, throughout western and central Europe, and particularly amongst the landowning and professional classes, a new participatory political culture had been created; it survived repeated waves of repression. The year 1830 both satisfied some of the more moderate reformist demands and encouraged more far-reaching proposals that would enjoy wider support. The disparate character of political opposition, then and later, should, however, be noted. It included both liberals interested in limited constitutional change to ensure the rule of law, and radicals committed to manhood suffrage and vague measures of social reform.

In France the accession of Charles X in 1824 would in any case have caused a crisis. He was not merely unwilling to contemplate liberal reforms, he also introduced a series of repressive measures; these culminated in the dismissal of a newly elected Parliament in 1830 and the use of emergency decree powers to issue *ordonnances* revising electoral procedures and reducing the size of the electorate. This seemed to confirm the worst fears of liberals that a reactionary *coup d'état* in favour of the aristocracy and the church was intended. In Paris and many provincial towns committees, which included liberal nobles but were mainly made up of non-noble landowners and professional men, called for resistance. They used rather ambiguous and universalistic terms, not wanting revolution, but which had the effect of mobilizing a disparate coalition determined to oppose the government.

Again in 1847 the government rejected an extension of the franchise beyond the levels established after the 1830 Revolution. This encouraged those active politicians who despaired of winning electoral victory under the existing system to seek the support of unenfranchised representatives of the professional classes. They organized protest in the form of a banquet campaign in order to evade laws prohibiting public meetings, and were able to mobilize substantial popular support. Yet again they were not revolutionaries, but they helped to create a situation in which violent conflict became a possibility because of the arousal of political passions. The limited nature of the reforms which had followed the 1830 Revolution, and the continued unwillingness of Louis-Philippe and his ministers to accept constitutional change, together with growing awareness of the 'social problem' created by urban-industrial development, had moreover reinforced support for democratic reforms, and, amongst a radical minority, for the re-establishment of the Republic.

Events in France, both in 1830 and 1848, provided a major stimulus to liberal demands elsewhere in Europe. Even where concessions had been made to liberalism, as in the Netherlands, or Baden and Bavaria after 1815 or in 1830, these had been extremely limited. By 1848 discontent was far more obvious throughout the German states and in the Austrian Empire. There the situation was further complicated by the emergence, again particularly amongst the educated landowning and professional classes, of national sentiment. In Germany this was expressed by demands for some form of unity, in the Austrian Empire by a growing will to question the decisions of a largely Germanic bureaucracy and in Italy, Hungary and Bohemia by the assertion of claims to linguistic and cultural equality.

The effect of growing political discontent to a large extent depended upon the way in which the various governments responded. Revolutions occurred, in both 1830 and 1848, when governments failed to make timely concessions which might have satisfied at least some opposition groups, and when they were at the same time unable to prevent the continued discussion of grievances. The inherent weakness of monarchical government, overtly dependent as it was on the character and qualities of individuals holding power often for long periods, was revealed by the inept crisis management of Charles X and his chief minister Polignac in 1829–30, of Louis-Philippe and Guizot in 1847–8, by William I's feeble efforts to reduce discontent in the southern (Belgian) provinces of his kingdom, and the paralysis which affected both the Austrian and Prussian regimes in 1848 as the news of the February revolution in Paris encouraged internal discontents. Monarchs such as Friedrich Wilhelm IV, the Prussian king, convinced of their divine right to rule and dependent on the advice of a narrow circle of court nobles, were not likely to make timely concessions. In 1830–2 moderate constitutional reform in some of the states of northern and central Germany, in Denmark and in Britain, successfully conciliated middle-class liberals. However, in the German cases the subsequent withdrawal of most of these concessions only increased distrust of government and reduced the likelihood that subsequent protest would adopt, as in Britain, legal and institutional forms. There was widespread and growing resentment of the arbitrariness and petty tyranny exercised by state officials.

More than any other individual, the Austrian Chancellor Metternich has been associated with the political repression designed to preserve monarchical absolutism and aristocratic power against further revolution, both within the empire and the German states, throughout the period from 1815 to 1848. Indeed, convinced that a secret committee of revolutionaries was plotting to plunge the continent into another era of revolution and war, Metternich sought to persuade European governments to co-operate in maintaining the status quo. The effectiveness and influence of the imperial regime was however considerably reduced by its own continued lack of cohesion. Weak emperors were unable to impose a spirit of co-operation upon squabbling ministers. Constant financial difficulties made it impossible to sustain a strong and efficient bureaucracy and army. Whilst reforms that might have increased the efficiency of the administration were repeatedly postponed, efforts continued to reinforce administrative control over the disparate sections of the empire. This awoke growing resentment, especially in Hungary and Lombardy-Venetia. By late 1847 Radetzky, the military commander in northern Italy, was reporting that 'the whole social order . . . [is] . . . about to collapse . . . the Revolution will only be kept in check by fear'. If in reality only very small groups actively favoured revolution, governmental inertia in the various countries undoubtedly had the effect of undermining the legitimacy of existing regimes, and reducing the strength of support for the status quo.

A revolutionary situation can be said to exist where opponents of a government resort to demonstrating their opposition on the streets, and enter into conflict with police and troops whose responsibility is precisely to control the public highway and assert the authority of the established government. The potential for violence in this type of situation might develop beyond the point of no return, owing to an, often accidental, triggering incident. The revolutionary overthrow of a regime will however only occur if its military forces are actively defeated; the circumstances in which this occurred in 1830 and 1848 are obviously on our agenda. Moreover, in order to overcome the resistance of governments backed by military force, substantial mass participation is necessary. Discontent in itself, however, is not sufficient to lead to a revolution, particularly where, as in most of the cases which concern us, hardly anyone, at least initially, was actively planning revolt. Secret revolutionary societies certainly existed, but were small, internally divided and usually penetrated by the police. Not surprisingly they were most common in those areas such as Italy, Spain or Poland in which repression had been most extreme.

When looking at the geography of revolutions an obvious characteristic is that they began in capital cities – the foci for political activity, but also sites of rapid economic change and population growth – and only subsequently affected other towns and rural areas. In both 1830 and 1848 violence began with clashes between the military and crowds of demonstrators, after which the latter erected barricades both as a form of protection and to secure control of the city. Successful use of the army by governments to assert mastery depended on carefully planned tactics in order to maintain control over detachments of soldiers in the narrow streets of still largely medieval cities; a determination to use whatever force was necessary; and confidence in the outcome. In the rising spiral of violence the excessive dispersal of forces, supply failures, loss of contact with superiors, and hesitation in the use of firepower, could and did lead to disaster.

The two essential components of the revolutionary situation were thus the rise of opposition and the collapse of government. At the onset of periods of revolutionary violence, the call for protest and the demands for wider participation in politics were made largely by men already involved in the political system, and mainly drawn from the professional middle classes. Given that they had not wanted revolution, it is hardly surprising that they were rarely found amongst those killed on the barricades (concerning whom we have statistical information). Those who fought in the streets were not, as the conservative press so often claimed, the unemployed, semi-criminal elements common in the pre-industrial city, but mainly representative of the lower-middle classes (small tradesmen and workshop owners) and, especially, skilled workers from the small workshops and building industries. In Paris in the July Revolution an estimated 200 troops had been killed and 800 wounded; the insurgents suffered some 800 dead and 4,000 wounded. David Pinkney's (1988) analysis of 1,538 individuals killed or wounded reveals that just under 300 were labourers and servants, 85 members of the liberal professions, 54 shopkeepers and almost 1,000 artisans and skilled workers. They were motivated by a desire for greater material security and an enhanced social status, and by resentment of those (employers, wholesale merchants, landlords, politicians) who exploited them and excluded them from political debate. These were men politicized by discussion at work, in the bar, at meetings of friendly societies and, with their high literacy levels, by reading; and attracted by simple slogans in favour of liberty, producers' co-operatives and democratic rights.

In the spread of revolution across Europe the 'domino effect' was to be of some significance in 1830, when debate on the reform issue in the British Parliament was clearly influenced by events in France, as were demonstrations in favour of reform in such German states as Brunswick, Hanover and Saxony. The effect was more clearly evident in 1848 when the news of events in Paris between 22 and 24 February stimulated protest which led to disorder in Vienna on 13 March, and this in its turn encouraged opposition in Milan and Venice, and in Berlin on 18 March. As a result of this the Austrian and Prussian monarchs, their confidence shattered, felt obliged to promise constitutional reform, afraid as they were of otherwise being dragged into an uncontrollable, continent-wide crisis. This inevitably weakened resistance to reform in the smaller German states which had looked to Austria and Prussia for support.

The course of revolution

The objective of some at least of the members of the revolutionary crowd was to replace the established government with another which it assumed would better represent their interests. In reality, however, a coalition of groups which had previously in common only their opposition to the deposed regime, was, once in power, likely to lead to instability. The groups which unexpectedly had achieved the one objective on which they agreed subsequently sought to define the aims of the new regime, and the limits to revolution, and so competed for positions of power in order to implement their diverse objectives. Unplanned revolution had created a power vacuum, into which those groups with at least a modicum of organization and authority might step. In France in 1830 this was a group of liberal parliamentarians (two bankers, two lawyers, a professor, two writers and five nobles), who were anxious above all to restore order and limit the impact of the revolution. Their reforms enfranchised mainly the well-off sectors of the middle classes and represented an attempt to reinforce social stability by integrating wider groups of property owners into the political system. Most people continued to be excluded because of their sex or inability to meet the tax qualification for voting. It was assumed that most of the population lacked wealth, education and independence – the virtues necessary to ensure an informed and rational involvement in political decision-making. Inevitably those groups disappointed with the outcome, but politicized by events, would form the basis for opposition to the new regime. In 1848, with monarchy apparently discredited, a small body of republicans, well known to the Paris public because of their political and journalistic activities, was able to seize power. Again the majority of moderate political leaders saw their role as essentially the preservation of order. Significantly, however, and indicative of the evolution of politics in the aftermath of 1830, they introduced manhood suffrage for the election of the Constituent Assembly that would draft the constitution of the Republic. In a major radicalizing move popular sovereignty was thus recognized. Nevertheless in France, and to an even greater extent in Austria and Prussia, where monarchs simply invited liberal politicians to participate in government, substantial elements of the previous regime remained intact. The moderates who had acceded to political power were anxious to avoid further violence and sought compromises acceptable to existing social élites, senior bureaucrats and military officers. Although they accepted the principle of constitutional reform to include parliamentary elections and limited ministerial changes the Emperor Ferdinand and King Friedrich Wilhelm IV retained considerable authority, and control of the bureaucracy and army. In France too, the fear of international complications, and the spread of internal disorders after the revolution, ensured that new ministers were sharply aware of their dependence on the military. The old élites also retained their property and much of their influence. But they were frightened. The future conservative minister Léon Faucher wrote from Paris to a British acquaintance that 'we live in the midst of permanent danger . . . A terrible tempest has smashed the social structure . . . The disorganization is complete . . . the workers are openly in revolt against the capitalists . . . houses have been pillaged and burnt, women threatened with violence and men with death'. Initially they were willing to accept liberal and moderate republican ministers in the hope of avoiding something worse, but in the longer term they were committed to political reaction.

In the meantime the new governments faced major problems, notably those of securing recognition of their authority and achieving a constitutional settlement. In Germany in 1848 this involved not only liberal reform in the individual states but responding to the liberals' demand for greater national unity. Meeting in late March as a *Vorparlament* in Frankfurt, they wanted elections for an assembly to prepare a federal German constitution. There was a need also to respond to demands made by a variety of groups sharing in the often almost Utopian sense of expectancy of social change created by the revolutions. These included the large numbers thrown out of work because of the renewed crisis of confidence amongst businessmen caused by the revolution. They wanted the restoration of prosperity and in the meantime assistance. A small, but growing, minority proved susceptible to socialist calls for a permanent reorganization of work on the basis of producers' co-operatives. In many regions peasants reacted against the growing capitalist commercialization of agriculture and demanded the restoration of customary rights of usage in forests and on common lands. In eastern Germany and the Austrian Empire they demanded the abolition of the last vestiges of serfdom. In Prussia and Austria an additional problem was the demand for greater autonomy articulated by Polish, Czech and Romanian landowners and intellectuals.

In the cities politics was transformed by the political mobilization of the masses sustained by a newly free press, by numerous political clubs and meetings and frequent demonstrations. Foremost in these developments were skilled artisans, already organized at the level of their trades, and suffering from changes in economic structures, and from intensified competition caused by industrialization. This threatened not only their livelihoods but their entire way of life. They were anxious to assert their status both as creators of wealth and members of the political community Although enthusiasm soon declined, the experience gained in 1830, and particularly in 1848, provided a major stimulus to the development of a political awareness, especially amongst skilled workers in the major cities where political propaganda was most intense. Even as governments sought to reassert their authority and regain control of the streets in the major cities, such democratic organizations dominated by professional men, intellectuals and artisans as *Solidarité républicaine* in France or the *Zentralmärzverein* in Germany continued to organize and propagandize in provincial cities, market towns and increasingly even in the countryside.

The instability caused by competition for power within governments constituted by informal coalitions was thus reinforced by the efforts of members of a variety of social and political groups to exert influence and put pressure upon political leaders. As the new governments sought to impose control, and secure recognition of their legitimacy, it was likely that disorder and violence would become increasingly widespread, and that inexperienced ministers would have little alternative but to rely upon the bureaucratic and military machines inherited from the old regimes.

Revolution, or simply apparent governmental weakness, had appeared to inaugurate a new era of liberty which encouraged all manner of demonstrations by groups with grievances or aspirations. Widespread protest occurred in rural areas; in the Rhineland and much of central Germany in the summer and early autumn of 1830, rent, tax and conscription records were burnt. Similar disorders occurred in many parts of France, and were paralleled in some urban centres by demonstrations and strikes by workers. In Paris in particular, encouraged by the leading part they had played in overthrowing the Bourbons, and by the apparent establishment of liberty, workers were mobilized in August and September 1830 to take part in street demonstrations demanding amongst other things the trial of Charles X's ministers, increased wages and a shorter working day. They hoped that the new regime would guarantee them work at a decent wage, but were rapidly disabused by the incomprehension and hostility with which their demands were met and by growing official repression. This, together with the restrictive conditions imposed by a new electoral law (the tax qualification for voting was only reduced from 300 to 200 francs) stimulated a rebirth of political opposition amongst some liberals and republicans. The ability of the well-organized workers in the Lyon silk trade to seize control of the city in

November 1831 impressed conservative opinion throughout Europe. The journalist St Marc Girardin saw it as revealing the 'grave secret' of the times, that 'the Barbarians who threaten society are not in the Caucasus, nor on the Steppes of Tartary; they are in the suburbs of our manufacturing cities'. This post-revolutionary period lasted from July 1830 to 1834, when it was cut short by the repressive measures stimulated by this kind of fear, such as the law banning association. In France at least it was central to the development of a class consciousness and interest in republican politics amongst some sections of the lower middle classes and skilled workers.

From the point of view of governments and conservatives, the situation was far worse in 1848, the crisis of government deeper, the demonstrations more widespread, the aspirations of peasants and workers more substantial, and more politicized. In much of Germany, and in the Austrian Empire, rural discontent was calmed by the attenuation or abolition of surviving seigneurial rights. In France a similar political result, the isolation of the urban revolutionaries, was achieved by the government's concern to pay for the 'national workshops', established to provide work for the unemployed, and balance the budget. This led it to impose a 45 per cent surcharge on the land tax – not a very effective means of winning peasant for the Republic. In the cities political debate was stimulated by the multitude of new newspapers, pamphlets, associations and political clubs which were created in the new freedom, by the extension of the franchise to all adult males and by preparations for elections. Once again the revolution had broken the habit of obedience to authority and created a sense of expectancy. Radical republicans and worker militants were determined on this occasion to avoid a repetition of the 'betrayal' of 1830 and to secure meaningful social reform. The manifesto of the *Club de la révolution* in Paris, for example, announced that 'we still have only the name of the Republic, we need the real thing. Political reform is only the instrument of social reform.' The French Provisional Government felt obliged to make concessions; its decree of 25 February proclaimed the right to work but promised far more than was intended. The National Workshops created in Paris and many other towns were merely an extension of the charity workshops traditionally established in periods of high unemployment to provide poorly paid work relief on public work projects. It was most certainly not intended to establish the producers' co-operatives which militants believed would bring to an end 'the exploitation of man by man'. A government composed of moderate republicans was primarily concerned to promote economic recovery and the restoration of order by means of the re-establishment of business confidence. This required the avoidance of any 'socialistic' measures. In the German states and Austria the appointment of liberal ministers, most obviously Camphausen and Hansemann in Prussia, although it might appear to herald constitutional change, did not reduce the absolute commitment in government circles to the preservation of the existing social system.

In Germany and Austria it rapidly became clear that the other main concern of both ministers and the majority of liberal politicians was, in the one case, the question of German unity, and in the other, the preservation of the unitary empire. The French Revolution and its aftermath had stimulated national sentiment throughout Europe. In the succeeding years this had been reinforced by romanticism and by the development of a cultural nationalism reinforced by the writing of national histories. These sentiments were particularly strong amongst the educated classes in Germany and northern Italy, whilst the popular classes often remained indifferent or motivated by strong local loyalties. Already in 1830 the power of nationalism had been revealed by the collapse of the United Netherlands and the establishment of the Belgian state. Resistance to Dutch rule was stimulated in those areas that had constituted the Austrian Netherlands before 1789, and had subsequently been incorporated into France, by tax and tariff structures seeming to favour the Dutch. To this were added grievances over education, language and the respective shares in political power. In Poland a mixture of economic grievances and patriotic feelings amongst the numerous gentry families, stimulated by the news from France, encouraged sections of the Polish army, maintained under Russian rule, to revolt. Although the movement enjoyed some support from the urban middle classes, the unwillingness of the gentry to attract peasant support by promises of agrarian reform isolated them and so ensured Russian victory. Rather than a war of 'national liberation', in 1830–1 Italy experienced revolts in protest against maladministration, most notably in the Papal States. However, resentment of the

'Germans', as the Austrians were called, was widespread and further intensified by the Austrian occupation of Modena, Parma and Ferrara in support of their rulers' resistance to liberal reform.

The year 1848 saw national movements in much of central and eastern Europe. In Germany, following an initiative taken by a group of fifty-one liberals meeting at Heidelberg on 5 March, a *Vorparlament* made up of 600 members of existing state assemblies gathered at Frankfurt on 30 March and agreed that elections should be held to elect an assembly to prepare a German constitution. With the exception of a small minority they were clearly anxious to proceed by means of compromise with the existing state authorities. The Parliament which convened in the Paulskirche in Frankfurt in May was dominated by jurists and officials. Its members were determined to assert their authority and rapidly established a responsible ministry under the Austrian Archduke John, a man acceptable to both the Austrian and Prussian monarchs. From the beginning major divisions were apparent on such matters as whether to include Austria, with its non-German peoples, within the new German Empire, on the franchise qualification, and on social reform. It moreover quickly became clear that the implementation of constitutional measures depended upon the good will of the major states. When, by April 1849, agreement was finally reached to establish a federal union (excluding Austria and its Slavs) with an elected diet, responsible ministers and an emperor with substantial executive power, Friedrich Wilhelm, the most favoured candidate, was determined to reject the crown offered by an elected assembly. In this situation, with most of its members, like other men of property, unwilling to call for resistance to the monarchy and risk radical rebellion, there was little to do but go home.

Significantly, German and Austro-German liberals were unable to accept that to non-Germans 'freedom' and 'unity' might mean the end of German dominance. Efforts by the Poles in Posen, and by Czechs in Prague to claim greater autonomy were suppressed with relative ease. The Austrian command responded to an uprising in Prague in June 1848, involving some 1,200–1,500 insurgents, with an artillery bombardment. Far more serious for the Austrian regime were events in Italy and Hungary, where the opposition was composed of regular troops as well as civilian insurgents, and where, following initial revolution, full-scale wars of national liberation, were fought.

After bitter street fighting between 18 and 23 March 1848 crowds inspired by the news from Paris and Vienna drove the Austrian army out of Milan. This was followed by the humiliating capitulation of the Venice garrison and by the intervention of Piedmont, the Papacy and Naples in the struggle for a united Italy. The Italian effort had however rapidly turned into a fiasco. It was marred by mutual suspicion between its leaders and their shared fear that political radicals might usurp their authority. This in fact happened in Rome after Pius IX's decision to denounce the war. The main armed force, the Piedmontese army, was defeated by the Austrians under Radetzky at Custozza in July 1848, and again, following an armistice, at Novara in March 1849. This finally allowed the Austrians to reimpose control over Lombardy-Venetia.

Hungarian political leaders, most notably Széchenyi and Kossuth, had also seen the collapse of the central government in Vienna as an opportunity to gain greater autonomy, and with much of the imperial army tied down in Italy, enjoyed considerable initial success in forcing concessions from the beleagured Habsburg regime. Their own growing assertiveness and efforts to impose linguistic and administrative uniformity soon, however, led to uprisings by non-Magyar groups and particularly the Croats and Transylvanian Romanians. Moreover, once the imperial government felt strong enough to take the military initiative, conflict was inevitable. The authorities were determined to avoid the dismemberment of the empire. Indeed in every European capital, regardless of their political affiliations, aristocratic and upper-middle-class ministers, officials and army officers determined to resist the pressure for social reform. The former supporters of liberal constitutional change were increasingly thrown back into alliance with conservative groups, and into dependence on the military. They had wanted nothing more than limited political reform. The threat to order posed by crowds demonstrating for social reform now transformed them into the ardent defenders of private property and 'Christian civilization'.

The growth of reaction

The year 1830 confirmed for conservatives that the revolutionary monster created in 1789 had not been slain. The disorders provoked by economic crisis and political unrest had briefly threatened social order, and it had been widely agreed, even by the Legitimists who had so recently lost power in France, that determined governmental repression was necessary. A much greater threat was presented in 1848. Once concessions were made to liberal demands a political realignment commenced as the more moderate, especially amongst the better-off and economically secure, affirmed their fundamental desire to avoid social change. In France this was evident from as early as the April 1848 elections. These, the first elections held under universal male suffrage, had seemed to present such a threat to social stability. The results were reassuring. Traditional élites, including the clergy, were able to exert a considerable influence amongst an inexperienced electorate. Of nearly 900 deputies, only a minority of around 300 appear to have been republicans before 1848, and only 70 to 80 of these later revealed some degree of sympathy for measures of social reform. The remainder were monarchists, most of whom temporarily adopted a republican label. Socially this was an assembly of wealthy, provincial notables. In Prussia, where liberals enjoyed some success in the May 1848 local elections, conservative landowners responded by organizing an 'Association for the Protection of Property and the Advancement of the Welfare of all Classes'. There and in German Austria they combined concessions to 'their' peasants, with exaggerated accounts of the threat posed by the Left to property, to religion, the family and the nation. If this appeal failed intimidation was usually possible.

The return to military repression was indeed surprisingly rapid. In France, a mass insurrection occurred in June following the government's announcement of its intention to close the Paris National Workshops. This decision seemed not only to threaten the existence of the large numbers of unemployed workers and their families, but also had considerable symbolic value. The February Revolution had created an immense sense of expectancy. The workshops had appeared to represent the first step in a programme of social reform, all hope of which would now disappear. Thus many insurgents felt justified in resorting to violence in spite of the existence of the democratically elected Constituent Assembly and its ministers. Against them the moderate republican General Cavaignac deployed the army, civilian National Guards, mainly from middle-class districts but including many workers, and the Mobile Guard recruited from amongst young unemployed workers. Given determined leadership and ruthless tactics, the success of the forces of order against mainly unprepared insurgents was inevitable. This was however a revolt which impressed and frightened the whole of Europe. It was described by de Tocqueville as a, 'brutal, blind but powerful attempt by the workers to escape from the necessities of their condition' and by Marx as, 'the first great battle . . . between the two classes that split modern society'. The insurgents were in fact drawn from the small workshops and building sites of the capital. In terms of their social profile they had more in common with the *sans-culotte* of 1789 than with a modern factory workforce. In any case the victory of the 'forces of order' was acclaimed by conservatives everywhere. In the same month the Austrian General Windischgrätz regained control of Prague. September saw the return of the army to Berlin, October the deaths of 2,000–5,000 insurgents in Vienna as the army re-entered the city. As a result, in 1849 it was possible for the Austrians to deploy substantial forces, first in northern Italy and subsequently in Hungary, where, with Russian help, resistance was finally crushed between August and October, with an estimated 50,000 dead on both sides.

In spite of these successes, conservatives remained gravely concerned. Military repression was not enough entirely to restore self-confidence. Such events as the January 1849 elections in Prussia, and those of May in France, in which liberals in the first case and the radical *démocrate-socialistes* in the second, appeared to be gaining ground, suggested that opposition groups might one day secure an electoral majority. There was, it seemed to the vast majority of both conservatives and liberals, an urgent need to ensure that electoral systems were modified in order to prevent this outcome, and that the powers of parliamentary institutions were restricted. The June insurrection in Paris had seemed to confirm the worst fears about the revolutionary threat to the social system. It justified reaction in various forms, such as a whole variety of measures aimed to secure the political demobilization of the masses: police repression, the closure of political associations, bans on meetings and censorship of the press. The measures enjoyed considerable success. Opponents of reaction either gave up political activity from disillusionment or fear, or were forced to continue in a clandestine, and less effective manner.

In France the election of Louis-Napoléon Bonaparte as President of the Republic in December 1848, with the support of most conservative notables, was part of this drive to restore social order, but also represented a far more widespread popular desire for prosperity and security. With substantial support from all social groups Bonaparte launched a *coup d'état* in December 1851, with the dual objectives of finally ending radical agitation and ensuring that there would be no *démocrate-socialiste* electoral triumph in 1852, as well as taking a major step towards the re-establishment of the empire. Unexpectedly the *coup* met with widespread resistance, mainly from artisans and peasants with middle-class leaders, in rural areas of the south-east. This provided both justification of the *coup* as an essentially preventive measure and an excuse for widespread arrests. Similar movements in Germany in May-June 1849 occurred in protest against political reaction and the sense amongst democrats of betrayal by the princes and liberal bourgeoisie, after Friedrich Wilhelm refused to recognize the imperial constitution prepared by the Frankfurt Assembly. Risings took place, mainly in the south-west, organized by the popular political societies, and in Baden supported by part of the army. Fighting also occurred around the textile centre of Elberfeld in the Prussian Rhineland and in Dresden where 8,000–10,000 insurgents fought Saxon troops hurriedly reinforced by Prussians. In all these cases 1848 radicalized large numbers of artisans suffering from economic crises and the longer-term intensification of competitive pressures. At the same time, and largely in reaction, the established commitment of the liberal middle classes to social order was substantially reinforced. The experience of revolution created a willingness to accept strong monarchical government at the expense of liberal institutions as the essential means of safeguarding a social system based on private property. To obtain this goal even the use of brutal military violence was welcome. It was a situation in which the crucially important role of the army as a conservative social institution was made abundantly clear.

Military repression was accompanied by the return to absolutist forms of government – seen for example in the appointment of ministers who did not enjoy the confidence of parliaments. In Austria Prince Felix Schwarzenberg, who became Chancellor in November 1848, was a man dedicated to the modernization, centralization and Germanization of the monarchy. His appointment was followed in December by the announcement of the abdication of the Emperor Ferdinand in favour of the youthful Franz Joseph, a change which made the disavowal of earlier concessions all the easier, since the new Emperor had not sworn to uphold them. Symbolically he styled himself 'Emperor by the Grace of God', a form which had been abandoned in March. The Austrian Parliament, exiled to the little Moravian town of Kremsier where it continued to prepare a new imperial constitution, was increasingly ignored, until its final dissolution on 7 March 1849. On the same day a new constitution, imposed by the Emperor, was introduced. This maintained the Emperor's right to veto legislation, rejected ministerial responsibility to parliament, restricted the franchise, reduced Hungarian autonomy and reinforced the powers of the central administration.

In Prussia too the return of the army to Berlin was followed by a reaffirmation of non-parliamentary government and the exiling of the Prussian assembly to the provinces until its dissolution in December. Although these reactionary measures taken in France, Austria and Prussia and emulated in the minor German states were accepted by most citizens as necessary to the restoration of order, the various governments still recognized the advisability of concessions to liberal and, in France, even to democratic opinion. In Austria this phase was short-lived, with the new Emperor asserting himself to eliminate representative institutions by decree in December 1851. In France the franchise, restricted in May 1850, was restored as one of the measures accompanying the *coup d'état*; in the other states equality before the law was reinforced and in Prussia too a wide franchise maintained. The electoral law of 30 May 1849, however, established a three class system of voting, which sought to relate voting rights to wealth (signified by taxation) and status. Each of the classes, which made up 5, 12 and 83 per cent of the electorate, elected an equal number of deputies. In France the impact of mass enfranchisement was negated by a system of official candidature whereby candidates for election selected by government officials were given every assistance, and opponents subjected to intimidation and obstruction. This combined with administrative repression to create a system of guided democracy which survived well into the 1860s.

If in the short term the measures taken involved the use of military and administrative repression, governments did not lose sight of the need to ensure stability in the longer term. In this they were assisted by the more prosperous economic conditions of the 1850s, but stress should also be placed on the renewed interest in mass education. The Falloux Law of 1850 in France and the Concordat of 1855 between the Austrian regime and the Papacy were measures intended to increase the influence of the church in the schools. Conservative Christian teaching would, it was assumed, serve as a means of socialization, persuading the poor and unprivileged to accept the place in society which God had ordained for them.

Conclusion

This short essay can in no way do justice to the complexity of political behaviour. It would be a gross over-simplification to read the history of the revolutions of 1830 and of 1848 simply in terms of class conflict. Diverse communities and social and cultural groups responded to complex crises in order to protect their particular interests; they employed forms of political behaviour suggested both by tradition and the rapid diffusion of new, more modern political organizations. At the risk of simplification, it is possible to suggest that in the early stages of the revolutions, members of a variety of interest groups sought to make use of the unexpected opportunity presented by government collapse, to fulfil objectives already largely formulated by the small groups of pre-revolutionary political militants. Whilst members of the middle classes were particularly interested in political representation, workers and peasants sought, above all, economic security. Subsequently, when political disorder disrupted the economy, and it appeared as if the entire social system with its hierarchy based on the ownership of property was threatened, many came to desire a return to 'normal'. This strengthened the anyway powerful capacity for resistance possessed by the military and by established élite groups entrenched in state bureaucracies. German historians have tended to dwell on the failure of the middle classes in 1848 to press for the creation of a liberal state, and have seen this as a sign of the uniqueness of German history (the *Sonderweg*). However, it would seem that this 'treachery against the people' and willingness to 'compromise with the crowned representatives of the old society' (Marx) was a character-istic of the property-owning classes throughout the continent. Analyses which compare German political and economic develop-ment with an idealized version of the British experience, or pose a conception of the *real* interests of the bourgeoisie which they are supposed to have betrayed, are fundamentally ahistorical.

The opposition to reaction came from minorities amongst in particular the professional middle classes, skilled workers and peasants. Popular commitment was especially apparent in its more violent manifestations. These movements, in spite of the participation of workers from modern factories and engineering workshops in Paris in June 1848 or Vienna in October, would appear, in terms both of involvement and objectives, to have more in common with the *sans-culotte* of the French revolution than with twentieth-century socialism. In the transition societies of mid-nineteenth-century Europe, those involved in protest were likely to be the relatively privileged artisans and skilled workers and peasants – those with traditions and a capacity for organiza-tion but whose way of life seemed threatened by economic and social change; less likely was the involvement of the impoverished factory proletariat that a reading of some Marxist texts would seem to suggest. Moreover the former were searching for a compromise with other social groups rather than revolutionary change. That in some circumstances they were driven to revolt was owing to the intransigence of social élites. In any case the experience of 1848 and its aftermath must have been profoundly disillusioning.

However, this should not lead us to underestimate the significance of the nineteenth-century revolutions. They were important stages in the development of mass politicization. As such they heightened the sense of anxiety felt by existing élites, which had largely been created by the experience of the revolu-tionary and imperial wars, and which was substantially reinforced by accelerating economic and social changes. The experience promoted efforts by the various state administrations to develop both more effective means of repression, and, in collaboration with the church, of socialization. These measures enjoyed a considerable degree of success. Even in France, where the social and political rivalries created after 1789 had formed a more combative political culture, the competition for power was subsequently more restrained. When, as in the closing years of the Second Empire, radical republican opposition re-emerged, and the 'red menace' again appeared to threaten, a process of political polarization similar to that of 1848 recurred. Liberals and moderate republicans allied with conservatives in defence of the principles of order. The danger appeared greater than ever when military defeat by Prussia in 1870 destroyed the legitimacy of the Second Empire. This weakening of the central state was accompanied by the establishment, in the hot-house conditions created by the siege of Paris in 1870–1, of the Commune; this was subject to radical and socialist influences, and supported by a civilian National Guard which challenged the state monopoly of armed force. Once again the response of men of property to the threat to their privileges was the employment of brutal military force.

The circumstances were, however, different from those of 1848. In the intervening decades the capacity of established states to respond to discontent had been substantially increased. The construction of the telegraph and railway allowed the swift diffusion of information and movement of military reinforcements. Mass discontent had been reduced by improvements in living standards and a reduction in insecurity. The communications revolution had also ensured the disappearance of the food shortages which had been such a prominent feature of the pre-revolutionary crises of 1789, 1830 and 1848. Major steps had furthermore been taken in the development of both mass education and the mass media as fundamentally conservative institutions of socialization. Therefore, as long as existing state and social systems could preserve their aura of legitimacy by protecting order and prosperity (particularly if this was accompanied by minor concessions of political rights) and their capacity for occasional repression, then revolution was unlikely. War, as the collapse of the Second Empire and the Paris Commune revealed, was the main threat to this stability. Paradoxically in central and eastern Europe it was to be another legacy of 1848 – growing national discontent – which was to cause the major internal and international tensions that eventually led, in 1914, to the war which destroyed the social order created in and after 1848.

Note

1. E. Labrousse, 'Comment naissent les révolutions – 1848 – 1830 – 1789', in *Actes du congrès historique du centenaire de la Révolution de 1848* (Paris, 1948).

Further reading

GENERAL BOOKS

C. H. Church, *Europe in 1830: Revolution and Political Change* (London, 1983); R. J. Goldstein, *Political Repression in Nineteenth Century Europe* (London, 1983); P. Jones, *The 1848 Revolutions* (London, 1981); K. Marx and F. Engels, *The Revolution of 1848* (Harmondsworth, 1973); R. Price, *The Revolutions of 1848* (London, 1988); P. N. Stearns, *Eighteen Forty-Eight* (New York, 1974); M. Traugott, 'The mid-nineteenth-century crisis in England and France', *Theory and Society*, vol. 12 (1983); J. Sperber, *The European Revolutions, 1848–1851* (Cambridge, 1994).

FRANCE

M. Agulhon, *The Republic in the Village: the People of the Var from the French Revolution to the Second Republic* (Cambridge, 1982) and *The Republican Experiment, 1848–1852* (Cambridge, 1983); P. Amann, *Revolution and Mass Democracy: the Paris Club Movement in 1848 France* (Princeton, NJ, 1975); H. A. C. Collingham, *The July Monarchy, 1830–1848* (London, 1988); W. Fortescue, *Revolution and Counter-Revolution in France, 1815–1852* (Oxford, 1988); F. A. de Luna, *The French Republic under Cavaignac, 1848* (Princeton, NJ, 1969); P. McPhee, *The Politics of Rural Life: Political Mobilization in the French Countryside 1846–1852* (Oxford, 1992); T. Margadant, *French Peasants in Revolt: the Insurrection of 1851* (Princeton, NJ, 1979); J. M. Merriman, *The Agony of the Republic: the Repression of the Left in Revolutionary France, 1848–51* (London, 1978); D. Pinkney, *La Révolution de 1830 en France* (Paris, 1988), a revised version of *The French Revolution of 1830* (Princeton, NJ, 1972); R. Price, *The French Second Republic: a Social History* (London, 1972); R. Price (ed.), *Revolution and Reaction: 1848 and the Second French Republic* (London, 1975) and *1848 in France* (London, 1975); M. Traugott, *Armies of the Poor: Determinants of Working-Class Participation in the Parisian Insurrection of June 1848* (Princeton, NJ, 1985).

GERMANY

F. Eyck, *The Frankfurt Parliament, 1848–49* (London, 1968); J. R. Gillis, *The Prussian Bureaucracy in Crisis: 1840–1860* (Stanford, CA, 1971); E. Hahn, 'German parliamentary national aims in 1848–49; a legacy reassessed', in *Central European History*, vol. 13 (1980); T. S. Hamerow, *Restoration, Revolution, Reaction* (Princeton, NJ, 1958) and '1848', in L. Krieger and F. Stern, *The Responsibility of Power* (London, 1968); D. J. Mattheisen, 'History as current events: recent works on the German Revolution of 1848', *American Historical Review*, vol. 88 (1983); P. H. Noyes, *Organization and Revolution: Working Class Associations in the German Revolution of 1848–49* (Princeton, NJ, 1966); L. O'Boyle, 'The Democratic Left in Germany, 1848', *Journal of Modern History*, vol. 33 (1961); W. J. Orr, 'East Prussia and the Revolution of 1848', *Central European History*, vol. 13 (1980); J. Sheehan, *German Liberalism in the Nineteenth Century* (Chicago, Il., 1978); W. Siemann, *Die deutsche Revolution von 1848–49* (Frankfurt, 1985); J. Sperber, *Rhineland Radicals: The Democratic Movement and the Revolution of 1848–1849* (Princeton, NJ, 1991).

THE HABSBURG EMPIRE

R. A. Austensen, 'The making of Austria's Prussian policy, 1848–52', *Historical Journal*, vol. 27 (1984); I. Deák, 'Destruction, revolution or reform: Hungary on the eve of 1848', *Austrian History Yearbook*, vol. 12–13 (1976–7), 'An army divided: the loyalty crisis of the Habsburg officer corps in 1848–1849', *Jahrbuch des Instituts für deutsche Geschichte*, vol. 8 (1979) and *The Lawful Revolution: Louis Kossuth and the Hungarians, 1848–49* (New York, 1979); B. H. Király (ed.), *East Central European Society and War in the Era of Revolutions, 1775–1866* (New York, 1984); S. Z. Pech, *The Czech Revolution of 1848* (Chapel Hill, NC, 1969); R. J. Rath, *The Viennese Revolution of 1848* (Austin, Tex., 1957); A. Sked, *The Survival of the Habsburg Empire: Radetzky, the Imperial Army and the Class War, 1848* (London, 1979).

ITALY

J. Davis, *Conflict and Control. Law and Order in Nineteenth-Century Italy* (London, 1988); P. Ginsborg, *Daniele Manin and the Venetian Revolution of 1848–1849* (Cambridge, 1979); H. Hearder, 'The making of the Roman Republic, 1848–1849', *History*, vol. 60 (1975) and *Italy in the Age of the Risorgimento* (London, 1983); S. Woolf, *A History of Italy, 1700–1860: the Social Constraints of Political Change* (London, 1979).

2

France: the search for stability, 1830–90

ROGER PRICE

Introduction

This is not an exercise in narrative history; instead I want to
examine such fundamental questions as: Who ruled nineteenth-
century France, in whose interests and how? Why can small
groups dominate the mass of the population? These questions
about the nature of politics and the role of the state are frequently
addressed only obliquely by political historians.

Politics involves a struggle for control of the state, the social
institution through which power can be exercised most effectively.
Those who possess it seek to promote wider acceptance of their
own social and political values. The state, therefore, should not
be regarded as politically neutral, a claim frequently made by
conservatives. In France throughout the nineteenth century, in
spite of the revolutionary disorders upon which historians focus,
the social origins and objectives of the bureaucracy changed very
little. This strengthened conservative forces in French society;
their perception of a revolutionary threat inspired a constant
search for the means of reinforcing order and stability and of
minimizing the impact of politics.

A crucial determinant of political behaviour throughout the
century was the experience of the French Revolution, and of the
sustained political mobilization which had occurred in its aftermath. Those who had directly experienced the revolution
transmitted durable mental habits to their children. A new
political culture had been created. The hopes and fears this
represented, interrelated with older social divisions and religious

differences in complex and changing fashion, in numerous distinct communities, to produce a variety of political responses. The establishment of legal equality in 1789 had recognized wealth as the primary social distinction. Throughout the period of constitutional monarchy (1815–48) electoral legislation, which based the franchise on the ability to pay taxes on property, accorded legal recognition to a social élite composed both of nobles and a majority of non-nobles. They opposed the extension of political rights to the poorer classes and with even greater determination resisted every threat, real or supposed, to their rights as owners of property. Access to multi-faceted means of exercising pressure and influence – as officials, landowners, employers and dispensers of charity (in a pre-welfare state) – gave them massive advantages in the political game. Yet nineteenth-century France was beset by revolution. If a sense of unease survived amongst those privileged groups whose property, status or beliefs had been threatened in or after 1789, the same events had left others disappointed by what they felt was incomplete political or social change. A wide diversity of political options emerged including reactionary Catholic monarchism, commitment to the liberal principles of 1789, *sans-culotte* egalitarianism, Jacobin nationalism, and Bonapartism. Each of these signified adherence to highly selective references and images of the revolution (the Declaration of the Rights of Man, the execution of the king, Robespierre, Bonaparte, and so on), indeed to fundamentally different value systems around which political 'parties' (not organized bodies) coalesced and wider support could be mobilized. In effect the way people perceived reality, and thus behaved, continued to be substantially influenced by their conceptions of the revolutionary and imperial period, even when large parts of the urban and particularly rural masses did not consciously adhere to any clearly formulated political ideology.

The return of Louis XVIII in 1815 was generally welcomed because of the prospect of peace. Moreover, the new king realistically accepted the need for compromise with established élites and granted a constitution. Significantly, however, his title stated that he was *par la grâce de Dieu, Roi de France*; his authority derived not from the constitution, but from divine intercession. The liberal heritage of the revolution ensured that stability was to be short-lived. A variety of oppositions criticized government and more fundamentally the favouritism shown to nobles. Fear that Charles X, who became king in 1824, would engineer a *coup d'état* strengthened this opposition, particularly amongst the educated property-owning classes. In July 1830 an ambiguous call for resistance from liberal leaders, which brought lower middle- and working-class opponents of privilege on to the streets in Paris, led to the collapse of a regime which was unprepared for a mass rising. In the aftermath of revolution these liberal politicians were anxious to restore order and avoid social change, so they agreed on a constitution which preserved strong government under Louis-Philippe, secured parliamentary rights and somewhat widened the franchise. These changes satisfied some, but not all, of the critics of the previous regime. Once again those who felt excluded turned to opposition. Significantly, too, the 1830 Revolution, occurring in a period of economic crisis, had awakened the aspirations of the lower-middle classes and workers. The masses re-entered the political arena from which they had largely been excluded since the fall of the Jacobins. In the 1840s, the acceleration of industrial development and of urbanization further stimulated a new awareness of the 'social question'.

Another political crisis in the late 1840s transformed political life. The success of government supporters in the 1846 elections had created a feeling even amongst its parliamentary opponents that only by changing the electoral system did they stand any chance of gaining power. Once again politicians mobilized extra-parliamentary support which led to the collapse of the regime. Moreover, the February 1848 Revolution was followed by the establishment of a republic with manhood suffrage. In this situation, the search for stability took on a new urgency for the social élites which had formerly monopolized political power. Alexis de Tocqueville later remembered Paris, 'in the sole hands of those who owned nothing . . . Consequently the terror felt by all the other classes was extreme; . . . the only comparison was with the feelings of the civilized cities of the Roman world when they suddenly found themselves in the power of the Vandals or Goths.' Léon Faucher and conservatives like him totally rejected the popular demand for social reform, for recognition of the 'right to work' and any criticism of a social order based upon property and 'founded by God himself'. In June the government agreed on the closure of the Paris National Workshops, established in February, which had seemed to promise social reform and greater security for the city's labouring classes. To a large majority of the socially conservative deputies elected in April these had come to symbolize the threat of social revolution. Not surprisingly the workers reacted with insurrection. It seemed as though the revolution for which many of them had fought in February was betrayed. On this occasion, though, they met with a ruthless military response. Even so a *démocrate-socialiste* alliance was subsequently established which attracted considerable support in the general election of May 1849. The old political élites were increasingly afraid that manhood suffrage, which in April 1848 had produced, for them, a satisfactory result, might one day yield a radical parliamentary majority. Increasingly the answer appeared to lie in strong government, preferably through a re-established monarchy. In December 1848 Louis-Napoléon Bonaparte, the great Emperor's nephew, had been elected President of the Republic by a massive majority. After this, when he sought to strengthen his position further by mounting a *coup d'état* in December 1851, conservative notables supported or at least tacitly accepted what was undoubtedly a prelude to the restoration of the Empire. They were encouraged to do so by a rising, especially in the rural south-east, of artisans and peasants who believed that in 1852 they would have secured the election of a Parliament committed to a social and democratic republic. Once again, as in June 1848, military action destroyed hope of a better world. For the conservatives, the 'red spectre' finally seemed to have disappeared.

Conservative élites had been prepared to abdicate political power in favour of dictatorship, but soon they once again demanded a share of power. They could hardly be ignored. Ultimately the regime depended upon their ready compliance as candidates for political and administrative office. The concessions finally made to them, culminating in the establishment of the liberal Empire in 1870, satisfied most but military disaster destroyed the Empire's legitimacy. The republicans seized power in Paris on 4 September 1870. Their commitment to a hopeless war was however rejected by the electorate in February 1871. In the aftermath of this defeat a combination of deliberate provocation and incompetence on the part of the conservative liberal administration headed by Thiers led to another Parisian insurrection and to the Commune which reinforced fear of social revolution. It was, as the moderate and socially conservative republican Jules Simon insisted, 'June 1848, March 1871 – the same struggle', and with the same outcome – a bloodbath in Paris, followed by a search for constitutional arrangements which it was hoped would provide peace and order. From this a republic eventually emerged based on popular sovereignty. The provision of institutionalized channels for expressing grievances helped marginalize violent protest. This was part of a combination of factors which reduced the revolutionary spirit. These included more effective policing, improved living standards due to economic growth, and the continued development of mass education. This facilitated the socialization of the vast majority of French men and women into a national society, which they were taught represented the best possible of all worlds. Thus, by the late 1870s a functioning bourgeois liberal democracy had been created. Although political participation had been extended to wider social groups, power remained essentially the preserve of well-off and well-educated bourgeois, and the threat posed from the 1880s onwards by the rise of organized socialism only renewed their determination to maintain their social privileges.

The revolutionary movements of 1830, 1848 and 1871 resulted from complex economic, social and political crises causing discontent even within élites. In each case these were rapidly followed by the creation of conservative alliances, in which men of property and influence, reactionary monarchists, liberals, and republicans reaffirmed their dedication to the existing social system with all its inequalities, and their willingness to use the state to crush opposition. In the short term, order was restored on the streets by violent repression, and in the longer term it was hoped that 'moral order' and conformist behaviour would be revived, using the church and schools. The historian's fascination with revolution has often obscured the perhaps more fundamental fact that throughout the century France was ruled by men who – whatever their political labels – were committed above all to maintaining social order and the social system. They might disagree on means – and this was a major reason for revolution – but far less on ends. As we shall see, although a gradual extension of the ruling élites occurred, this remained limited by the expensive educational and cultural qualifications which alone allowed access to high office.

Who ruled?

In constitutional terms there occurred a gradual (but not linear) shift in the balance of power from the head of state (monarch or president) towards Parliament and government by elected ministers. Nevertheless until 1870, with the exception of the brief, but crucially important, formative years of the Second Republic (1848–52), substantial power rested with monarchy. Louis XVIII (1815–24), Charles X (1824–30), Louis-Philippe (1830–48) and Napoléon III (President 1848–52, Emperor 1852–70) were men of varying ability who shared a determination to rule. This frequently led to disputes with political groups who felt that their vital interests were neglected, and who sought in response to strengthen the powers of representative institutions. The dangers caused by tension between the authoritarian aspirations of monarchs and the liberal tendencies of many *notables* were clearly revealed in 1830 and 1848, when appeals for the defence of 'liberty' by liberal politicians couched in universalistic terms encouraged mass participation in politics. These revolutions, and that of 1871, encouraged conservative, liberal and many republican politicians to reaffirm their support of strong government – a cycle of revolution and reaction broken only with the establishment of the Third Republic in the 1870s. Another feature of the period – a response both to the desire for political and social stability, and the growing difficulties caused by industrialization and urbanization – was the growth of bureaucracy. In part this essay is concerned with interaction between the state, conceived of as an evolving complex of institutions, and a social system itself undergoing increasingly rapid change. More immediately, we shall examine changes in the balance of power between the various arms of government: executive, legislative and administrative/judicial.

Executive power

The constitutional charter of 1814 was influenced both by British ideas and those of the constitutional monarchists of 1789. It guaranteed equality before the law and the preservation of those liberties central to political debate. It limited the arbitrary power of the monarch by establishing an elected assembly. It also sought, however, to provide for a strong executive power capable of maintaining order, with sole authority to initiate and implement legislation and important exceptional powers for emergency situations. The Chamber of Peers (its members initially named by the king and thereafter hereditary) and of Deputies possessed limited powers, most significantly those of refusing the budget and other legislation. These bodies did, however, serve as major forums for political debate and represented the social élite whose members it would be unwise for any monarch to alienate.

The growth of a liberal opposition determined to ensure that ministers were responsible to Parliament as well as to the king and reflecting dwindling confidence in the government, led to a major constitutional crisis in 1830, and in an ill-judged move Charles X and his ministers reaffirmed monarchical authority by means of ordinances limiting public rights of discussion and further restricting the electorate. The development of this and other crises illustrates two basic points. First, subjects had certain (evolving) expectations of rulers. Continued recognition of the legitimacy of kings depended in large part on their ability to satisfy these expectations. Second, the power of any ruler was diminished by the need to delegate to subordinates upon whose capacity and willingness to co-operate he depended.

The 1830 Revolution altered the balance of power between king and Parliament. The crown was offered to Louis-Philippe after meetings of the Chamber of Deputies and the Chamber of Peers. At the former there were only 252 members (of the 430 eligible) of whom 219 supported revision of the constitutional charter; the latter was even more thinly attended: of the 114 present (of 365 eligible) 89 supported revision. There can be no doubt that the leaders of the liberal majority were anxious to avoid an inter-regnum which might allow radical republican protest, or else a movement in the provinces in support of the deposed king. The charter was to become a right of the nation, not a gift of the Crown; the possibility that the king might again attempt to take advantage of his emergency powers was strictly limited, and the responsi-bilities of Parliament in such matters as the initiation of legislation (formerly reserved to the Crown) greatly enlarged. In spite of efforts by the new king to maintain his authority, particularly in questions of foreign policy, there was a much greater awareness of its practical limits. The changed conception of the nature of government can be seen from revised perceptions of the role of ministers. During the Restoration and especially the reign of Charles X, ministers were essentially servants of the king, functionaries rather than politicians; during the July Monarchy, of 60 ministers, only 4 were not already members of Parliament (20 peers, 36 deputies) and the exceptions hurried to become parliamentarians. It ought to be noted, however, in partial contradiction of this trend that 36 of these ministers were by profession state officials.[1] Office holders appointed in the king's name continued to play a major role in Parliament.

The July Monarchy was succeeded by an experiment in democratic rule following the February Revolution of 1848, and the introduction of manhood suffrage. But the Constituent Assembly elected in April, made up mainly of well-off property-owners, was, particularly after the Parisian insurrection in June, especially anxious to restore strong government. Its constitution provided for the election of a president with substantial powers. In December a large majority voted for a *Prince-President*, Louis-Napoléon Bonaparte, who soon revealed his determination to maximize this authority. On 31 October 1849 a ministry composed of leading parliamentarians was replaced by a team clearly dependent on Bonaparte – an affirmation of presidential government which was a major step towards the re-establishment of an Empire.

The *coup d'état* in December 1851 inaugurated a period of extraordinary and repressive government by decree, ended by the promulgation of the constitution of 14 January 1852. It was based on that of the Year VIII, with the vital addition of universal male suffrage, but with the practical significance of this limited by political censorship and repression. It required little amendment to serve as the constitution of the Empire. It provided for the responsibility of ministers (on an individual, not a collective, basis) to the President (in office for ten years) and subsequently to the Emperor, who alone might initiate laws; for a *Conseil d'État* (its 40–50 members were senior state officials) to prepare and discuss proposals for legislation, which were then to be presented to a *Corps législatif*, elected by universal male suffrage (but meeting only for some three months each year and convoked, adjourned and dissolved almost at will by the Emperor), and a senate made up of members nominated for life (and richly endowed) by the Emperor, which was to interpret the constitution and to be consulted in case of proposed changes. These assemblies were not constitutional checks on authoritarian government, but rather functional parts of that government. The only real power exercised by Parliament was through the examination and vote of the budget and it was some years before it began to make use of this. The Emperor was responsible not to Parliament, but to the 'sovereign people', which would exercise its rights by means of periodic plebiscites – which, however, only he could call.

Not only officials, but deputies and senators, were obliged to swear an oath of loyalty to the constitution and to the Emperor. Louis-Napoléon was determined to eliminate what he regarded as divisive party political squabbling and to maintain effective control over the administration, as a means of promoting economic and social modernization. His was to be a regime above parties, concerned to reconcile all social groups by establishing the conditions for prosperity and social order. Thus, during the 1850s, most major decisions appear to have been taken by the Emperor, usually, but not always, after discussion with individual ministers. These were drawn from a narrow and very wealthy Parisian milieu (one-third nobles and the rest wealthy *haut bourgeois*). They were essentially the Emperor's agents, technocrats, convoked in Council twice a week to discuss an agenda drawn up by him. In a very real sense this was personal government, with the advantage of rapid decisions whenever the Emperor, a man with a sense of mission, determined to 'close the revolutionary era by satisfying the legitimate needs of the people' (proclamation of 2 December 1851), had strong views. It also suffered from the corresponding disadvantage of dependence on the sagacity and health of an individual.

In practice the executive and legislative powers assumed by the Emperor, and the lack of collective ministerial responsibility, meant that members of the disparate group close to Napoleon were able to exert considerable and often undocumented influence. Further confusion was ensured by the opposition and inertia of many senior administrators, most of whom were traditional conservatives. This appreciably limited the Emperor's absolutist pretensions. As Theodore Zeldin has stressed, 'He inherited institutions, customs and legal practices from his predecessors, so that this was a modified rather than a completely reshaped version of previous governments.'

Increasingly, moreover, as their fear of revolution declined, the government required the co-operation of traditional élites, and therefore had to make concessions to their elected representatives in the *Corps législatif*. Unlike his predecessors, Napoléon III appears to have intended to liberalize the political system once the threat of social disorder had declined. He did not however, intend to restore fully the parliamentary regime. Whilst increasing the role of the *Corps législatif* in the formulation and discussion of legislation, the constitutional amendments of the 1860s and the new constitution of 1870 thus preserved considerable prerogative powers for the Emperor, particularly over foreign policy and military affairs, and in the last resort his right of appeal to the people over the head of Parliament through the plebiscite.

The collapse of the Empire, in September 1870, followed by elections in February 1871 on the issue of war or peace, led to an Assembly with a majority of monarchists whose factions could not agree, however, on the constitutional form of another Bourbon restoration. They were thus forced to tolerate as an interim measure the establishment of a politically repressive conservative Republic. After the use made by Louis-Napoléon of the executive powers of the presidency it was however decided that these ought to be severely limited. So the constitution of 1875 established a parliamentary regime with the clear statement that, 'ministers are collectively responsible to the Chambers'. The President was to be elected by Parliament in the hope that he would have very little authority against it. Even though the right to appoint a prime minister gave him potential power, President MacMahon failed in May 1877 to form a government (because he lacked the confidence of what had, by then, become a republican parliamentary majority), making the limits clear. Although, especially in foreign affairs and through regular attendance at cabinet meetings, some presidents were able to exert substantial influence, throughout the Third Republic the effective head of government was the Prime Minister (*Président du Conseil*), presiding over – with more or less authority – a cabinet of ministers. In the 1870s–80s these continued to be drawn from a narrow social circle composed of landowners and *hautes fonctionnaires* (wealthy nobles and non-nobles), with smaller contingents of financiers and lawyers, including most notably Orléanist financiers, in other words, men who personally represented the fusion of the old and new political and socio-economic élites. Only subsequently, as a recent study of members of cabinets between 1870 and 1914 indicates, did a gradual and limited democratization of recruitment occur, with two decisive moments of change: the first in 1887 after the electoral success of the opportunist republicans, and the second in 1902 with the election victory of the radicals.[2]

The sons of bourgeois professional families gradually replaced those of large landowners and capitalistic entrepreneurs, and a marked professionalization of politics occurred. The former were less wealthy, but still very comfortably off – 42 per cent of them were in the legal professions (indicating the advantages conferred by knowledge of the law, practice in public speaking, and the benefits of a legal career for political notoriety) and some were co-opted by major enterprises anxious to promote links with government. To an important extent a shared culture and a commitment to private property united groups 4, 5 and 6 in Table 2.1. Nevertheless, it is worth stressing the growing social gulf between this politically dominant group and a wealth-owning élite. This development had the advantage however of creating an illusion of social democratization which republican ministers sought to reinforce by appeals for justice and equality.

Table 2.1   Professions of fathers of 320 ministers (1871–1914)

		% in active male population (1851 census)	% amongst ministers' fathers
1	Workers, farmers, clerks	78	6.5
2	Primary teachers, public officials, master artisans	10.4	9.7
3	Property-owning petty bourgeoisie	5.2	10
4	Professional bourgeoisie	1.8	37.8
5	Senior state officials	0.1	8.4
6	Landowners	5.1	25.9

Parliament

The decline in the authority of the titular head of state was matched by the growing importance of Parliament, with final recognition in the 1870s that governments were responsible to democratically elected bodies. Parliament served as a forum for particular interest groups, facilitating mediation between their conflicting claims but on a very unequal basis. It reflected differences in social power and influence even after the establishment of universal male suffrage.

If the question of parliamentary authority was one major element in political debate for most of the century, so too was the question of the electoral franchise. The 1814 charter sought to provide both strong royal government and to allow consultation of the 'nation'. Responsibility for the initiation of legislation therefore lay with the Crown, and Parliament's role was limited to discussion and voting without right of amendment. Moreover, the Restoration sought to reinforce the influence of traditional élites. Thus the Chamber of Peers was accorded great dignity and equal position to the lower house in the legislative process. However, it was rarely able to influence public opinion. Its members were clearly dependent on the king for their titles and pensions and its meetings received little publicity. For the election of deputies the right to vote was limited in 1817 to those paying 300 francs in direct taxation. In a predominantly rural society the electorate was composed primarily of landowners, together with, particularly in the economically active regions of the north, significant numbers of professional men, merchants and manufacturers. The illiberal character of the system was reinforced by electoral manipulation and outright repression, especially of unenfranchised groups. In addition, candidates for election had to be at least 40, and had to pay 1,000 francs per annum in direct taxes. Deputies were obviously men of independent means. Yet because there was no incompatibility between the mandate of deputy and administrative functions, governments were encouraged to attempt to construct reliable majorities through the use of patronage. Of the 430 deputies in 1829, 38.5 per cent were officials; 41.5 per cent large landowners; 14.8 per cent were in economic professions and 5.2 per cent liberal professions, although there was considerable overlap between these categories. In particular many officials were also landowners, and many of the latter had served the state in some capacity. Significantly too, some 40 per cent of deputies were nobles (58 per cent in 1821).[3] Although not politically homogeneous these provided the most steadfast supporters for conservative and reactionary policies. In practice, during the Restoration and to an even greater degree in the July Monarchy, Parliament represented an élite experiencing the transition from a land-based society of orders to an urban-industrial class structure.

Each year during the Restoration parliamentary sessions lasted six months – from November/January to, at the latest, July – and during this period speeches received extensive coverage in the press, particularly as they were uncensored. In spite of restrictions, the charter guaranteed certain liberties essential to the develop-ment of political life, so that the liberal opponents of Charles X, frustrated by their limited influence on government policy, were able to mobilize public opinion in their favour. During the 1830 political crisis the king and his ministers were thus led to implement measures designed to reduce the electorate in the hope of confining it to the wealthiest and generally most conservative groups in society, measures which provoked protest, revolution and substantial modification of the constitution. This left the Chamber of Peers with very little constitutional power, although the economic, social and political significance of its members as part of the social élite should not be ignored. The hereditary peerage was abolished so that membership came to depend on royal nomination. Most significant, however, was the reduction in the tax qualification required of candidates for the lower house and for their electors to 500 francs and 200 francs respectively. This roughly doubled the number of voters to 200,000, with some 56,000 eligible for election by 1840. Nationally one in every 170 inhabitants could vote (compared with one in 25 in Britain after 1832). Voting remained a prerogative of those with the intellectual capacity and stake in society which possession of property was assumed to signify, although the number of voters was gradually allowed to increase as a result of economic growth.

In a rural area like Loir-et-Cher there were, by 1847, 1,947 electors of whom 54 were very rich landowners (including 23 nobles) paying over 2,000 francs in direct taxes; 447, mainly landowners, paying over 500 francs; and the 1,446 others (paying 200–500 francs) included landowners (about 400), well-off peasants (about 400), members of the liberal professions (including 94 notaries, 10 solicitors, 30 barristers, 50 doctors) and of the economic professions (100 millers, 50 innkeepers, 100 shopkeepers and 50 artisans).[4] Most electors appear to have been subject to the influence of the large landowners. A small electorate inevitably made for highly personalized electoral campaigns in which a variety of influences could be brought to bear. In 1839, the election during the July Monarchy in which most seats were contested, 138 deputies were elected with fewer than 150 votes, 27 with fewer than 100. In many departments elections were dominated by the competition for power and status between a few wealthy families and their clienteles.

The extension of the franchise in 1830, together with the rejection by many nobles of the new regime, seems to have had a limited but significant effect on the composition of the Chamber due to the more substantial representation both of business (although this was not sustained) and professional men (the latter having more in common with office-holders than with business-men). Nevertheless, landowners together with office-holders, that is, the more traditional social groups, continued to dominate Parliament. Indeed regardless of socio-professional categorization most deputies owned land.

In the Chamber of 1840, 38 per cent of the deputies were officials; 29 per cent landowners without other professions although most had at one time had a profession; 19 per cent members of the liberal professions, mainly lawyers; and 13 per cent of economic professions. It remained the domain of a pre-industrial élite although only 13 per cent had *ancien régime* titles. By 1846 the Chamber had become rather more aristocratic. Over 25 per cent of deputies were members of the *ancien régime* nobility and another 9.3 per cent imperial nobles, indicating that the retreat of the aristocracy in 1830 was not definitive.[6] However, if there were

Table 2.2   Composition of the Chamber of Deputies (percentages)[5]

	1829	1831
Businessmen (*grande bourgeoisie*)	14	17
Professional men	5	12
Public office holders	40	38
Proprietors	31	23
Unidentified	10	10

relatively few businessmen in the Assembly a growing number of deputies belonging to the other socio-professional categories had business interests.

Rather than any deep-seated ideological divisions what is striking about debates in the Chamber throughout the July Monarchy is the concern of deputies with the preservation of social order and the representation of local and regional economic interests, on questions of customs tariffs and taxes, for example. Once the threat of further revolution had passed (by around 1834) parliamentary politics was reduced to a constant struggle between personalities and between 'ins' and 'outs' for control of official patronage – a means of winning elections as well as of reinforcing social status. Not surprisingly most deputies and probably most electors opposed a wider franchise; it would have threatened their exclusive position. However, some individuals were alienated from the regime because of their failure to secure election or government office, and larger numbers were disillusioned by the narrowness of the electorate and by accusations of corruption which served to discredit the regime and build up pressures for reform. Even amongst the privileged members of the electorate there was considerable discontent about a situation in which of 459 deputies elected in 1846, 287 were government officials. Most of these supported the ministers in power who themselves did not hesitate to use dismissal and promotion to influence voting behaviour.

After the February Revolution in 1848 the constraints on electoral participation were suddenly lifted, and manhood suffrage and freedom of the press and of assembly were established. There was also a substantial decline in electoral manipulation by government agents. The Constituent Assembly elected in April, however, differed little in social composition from the assemblies of the July Monarchy, although the numbers of both business and professional men seem to have increased. Candidates continued to be selected by small, politically versed oligarchies. Subsequently, fear of social revolution engendered a conservative reaction involving growing restraints upon political freedom. And, during the legislative assembly elected in May 1849, efforts to limit the franchise through a three-year residence qualification removed some three million voters from the electoral register. Even this, however, could not eliminate conservative

anxiety that the Left might gain electoral victories in the 1852
presidential and legislative elections. This explains the support of
conservative and liberal politicians for Louis-Napoléon's *coup
d'état* in December 1851. Guizot, Prime Minister during the July
Monarchy, regretted that 'We have not known how to safeguard
free government; we must now support the necessary power; it
has today a mission of flagellation, expiation, repression of
anarchy which none other could accomplish'. The original mark
of this dictatorship was the restoration of universal male suffrage.
It also, however, substantially altered the rules of the political
game by greatly reducing the powers of Parliament. Indicative of
this was the provision of the Constitution of 14 January 1852 that
the Emperor was personally 'responsible to the French people' –
a responsibility sanctioned by the plebiscite, a means of consulting
the population on essential decisions (although it was not
employed between 1852 and 1870 because of the risk that a
majority insufficiently vast would damage the regime's prestige).
To underline the fundamental separation between the executive
and the legislature, ministers were forbidden to be members of the
Corps législatif (modified from 1860, when three ministers
without portfolio attended to explain and defend government
proposals). They were to be responsible to the Emperor alone.

The object – in the wake of 1848 – was to combine democracy
and strong monarchical government, with the plebiscite and
elections serving to mobilize public support for the regime and to
legitimize its actions. Louis-Napoléon was determined to end the
'perpetual effervescence' of his contemporaries and to depoliticize
questions of national interest. The constitution provided for a
senate of 180, made up of senators named for life who were to
include senior army officers and state officials, representatives of
the Church and of industry and banking, together with the
imperial princes and other dignitaries of the regime. Their
permanence was supposed to guarantee independence. The main
functions of the senate were to oppose laws contrary to the
constitution, to religion, morality, individual liberty and equality,
the sanctity of private property and the security of France; and
through the *senatus consultum* to interpret and amend the
constitution. The senate was thus the guardian of liberty, and
appeared to possess considerable power; but in practice this
gathering of aged pensioners of the state showed little desire to

oppose the government. The lower house, the *Corps législatif*, with just over 260 deputies elected by universal male suffrage, voted on legislative proposals and taxes, and by rejecting these might exercise real influence over the government. It was in consequence important for the regime to determine its membership, which it attempted to do by refining the system of government-sponsored candidatures typical of its predecessors.

Official candidates were usually selected by the prefect from amongst local *notables*. Once selected they were supported by the entire administrative machine. As the opposition newspaper *L'Atelier du Gers* complained in 1868, 'In each commune the official candidate has the services of ten civil servants, free and disciplined agents who put up his papers and distribute his ballot papers and his circulars; one mayor, one deputy-mayor, one school master, one constable, one road man, one bill sticker, one tax collector, one postman, one licensed innkeeper, one tobacconist, appointed, approved and authorised by the Prefect'. The government felt bound to 'enlighten' the electorate. Opponents met with every kind of obstruction. These tactics were especially successful in the still relatively unpoliticized countryside. If they failed, constituency boundaries could be 'gerrymandered'. But the regime could not create a Bonapartist party of dependent newcomers. It thus failed to escape from dependence upon established conservative élites. Napoleon's close associate Persigny lamented, 'We, who have our friends only down below, have abandoned Parliament to the upper classes'. Even in its most authoritarian phase the government was never able to ignore entirely the opinions of a parliamentary body composed of representatives of the social élite.

Although parliamentary consent was required for laws, deputies were unable to initiate legislation. Their essential power was to accept or reject projected laws *en bloc*, something which, particularly in the case of the budget, deputies were rarely willing to consider, given that total rejection would paralyse the state. The responsibility for drafting laws and administrative regulations, for discussing amendments proposed by Parliament and, until 1860, for defending government proposals, rested with the forty to fifty members, mainly jurists, of the *Conseil d'Etat*. This was the supreme administrative tribunal, which now received considerable political power, although it remained clearly subordinate to a government which could dismiss its members at will, depriving them of large salaries and good career prospects. The inevitable lack of authority of such a body was reinforced by the hostility towards it of the ministers, bureaucrats and deputies whose legislation and amendments it criticized. This eventually forced the government to establish a direct relationship between itself and the *Corps législatif* in 1860, by means of ministers without portfolio who explained and defended its proposals in Parliament. Thus Parliament gradually increased its influence over government decisions partly by means of the publicity accorded to its debates.

These developments highlighted the essential problem of the Bonapartist regime – its inability to escape from dependence on the traditional social élite, men who politically were more likely to be conservative liberals than Bonapartists even when they served in such key institutions as the *Conseil d'Etat*. Although the proportion of businessmen in Parliament was slightly higher than before, most official candidates were landowners and members of the liberal professions, with the necessary wealth and leisure to serve as virtually unpaid deputies. Moreover it was now accepted that the holding of administrative office was incompatible with the mandate of deputy; and this deprived the government of a means of influence which it had used to some effect during the July Monarchy.

Table 2.3   Occupation of Second Empire deputies[7]

Businessmen	24%
Lawyers and other liberal professions	20%
Former government officials	26%
Landowners (without other profession)	19%
Retired soldiers	8%

Whatever their political divisions most parliamentarians shared a fear of democracy, a desire for cheap government and for the preservation of their own local and ultimately national influence. Inevitably their support for the regime was conditional. The establishment of the Emperor's strong personal power was widely acceptable in the face of a revolutionary threat but became less so as the menace diminished. Politicians began to demand the return to a parliamentary system as the only means of controlling a

regime which seemed financially extravagant and too adventurous in foreign policy. After 1860 concessions from the Emperor
gradually strengthened parliamentary financial control, and in
May 1869 substantially enlarged the freedom of the press and
meeting. Even the system of official candidature was virtually
abandoned in many areas in 1869, in the face of growing resentment of governmental interference in electoral decisions. The final
act of liberalization in 1870 considerably increased the powers of
Parliament, and allowed deputies to initiate legislation and question
ministers. This was still not a parliamentary regime given that
ministers were responsible to the Emperor alone, but for government to work the support of Parliament was necessary. Considerable concessions had thus been made, although substantial
dissatisfaction remained amongst liberals (including the new
Président du Conseil, Ollivier himself), particularly with the
ambiguous position of ministers.

　　The collapse of the Empire, followed by an election fought on
the issue of war or peace, led to a National Assembly dominated
by conservatives and monarchists determined to preserve social
order. The regime of *ordre moral* borrowed many of its predecessor's
forms of political repression and manipulation, but could not
prevent a gradual republicanization of the assembly. This took
place at the level of representation; successive elections shifted the
balance of support within Parliament in favour of moderate
republicans committed to social order and away from the
supporters of already discredited monarchist pretenders. At the
constitutional level a series of laws in 1875 established collective
ministerial responsibility to Parliament in spite of the resistance of
the monarchist President Marshal MacMahon. The new authority
of Parliament can be seen in such developments as the extension
of sessions, the continued questioning of ministers, the numerous
bills and amendments proposed by deputies, the increased
importance of permanent parliamentary commissions, and
frequent ministerial changes. However, the effectiveness of
parliamentary control continued to be limited by the shortness of
parliamentary sessions (around 450 hours per year even in the
1900s), by an anarchical procedure which allowed an excessive
number of questions and interminable discussions, and by the
representation of a number of poorly disciplined party groups and
the ease with which governments were brought down. Ministers

spent much of their time doing favours for deputies and their constituents in an effort to safeguard their places. The 'good' minister, in the eyes of deputies, was always available. Ministers were also subject to constant pressure from multi-party groups of deputies interested in particular issues. In 1900 around 218 deputies belonged to the *groupe agricole*, 109 to the colonial group, 175 were interested in lay education, and 56 in industry, commerce, etc. Deputies themselves constantly intervened on behalf of constituents, hoping to build a grateful clientele and safeguard their seats. The protection of local interests frequently outweighed party loyalty.

In this period too the social origins of parliamentary deputies began to change. A slow 'democratization' of political personnel occurred with an influx of *moyen bourgeois* and especially members of the liberal professions who replaced traditional *notables* and particularly landowners. Even so, Parliament remained dominated by well-off bourgeois. In 1893 88 per cent were of *grand* or *moyen bourgeois* origin. Even in 1900 there were barely 30 deputies with peasant or working-class origins. Only the radical electoral victory in 1902 brought a more substantial influx of lower-middle-class personnel, reflecting the establishment of modern political parties and mass politics. Nevertheless most deputies remained property owners, many of them using politics not only as a means of access to political power but to new opportunities for income. These were major factors promoting economic and social immobility throughout the Third Republic, with the conservatism of the lower house reinforced by that of a senate elected by the representatives of communes and thus mainly designed to represent rural interests. Senators were primarily retired deputies and civil servants, and consistently obstructed proposals for income tax, old age pensions, the improvement of factory conditions, etc. Thus in spite of the changing social characteristics of Parliament and the widening gap between political and economic power, the interests of the old social élite were safeguarded, along with those of the new political élite.

How?

Bureaucracy

Identification of the key political decision-makers is the essential first stage in an examination of the process of government. The next is to look at the role of the bureaucracy, and at the judges and police, who acted as intermediaries between the law-makers and the rest of the population. At the higher levels, senior officials exercised a major influence on policy. Further down the hierarchy, at the level of the community, subordinate officials and the police represented authority for the mass of the population.

The French bureaucracy evolved slowly, but it was during the period of revolution and Empire that the institutions of the modern centralized state were largely created. At first the revolution had reacted against excessive centralization, but the exigencies of war and internal disorder soon forced a reversal and the creation of new state organizations. The traditional functions of the state had been waging war, maintaining internal order, and appropriating sufficient resources through taxation and recruitment to meet these objectives. The period with which we are concerned saw a considerable extension of the activities of state, in spite of the liberal non-interventionist ideologies favoured by the authorities. To a large degree this was because of the growing complexity of a modernizing society, and the need to support larger and more complex military establishments, as well as to ameliorate the social effects of industrialization and urbanization. Particularly significant in this context were efforts to improve communications (roads, rail, telegraph and literacy); this contributed to the more effective penetration of society by the state.

In consequence, one feature of the nineteenth century was the growth in the number of public servants. In 1830 there were 119,000; Parisian ministries employed no more than 5,000 people, including over 3,000 in the Ministry of Finance, and administrations annexed to it, but only 88 at Foreign Affairs and 87 at Justice. Paying them cost some 150 million francs (about 13 per cent of the budget). Then as always there were considerable complaints about the burden this imposed. Subsequently numbers rose precipitately – from 188,000 to 265,000 during the Second Empire, and to 776,000 in 1913, with the result that whilst there was one civil servant per 261 inhabitants in 1839, there was one per 85 in 1914.[8] Of these, perhaps 10,000 exercised significant authority. Who were these civil servants? The middle and lower classes provided willing recruits for the lower ranks despite low salaries and poor promotion prospects because of the status, security and pensions offered by the civil service. At the upper level they were men with the education and culture necessary for full membership of the social élite. Although technical, and particularly legal, qualifications were increasingly valued, wealth and the ability to adopt the proper life-style remained essential. It seems also to have been generally assumed that family traditions of service provided useful preparation for the future civil servant. The traditional bourgeoisie and nobles therefore continued to be attracted to state office rather than to business or the professions. It provided them with a respectable means of reinforcing their social status and a useful supplement to incomes which for some time continued to be primarily derived from land-ownership. In spite of political upheavals, followed by extensive purges as new regimes sought both to reward their supporters and to place trusted individuals in key offices, the habits and recruitment practices of the administration changed very little.

The recruitment of senior civil servants ensured that the same relatively small and cohesive social groups held considerable economic, political and administrative power throughout the century. This can be seen from an analysis of the social origins of senior officials during the Second Empire.[9]

Clearly strong family traditions of bureaucratic service existed. Adopting another form of classification indicates that 95, 82 and 87 per cent respectively of these officials were drawn from wealthy bourgeois or aristocratic families.

Table 2.4 Social origins of senior officials in the Second Empire

	Directors of Ministries	Conseillers d'Etat	Préfets
sons of:			
Politicians	2%	12%	4%
State officials	57%	53%	63%
Propriétaires	19%	14%	16%
Liberal professions	17%	21%	17%
Unknown	5%	–	–

During the Third Republic the social backgrounds of ministers and deputies and those of members of the administrative élites diverged to some extent, owing to the limited democratization of political recruitment. Even in 1900 two-thirds to three-quarters of a sample of individuals at the head of the various administrative hierarchies continued to be drawn from aristocratic and especially traditional wealthy bourgeois families. Such marginal change as had taken place since mid-century occurred partly for political reasons, partly because of the sheer expansion of the civil service, and partly because members of the old élites had been attracted towards more lucrative employment in large-scale private enterprise.

The *grand corps – Conseil d'Etat, Cour des comptes, Inspection des Finances*, the prefectoral and diplomatic corps – maintained their 'snob' appeal in part because of the socially élitist character of their recruitment. Patronage was another factor helping to preserve the character of the higher administration. Only very gradually did a modern bureaucracy with objective, meritocratic criteria for appointment and promotion develop. Competitive recruitment was slowly introduced. It emerged in the technical corps in the eighteenth century, in 1842 for the *Inspection des Finances*; for the *Cour des comptes* in 1856; for the Foreign Ministry in 1880. The establishment in April 1848 of an *Ecole nationale d'administration* showed a desire for more far-reaching reform but it soon disappeared in the face of conservative suspicion. Even with the advent of competitive recruitment the costs of a higher education, of an unremunerated *stage* in the administration, the unwritten requirements for style in dress and manners and the all-important contacts in the higher administration, all meant that most of the competitors, for a maximum of 500 high-level posts per annum at mid-century, were drawn from a restricted and homogeneous social milieu. Only as the size of the bureaucracy grew, particularly after 1880, was more space created for recruitment outside the social élite.

It is very much easier to describe the structure of an administrative system than to judge its effectiveness. For one thing so much has been deliberately concealed that there might be a considerable gulf between administrative regulations and daily practice, for another, criticism of bureaucracy as inefficient, over-staffed and too expensive is almost a reflex action in many political quarters.

Even so, if the development of bureaucratic routine was essential to the effective conduct of business, its reliance upon precedent could also be stultifying. Certainly the major purges in 1815, 1830, 1848 and in the 1870s involved not only the dismissal of experienced officials but, by creating considerable insecurity in the administration, discouraged initiative. More generally, centralized control over the system continued to be impeded by a weak tax base which placed a limit upon the numbers of professional officials; by the inertia and ill-will of many part-time local officials and particularly communal mayors; and by the slowness of communications by word of mouth, letter or semaphore prior to the advent of the railway and the electric telegraph in the 1840s and 1850s, and the telephone in the late 1880s. (The semaphore network, 5,000 kilometres long in 1844, had limited capacity.) These factors combined to leave central government poorly informed about local developments. Furthermore administrative techniques and training responded only slowly to the increasingly complex demands of a changing society.

The basis of the administrative system was the prefectoral corps, established in 1880. The prefect appointed by the Minister of the Interior was responsible for the maintenance of law and order, but also for all other state services in his department. These powers were reinforced by a decree of 25 March 1852 which remained in force until 1964. He also served as the eyes of the central government, providing the various ministries with regular reports. In effect his role was to serve as the crucial link between the central government and the provinces, his special status to be affirmed by his uniform, high salary and official residence. Paradoxically, for most of the century the resources available for performing these various tasks were pitifully slight. In 1816 an important prefecture such as that of Calvados functioned with 26 officials and 5 general labourers, at a total cost, including salaries, of 48,000 francs. The prefecture of Pas-de-Calais had a staff of 26 until the turn of the century; the numbers rose to 52 in 1914.[10] At the level of the *arrondissement*, the *sous-préfectures* had three to five personnel.

At least until the 1840–50s the slowness of communications allowed *préfets* considerable freedom of initiative, especially in a crisis. Career ambitions, however, enjoined caution. This can be seen in the regular reports which were the fundamental source of information (and misinformation) for the central government. The quality of reporting obviously depended upon the ability of individual prefects and their subordinates, but in general had serious shortcomings. The reports reflected an 'administrative attitude', presenting the common opinions of members of the socio-professional élite. Many prefects seem to have operated on the principle that voluminous reports were appreciated, and the golden rule was to tell superiors what they wanted to hear – a tactic likely to induce a sense of complacency. Another rule was to avoid succumbing to local influences. They were rarely posted to regions in which they had personal interests. However, their effectiveness to a large degree depended upon the establishment of good relationships with local *notables* and this might in certain circumstances lead to a conflict of loyalties. It also, particularly under the monarchies, required frequent (and expensive) entertaining (for which a wife was almost a necessity) and a constant round of visits to agricultural shows, learned societies, firemen's banquets, etc. The cost of maintaining 'appearances' and subscribing to local charities, could be a heavy burden on a prefect's private income.

Concepts of the role of prefects appear to have shifted over time. From the late 1840s, as the pace of economic and social change accelerated, a range of new problems increased their importance. Moreover, after the 1848 Revolution political surveillance was intensified, and the tasks of selecting official parliamentary candidates, and then of managing their election, developed into a fine art during the Second Empire. Success in this was regarded as the clearest proof of efficiency. These often competing demands nevertheless imposed strains upon the system. Many prefects adopted the habit of referring politically delicate decisions to Paris, and by the late 1860s the prefect was increasingly expected to be a competent all-round administrator rather than a political manipulator.

Interaction between government and society is best examined at the local level, at which it becomes relevant for most of the population. There centralized control through the hierarchical administration often broke down. For much of the century central government was forced by the small size of its own bureaucracy to rely upon the assistance of local *notables*. This was especially so outside the larger towns in which the representatives of the central bureaucracy were based. Finding suitable (politically reliable and competent) candidates for the key posts of mayor and deputy mayor in over 36,000 communes was a constant problem. The integration of communal administration within a hierarchy was nevertheless a major contribution of the revolutionary-imperial period to increasing efficiency and centralized control, and at the same time a limitation on the capacity of local communities for collective opposition to the state. Gradually the central authorities increased their control. This shift in the balance between the centre and the locality occurred as part of a broad process involving greater state intervention in the economy, the development of representative government, urbanization and cultural integration, and the more successful co-option of local élites by the central power. All of these developments contributed to more effective penetration of the local community by representatives of the state.

The selection of a mayor was crucial. He had important functions within the administrative and police hierarchies, and as an electoral agent. Suitably qualified candidates were not always easy to find. In the early part of the century, and especially in isolated rural communes, prefects might even have to accept political opponents, providing that these did not push their opposition too far. The danger, from the point of view of Paris, was that, particularly in rural communes, where the mayor was the sole representative of the government, he would be parochial in outlook, or subject to pressure from important local families.

Another problem was the existence of communal councils. A law in 1800 had provided for prefectoral nomination of local councillors. Another law in 1831 created a municipal electorate of over two million, mainly bourgeois but including a minority of artisans and peasants (about one in four or five of the adult male population, compared with one in fifteen in legislative elections). It also provided for the selection of the mayor from the elected councillors. In 1848 the right to vote at municipal level was extended to all adult males. As a reflection of the importance of the office, until 1884 (except during the Second Republic) the mayors of towns with a population of over 2,500 continued to be appointed by the government, usually from the ranks of the municipal councillors. Thus in large cities mayors appointed were normally wealthy business or professional men. Existing local élites were clearly difficult to displace, even with manhood suffrage.

With the exception of large towns, municipal elections had more to do with local social structures than with political ideologies – and these, when present, often shrouded personal rivalries. During periods of political turbulence such as August 1830 or February-March 1848 substantial changes in personnel might occur. Initially municipal revolutions might be stimulated by the change in government in Paris, and local opposition groups might replace or impose themselves on existing councils. Subsequently personnel might change through election; and finally, during ensuing periods of political reaction prefects might suspend unreliable mayors or councils. Furthermore, a decree in 1852 (in force until 1866) provided for the selection of the mayor from outside the council if this were considered necessary. This represented a reaction against democratic election which, according to one *sous-préfet* 'makes objective surveillance of the rural communes almost impossible. Some mayors are pusillanimous and close their eyes; others, chosen by the masses, adhere to the principles of demagogy and socialism.' Clearly, the administrative and political roles were judged to be incompatible. The ideal mayor was a respectable and reasonably well-off landowner or professional man who obeyed prefectoral instructions.

In addition to dismissals, more subtle pressure could be exerted on local councils especially in impoverished rural communes through, for example, the provision of subsidies for road works or the construction of schools. More generally, however, the growing provision of a variety of services was accompanied by ever closer control by the prefect, particularly through insistence on minimum standards and supervision of local finances. From the 1840s, the large cities were supplied with water and gas, sewers, pavements, street lighting, their worst slums were demolished and increased schooling was provided, all of which contributed to a substantial growth in municipal expenditure and to a growing professionalization of municipal administration. Eventually socialist electoral victories in some towns in 1892 and 1896 posed a new threat to government control. Local initiatives were taken to democratize municipal finance, create municipal enterprises, improve the provision of public assistance, and to encourage efforts by workers to organize themselves. These, it was claimed, were the prelude to the establishment of a new form of administration within the bourgeois state. The central authority strove to prevent this by means of tighter prefectoral controls and if necessary by the suspension of socialist mayors.

Throughout the century Paris enjoyed a special status. Legislation during the Consulate had provided for two prefects, one the Prefect of Police, responsible for the maintenance of order, the other the Prefect of the Seine, for the remaining mayoral functions. In practice conflict over responsibilities was frequent. Members of the *Conseil général* of the Seine nominated by the senate were to act as a municipal council. Furthermore, the capital was divided into 12 *arrondissements*, each with a mayor whose functions were decorative rather than real. The establishment of an elected municipal council in 1834 did not significantly reduce prefectoral power, but did require more tact from the prefects. Louis-Napoléon, like his uncle, saw the city as the national capital, as a subject for government rather than municipal control. With his close collaborator Haussmann as Prefect of the Seine he sought to create a capital fit for the Empire and throughout the 1850s major public works were authorized simply by decree. The nominated municipal council proved docile. Then, when the Empire collapsed the cycle of democratization and the re-imposition of the central control of 1848 was repeated. The Paris Commune ensured that conservatives would reassert firm administrative control over the capital. Not until the 1880s did the prefects again experience difficulty with the Parisian city council.

The legal system

To an important degree the administration established a framework for daily life by means of decrees and laws. To an even greater extent, its own activities were determined by such a framework. The law in effect was both a major means of exercising state authority, and additionally – and this is of crucial significance – of legitimizing it. There was an increasingly widespread acceptance of the ideal of the state enforcing law and order in the interests of all. The legal system was also (particularly for those who could afford recourse to it) an important means of resolving private disputes. A range of important questions needs to be asked about the internal coherence and values of the legal system, and its development as a social institution. In particular it has to be considered whether and, to what degree, this legal system represented the interests of particular social groups. In addition it would be useful, if only space permitted, to consider the attitudes of citizens towards the law, the degree to which community custom and external legislation might conflict, and the extent to which citizens' own norms of behaviour were defined by outside authorities.

Although important continuities of personnel and procedure survived the revolution, the legal codes introduced between 1804 and 1810 replaced a common law based upon a confused mixture of legislation and precedent and ended the conflict of competences so characteristic of the *ancien régime*. Under the new system the three major courts of appeal – the *Conseil d'Etat, Cour de Cassation* and *Cour des Comptes* – were conceived as both the summits of the judicial hierarchy and as part of the state administration. This interpenetration of administration and justice and the legal training so common amongst civil servants imposed a legalistic outlook and concern with precedent on all sections of the bureaucracy. More significantly, perhaps, it produced a conception of the relationship between state and society which assumed that the law was an independent arbitrator and which largely ignored the reality of unequal access to the legal system.

In the crucially important area of property law the *code civil* was a compromise between custom and Roman law. This attempt to create a unitary system of law was most successful in those areas, such as Burgundy, in which the existing customary regime was quite similar. But even there it was necessary for some considerable time to respect existing customary practice in such matters as water rights, gleaning, etc. This innate conservatism was reinforced by the frequent recruitment of magistrates (judges, state prosecuting attorneys, *juges d'instruction* who supervised investigations, and justices of the peace) from amongst families with a legal tradition. In practice the costs of an education culminating in a *licence en droit*, of an apprenticeship as an unpaid (until 1910) substitute or *juge suppléant*, ensured that magistrates came from relatively well-off and generally landowning families. The importance of personal recommendation and co-option, rather than competition (definitively established only in 1906) reinforced this.

The key figures in the administration of justice were the government's senior prosecuting attorneys (*procureurs-généraux*) of whom there were 27 until 1860 and 28 thereafter, each responsible for a *ressort* of two to four departments (or seven in the case of Paris). They co-ordinated the activity of a network of *procureurs* at *arrondissement* level, and of justices of the peace – the latter with a limited competence for dealing with minor criminal and civil matters – at cantonal level. In addition to their judicial functions these officials all had important administrative and political roles in providing information of all kinds to their hierarchical superiors and were used as a means of supplementing and also of checking on the parallel hierarchy of the prefectoral corps. The political importance of the magistrature was made clear by the frequency with which its ranks were purged. Good cause was always found to remove those magistrates of too independent a spirit, even though their judgements and integrity were supposedly valued and their tenure theoretically protected. Their local influence and potential role in political repression meant that their offices were too important to be left in the hands of opponents. As part of the executive power, the public prosecutors were anyway not so protected. Substantial changes of personnel occurred at all levels in 1814–15, 1830, throughout the stormy years of the Second Republic when dismissal following the February Revolution was regarded as a good qualification for appointment in 1849–51, in 1870 and again in 1879–83, when a purge was accompanied by the mass resignation of Catholics unwilling to implement measures against the religious congregations. Moreover, personal rivalries and patronage resulted in a complex and continuing competition for office. By the 1880s, however, it was accepted that magistrates, to maintain public respect, must abstain from political activity altogether.

Legislation was formulated and implemented by members of the relatively well-off classes and inevitably reflected their social attitudes. It was administered so as to reward conformists and to punish deviants. Justice was often a myth masking injustice, a view immortalized by Daumier's unflattering caricatures of judges as birds of prey. The essential mission of justice, it was asserted – particularly in moments of social crisis – was to preserve certain 'eternal' social values and to defend the foundations of civilized society: property, the family and religion. A law in 1819 condemned 'all outrages against public religious morality'. This inspired the socialist Proudhon's prosecution in 1858 for such 'outrageous sarcasms' as his reference to Christ as the 'supposed son of God'. Subsequently legal reference to Christian morality was dropped, but the vague notion of an offence against 'public morality' remained a means of defending social and moral order.

The courts also assisted in the repression of political crimes and in action against members of illegal associations and strikers. In January 1849 the role of the *procureur-général* was publicly described as being to 'ensure the reign of law' by serving as 'the advance guard of a social order . . . of religion . . . the family and property against the threat of anarchy and the mad dreams of utopians'. As a result almost the entire magistrature, regardless of reservations about the rule of law, supported the military *coup d'état* of December 1851. As one of their number explained, 'the magistrate would badly misunderstand his mission, if in the midst of the universal peril . . . he refused to throw himself into the combat'. Over time the attitudes of magistrates and of the social milieu to which they belonged were modified, without being fundamentally transformed. Although the rule of law was enshrined in successive constitutional documents as the basis of individual liberty and security and as such served to legitimize state power, there were clearly considerable inequalities in the way in which the law was implemented. However, this is not to deny that in many cases judges committed to proper legal procedure safeguarded the interests of individuals with whom they had little personal sympathy and so checked over-zealous police repression.

Police

Another aspect of the growth of the state apparatus was the increase in the numbers and effectiveness of the police. For most of the century France was thinly policed. Only gradually, though with greater rapidity during the Second Empire, was the number of policemen increased and, particularly from the 1880s, their organization and training improved. In 1818 the Paris municipal police force included only 300 men (supported by 1,528 *gendarmerie*, a branch of the army); as late as 1857 Lille had only 44 municipal policemen and 16 *gendarmes*. The Parisian police force meanwhile had risen to 4,600 in 1860 (with 2,441 *gendarmes*) and to 8,600 in 1914, supported by 3,000 *gendarmes*.[11] In the countryside *gardes champêtres* (usually part-time and ill-regarded) served as a village police. These local policemen could, until its final suppression in 1871, call for support from the National Guard (a form of local militia) which was however usually poorly organized and lacking enthusiasm for its duties, and more especially from the *gendarmerie*.

In spite of the growing numbers of policemen effective co-ordination of these diverse agencies was a major problem. Even within Paris the difficulty of controlling an administrative and police system (which included responsibility not only for public order, but for food supplies, hygiene, lighting, etc.) and combating its internal traditions and prejudices proved extremely difficult. Prefects of Police were usually selected from the prefectoral corps and remained in the post for only short periods. Any inclinations towards reform they might have possessed were obstructed by powerful subordinates and by such rivals as the Prefect of the Seine or the Minister of the Interior. On a national scale, the problems of control were compounded. The absence of a large professional police force meant that even comparatively minor disturbances forced the authorities to rely upon the army to restore order. The army was in consequence a crucially important social and political institution. Its officer corps, whilst the most democratic in Europe in social composition, was nevertheless dominated by the propertied classes. Its rank and file were inspired by a sense of discipline and *esprit de corps*. As a result it was a reliable means of preserving order, provided that its civilian masters issued clear instructions, and were ruthless enough to make full use of its potential (as in June 1848 and 1871). The failure to prevent revolution in July 1830 and February 1848 has to be understood primarily in terms of a crisis of confidence within the political leadership.

At other times, until improved communications and market integration reduced the significance of these traditional forms of protest, the most frequent causes of unrest were high food prices (especially in 1817, 1832, 1839, 1846–7); and disputes over rights of usage in forests and tax collection (particularly in the aftermath of revolution). In the second part of the century, industrialization, politicization and, from the 1860s, a less repressive legal framework, led to the emergence of the strike and of political activity as the predominant forms of protest. In all these circumstances, regardless of their personal political outlook, senior military officers consistently collaborated with government and the magistrature in both preventive and repressive measures designed to intimidate or punish those who threatened public order. Throughout the century the basic principle of behaviour of officers and men was obedience to hierarchical superiors. The army became the instrument of every government, but was especially fond of strong regimes which guaranteed social order. The French army was above all a garrison force dedicated mainly to the maintenance of internal security. From the late 1840s its effectiveness as an internal police force was increased through the closer control and more rapid circulation of troops made possible by the electric telegraph and railway. Paradoxically at this very moment when military repression became potentially more effective, its very brutality and the likelihood that this might heighten levels of violence (as it had in July 1830 and February 1848) encouraged efforts both to improve the capacity of the police and *gendarmerie* to cope with popular disorder, and in particular to construct a consensus in favour of the existing society.

In whose interests?

Through its various agencies the state regulated social and political disputes. Because of its own involvement, and the social origins of its personnel, it was not an impartial actor. Yet this was precisely the claim made by its defenders in insisting upon the universality of the 'rule of law'. In this way they sought to establish the legitimacy of government policy, to negate critical actions and ideologies and to increase the capacity of the state for effective social management. In the last resort, however, coercion existed as a powerful deterrent to all those forms of behaviour from crime to political protest seen as a threat to the established order. This was particularly the case with organization and protest by workers. Policy fluctuated. Thus, during the Empire and especially the Restoration, workers' mutual aid societies were tolerated because of their practical utility and links with the pious fraternities of the *ancien régime*, although the Paris Prefect of Police evinced growing concern that they organized strikes. This anxiety was magnified by the disorders after the 1830 Revolution, which culminated in the Lyon revolt in November 1831. Guizot insisted on the need for urgent action, and legislation was introduced in March 1834 requiring administrative authorization for all forms of association. As if to confirm the authorities' worst fears there were risings in protest in Paris and Lyon, although they were easily crushed in a demonstration of the government's power and of the support for it from middle-class National Guards. Successive governments, afraid of revolution, were clearly prepared to use brutal repression; they did so in Paris in June 1848, and in crushing the Commune in 1871. In less dramatic circumstances the police frequently arrested suspected ring-leaders of strikes or demonstrations and members of illegal organizations. In these conditions it took courage to protest. A letter received in March 1870 by Varlin, a prominent member of the Workers' International, insisted on how difficult it was to attract workers into unions when, 'they are so frightened; confidence lacks everywhere because they see police spies on every corner'.

State action, more than any other single factor, probably explains the decentralized character of working-class organiza-tions and political action until the closing decades of the century. Trades unions were not legalized until 1884 and only in 1901 were laws amended to give them the same rights as other voluntary associations. This finally completed the extension of political liberties within the nineteenth-century bourgeois democratic political system. However, the role of the state had not previously been entirely negative. Indeed repression became increasingly rare and more selective. Within strict limits, various constructive and more attractive policies were put into effect. This can be seen in relation to the frequent economic crises. There was a danger that discontent might be politicized, as in 1830 and 1848, or at least lead to increased crime as desperate people sought to make ends meet. 'Respectable' citizens were certainly alarmed by what seemed to be the growing criminality of the urban population. The social philosophy of the *notables* was evident in their attitude towards assisting the poor. At the local level they favoured voluntary private charity (in other words, paternalistic measures), and the *bureaux de bienfaisance*, created in 1796. These were controlled primarily by the donors and proved a useful means of reinforcing the dependence of the poor. Benevolence, reinforced by the threat of repression, was an effective method of social control, although the activities of the *bureaux* were limited by insufficient funds, lack of co-ordination and arbitrary criteria for providing assistance. Only when private initiatives failed to cope with mounting social problems did support for state intervention spread both from humanitarian motives and a desire for more effective social control. Thus, in economic crises throughout the century, state aid in providing public works employment and charity was welcomed as a means of avoiding disorder. Until subsistence crises ceased in the 1850s, official intervention in the regulation of bread prices was also favoured, again as a measure of policing. Thus in 1817 one prefect commented that, 'it is a fine thing in theory, but it is to be feared that freedom of trade [in grain] would lead to the same disastrous results as freedom of the Press'. Only in 1863, as a result of improved communications and the end of the threat of dearth did the government complete the liberalization of the grain trade by ending controls over bread prices. At the same time, intervention to deal with other social problems became more regular, although progress was slow in comparison with Germany or even Britain.

Growing state intervention in the economy was in part designed to promote social order by establishing the conditions for greater economic prosperity. Slowly, with this objective in mind, politicians came to accept a more interventionist role. Traditionally the state had been viewed as guarantor of a social order threatened by the indiscipline of the lazy, the improvident and the immoral. For this reason intervention in work-place relationships – most notably by means of the 1841 law on child labour – had been bitterly opposed as likely to lead to increased costs for industry, a decline in family incomes, and to a reduction in the rights and responsibilities of parents. During the Second Empire, however, policies such as the reconstruction of central Paris (designed primarily to promote economic modernization) were also intended to create employment opportunities. In the 1880s, the return to high levels of tariff protection was in part intended to satisfy the grievances of small businessmen and peasant farmers.

Tariff policy was used as an important means of preserving the political and social consensus.

The establishment of the Third Republic initially had little effect. Moderate republicans were as concerned to preserve the individualist ethos of the old social order as were political conservatives. Only around the turn of the century did radicals such as Léon Bourgeois and independent socialists such as Millerand promote social reform, so as to maintain electoral support from the workers against competition from the socialists. However, their projects continued to be restrained by a reluctance to alienate other elements of their constituency (lower middle class and peasants) by increasing taxation. Nevertheless, as dissatisfaction with the arbitrary and inadequate provisions of the communal system of public assistance grew, the state began to accept obligations to particular categories of claimants. These were accorded a statutory right to aid: abandoned children and the insane in 1884; the indigent sick in 1893 (in 1912, 1,160,361 individuals were assisted); the aged poor in 1905 and large families in 1913. In 1910 a law on old-age pensions, based upon a contributory scheme, was introduced, but in 1912 only around 2,800,000 individuals of a potential of 18 million were actually covered. Despite these measures even radical governments remained committed to a basic economic liberalism, seen most dramatically in the use of the army to protect the *liberté du travail* during strikes. The scope of reform was severely limited. Its effects were circumscribed by exemptions, by the actual practice of judicial interpretation and administrative implementation, and by the resistance of such groups as employers to any hint of restrictions on their authority. There was thus no systematic social legislation before 1914.

Of far greater significance as a means of promoting social and political order was the development of primary education for which, particularly after the Guizot law of 1833, the state assumed growing responsibility. This required a teacher training college (*école normale*) in every department, a primary school in every commune and a supervisory inspectorate. At the same time economic development, urbanization and complex cultural change stimulated growing popular interest in education and even before attendance was made compulsory, in 1882, most school-age children attended school.

As well as the basic skills of literacy and numeracy, the school system provided deliberate indoctrination. The basic objective according to the *Statut des écoles primaires* of 1834 was 'constantly to tend to penetrate the souls of pupils with the sentiments and principles which are the safeguard of good morality and which are proper to inspire fear and love of God'. These provisions were reinforced in the aftermath of the 1848 Revolution by the *loi Falloux* of 1850. In certain key respects the republican political victory in the 1870s preserved the conservative, socializing objectives of the educational system. As secularization gradually occurred in the state schools, religion gave way to civic instruction, with an increasingly pronounced emphasis on patriotism. Throughout the century the teacher imposed the culture and ethics of the dominant social group upon children, stressing the ideals of self-discipline, honesty, thrift, the avoidance of vice, respect for the family, hard work, cleanliness, politeness and grateful acceptance of the established social order as the best possible of all worlds.

It would be a mistake to be too cynical and ignore the idealistic dedication of many republicans to democratic politics and their continuing hostility towards conservative and Catholic alternatives. They demanded political democracy and fundamental human rights. In addition, they legitimized a state which could be seen to derive its authority from the people. Democratic political institutions, together with mass education provided a set of integrative mechanisms. Even the political extremes, to Right and Left, could in the last resort find some virtue in a political system dedicated both to the protection of private property and to democracy.

Conclusion

A century which witnessed substantial industrialization and urbanization also saw the evolution of the political system from constitutional monarchy to liberal democracy, together with a substantial increase in the size and activities of the bureaucracy, police and army. An effectively centralized state only came into existence when improved communications allowed the central authority for the first time to receive information quickly from, and transmit instructions to, the provinces. At the same time it

possessed the means to ensure compliance through the rapid
intervention of its civil and military agents.

In any social system those who control the state possess
considerable power. It should not be assumed that consensus
always prevailed within social and political élites and that the state
authorities did not act at various times in a fashion which some
élite groups believed was contrary to their vital interests. Neither
should it be assumed that these authorities inevitably acted
against the interests of non-élites. Nevertheless, throughout the
nineteenth century the French state consistently behaved in a
broadly conservative manner in order to maintain 'order' and to
preserve existing economic and social relationships. Competition
for power could destabilize political life, particularly because of
the strength of the ideologies which inspired political action.
Pressure for the extension of political rights was another divisive
factor. To those who possessed power, therefore, it seemed
essential to impose restraints upon political conflict. These were
effective because those who took part in the political game,
whatever their political affiliations, came largely from relatively
narrow social groups whose wealth allowed them the education,
culture and leisure that were the prerequisites for sustained
participation in both politics and government. The vast majority
of politicians and bureaucrats were unwilling to contemplate more
than limited social reform and were prepared to use the repressive
capacity of the state against any who, individually through
criminal activity, or collectively by means of revolutionary
agitation, threatened social stability. This was especially evident
in 1830, 1848 and 1871 and in reaction to the rise of socialism at the
turn of the century. Yet it was not primarily repression but the
recognition of political 'liberties' and the creation of means for
peaceful protest which reduced the likelihood of violent conflict.
The legitimization of the political (and implicitly of the social)
system by the establishment of popular sovereignty was reinforced
by the extension of the schooling network and by appeal to such
values as 'law and order' and to patriotic sentiment. In practice,
however, the mechanisms by which parliamentarians and officials
were selected, dependent as they were upon unequal access to
education, to patronage, to the means of exercising influence and
ultimately to the possession of at least a modicum of wealth, made
certain that effective political power remained the preserve of

narrow groups. In its essentials this was bourgeois liberal democracy creating only the illusion of equality and opportunity, whilst political institutions in practice were manipulated in order to protect private property and privilege. But whatever the ideological and political differences between political practitioners, the majority of them, and possibly also their electors, did come to share a broadly based consensus in support of a pluralistic, liberal and property-owning society. This was the very real achievement of the much-maligned Third Republic.

Notes

1. C.-H. Pouthas, 'Les ministères de Louis-Philippe', *Revue d'histoire moderne et contemporaine*, Vol. 1 (1954), p. 102.
2. J. Estèbe, *Les Ministres de la République, 1871–1914* (Paris, 1982), p. 22.
3. G. de Bertier de Sauvigny, *The Bourbon Restoration* (Philadelphia, PA, 1966), pp. 290–1.
4. A. Jardin and A.-J. Tudesq, *Restoration and Reaction, 1815–1848* (Cambridge, 1984), p. 363.
5. D. H. Pinkney, 'The myth of the French Revolution of 1830', in D. H. Pinkney and T. Ropp (eds), *A Festschrift for Frederick B. Artz* (Durham, NC, 1964), pp. 56–7.
6. A.-J. Tudesq, *Les grands notables en France (1840–1849): étude historique d'une psychologie sociale*, Vol. I (Paris, 1964), pp. 365f; T. D. Beck, *French Legislators* (Berkeley, CA, 1974), p. 127.
7. T. Zeldin, *The Political System of Napoleon III* (London, 1958), p. 62; A. Plessis, *The Rise and Fall of the Second Empire, 1852–1871* (Cambridge, 1985), pp. 36f.
8. G. de Bertier de Sauvigny, op. cit. p. 275; G. Thuillier and J. Tulard, 'Conclusions', in *Histoire de l'administration française depuis 1800* (Geneva, 1975), p. 109.
9. C. Charle, *Les hautes fonctionnaires en France au 19ᵉ siècle* (Paris, 1980), p. 27, and 'Le recrutement des hautes fonctionnaires en 1901', *Annales*, vol. 35 (1980), pp. 381–3.
10. G. de Bertier de Sauvigny, op. cit., p. 277; B. Le Clère, 'La vie quotidienne des préfets au 19ᵉ siècle (1815–1914)', in J. Aubert *et al.*, *Les préfets en France (1800–1940)* (Geneva, 1978), p. 45.
11. Capitaine Saurel, *La gendarmerie dans la société de la Deuxième République et du Second Empire*, Doctorat d'État, Sorbonne, Paris (1957), p. 580.

Further reading

The most useful general introductions to the period are: W. Fortescue, *Revolution and Counter-Revolution in France, 1815–1852* (Oxford, 1988); A. Jardin and A.-J. Tudesq, *Restoration and Reaction, 1815–1848* (Cambridge, 1984); R. Magraw, *France, 1815–1914: The Bourgeois century* (London, 1983); J. Furet, *Revolutionary France: 1770–1880* (Oxford, 1992); M. Agulhon, *The French Republic: 1879–1992* (Oxford, 1993).

More restricted periods are covered in: M. Agulhon, *The Republican Experiment, 1848–1852* (Cambridge, 1983); G. de Bertier de Sauvigny, *The Bourbon Restoration* (Philadelphia, PA, 1966); H. A. C. Collingham, *The July Monarchy: a political history of France, 1830–1848* (London, 1988); J.-M. Mayeur and M. Reberioux, *The Third Republic from its Origins to the Great War, 1871–1914* (Cambridge, 1985); D. H. Pinkney, *The French Revolution of 1830* (Princeton, NJ, 1972), and especially the revised edition *La Révolution de 1830 en France* (Paris, 1988); A. Plessis, *The Rise and Fall of the Second Empire, 1852–1871* (Cambridge, 1985); R. Price, *The French Second Republic: a Social History* (London, 1972); J. McMillan, *Napoleon III* (London, 1990); P. Pilbeam, *The French Revolution of 1830* (London, 1991).

C. Charle, *A Social History of France in the Nineteenth Century* (Oxford 1994); P. McPhee, *A Social History of France, 1789–1880* (London, 1992) and R. Price, *A Social History of Nineteenth-Century France* (London, 1987) set the social context for political activity.

There is a paucity of works in English on the development of state institutions. Reference should be made to the works referred to in the notes and to such studies as B. Le Clère and V. Wright, *Les préfets du Second Empire* (Paris, 1973).

However, useful insights into the development of administrative and police systems are provided by: R. Holmes, *The Road to Sedan: the French army, 1866–1870* (London, 1984); J. M. Merriman, *The Agony of the Republic: the repression of the Left in revolutionary France, 1848–1851* (London, 1978); H. C. Payne, *The Police State of Louis Napoleon Bonaparte* (Seattle, WA, 1966); N. Richardson, *The French Prefectoral Corps, 1814–1830* (Cambridge, 1966); T. Zeldin, *The Political System of Napoleon III* (London, 1958).

The reactions of the authorities to particular intense crises are considered by J. M. House, H. Machin and V. Wright in R. Price (ed.), *Revolution and Reaction: 1848 and the Second French Republic* (London, 1975) and by R. Tombs, *The War against Paris, 1871* (Cambridge, 1981).

Changing patterns of popular protest are examined in R. Price, *The Modernization of Rural France* (London, 1983), C. Tilly, *The Contentious French* (Cambridge, MA, 1986) and P. McPhee, *The Politics of Rural Life* (Oxford, 1992).

3

Italy: independence and unification without power

B. A. HADDOCK

Among the political achievements of the nineteenth century, the emergence of a unitary state in Italy in 1861 must rank among the least likely. The settlement of 1815 had left Italy weak and divided. Lombardy and Venice had been restored to Habsburg rule; the political fortunes of the duchies of Tuscany, Parma and Modena were tied to the Habsburgs through dynastic alliances; meanwhile central and southern Italy endured the exquisite combination of obscurantism tempered only by inefficiency in the restored regimes of the papacy and the Bourbons. Only Piedmont retained its political independence. But as a geographically peripheral state, it displayed little interest in the wider affairs of the Italian peninsula until after 1840. Its ruling class concerned itself rather more with military than with political or administrative matters. And its general culture, so thoroughly French in ethos, gave little indication of the central role it would later play in the formation of an Italian state.

Yet politically articulate Italians had only to look back to the Napoleonic period to see the rudiments of a modern state established in their country. After his invasion in 1796 Napoleon had redrawn the map of Italy, leading to the adoption of new principles of political organization and administration. Very many intellectuals, far from resenting the imposition of foreign forms of rule, welcomed the opportunity to sweep away the remnants of the *ancien régime*. Whether or not republican principles were endorsed, there was a widespread feeling that the new scheme of things offered possibilities for modernization which would have been foreclosed under previous regimes. Political participation on a wider scale, the expectation of a career open to talents and the dismantling of aristocratic and ecclesiastical privilege, were prospects which fired the enthusiasm of the small class of intellectuals.

But these developments directly threatened powerful interests. With the defeat of France, the old order reasserted itself. Much of the upheaval of the revolutionary years had proved to be irreversible, especially in economic, administrative and legal spheres. Yet efforts could still be made to limit the political and social impact of the recent innovations. In 1815 the great powers, with Austria at their head, had been concerned to restore the political divisions of Europe as nearly as possible to their prerevolutionary condition. In accommodating past changes, the powers showed themselves to be in some measure flexible and pragmatic. With regard to the future, however, they were adamant. Austria, in particular, had learnt from experience of revolutionary turmoil that a local uprising could constitute a threat to the peace and stability of Europe as a whole and with it the security of her empire. What this meant, in effect, was that the settlement of 1815 was to be treated as a definitive solution to Europe's political problems. Attempts to placate liberal or nationalist pressures by piecemeal political or constitutional reforms would be precluded. Not the least of the paradoxes of these difficult years is that in treating local political issues as international problems, the powers had exaggerated their significance and contributed to the generation of the revolutionary pressures they had been so anxious to avoid.

The impact of the restoration on the politics of the Italian peninsula was decisive. Republican and Jacobin ideas and activities were suppressed. But moderates, too, found their political aspirations and expectations rudely interrupted. Hopes for the political modernization of Italy had, for the moment, to be set aside. Any suggestion that Italy should, in the longer term, strive towards independence was regarded as unrealistic and dangerously Utopian.

Restrictions on the style of political opposition varied from place to place. In Lombardy the journal *Il Conciliatore* (1818–19) could function briefly as a forum for intellectuals concerned with the economic and cultural regeneration of Italy. But if the Austrian authorities were prepared to tolerate discussion of the reform of industry and society, they could not turn a blind eye to arguments which defended a necessary link between economic progress and the extension of political liberties. To campaign even for the limited constitutional guarantees advanced by Benjamin Constant and his circle in France was regarded as a revolutionary threat to the status quo. Organized political opposition was thus forced to operate underground.

Secret political sects proliferated throughout Italy. In the north, Filippo Buonarroti's 'Sublime Perfect Masters' were dominant. Buonarroti, active in Jacobin circles in Paris in the 1790s, had been imprisoned after the failure of Babeuf's 'Conspiracy of Equals' in 1796. His organization in northern Italy followed the pattern of the conspiratorial tradition. Members were inducted into different levels of the federation, for the most part unaware of the long-term political goals of Buonarroti and his close associates. Buonarroti himself was intent upon the creation of a radically egalitarian republic through the dictatorship of a revolutionary élite. Lower ranking members of the federation, however, would generally have their attention focused on immediate political goals – the need to create a constitutional regime in northern Italy.

In the south the sects were rather more loosely organized. The *carboneria* had been in existence as a focus of opposition to French authoritarian rule since 1807. After 1815 the principal political target became instead the absolutist rule of Ferdinand I. Like Buonarroti's federation, the *carbonari* held to the most elaborate ritual in the conduct of their affairs. And the need for absolute secrecy meant that ideological aims could not be openly canvassed. The many carbonarist groups would thus often find themselves pursuing rather different political goals. But all would be committed to the creation of a secular, constitutionally-based regime. Just how far they constituted a genuine threat to Ferdinand's rule is a much disputed question, though the initial success of the Neapolitan revolution of 1820 is indicative of their capacity to act if occasion arose. The point to stress here, however, is that political opposition of any kind in Italy had been forced to assume a conspiratorial and revolutionary form. Indeed the failure of the authorities in the various Italian states to establish a *modus vivendi* with their moderate opponents would ultimately prove to be their undoing.

The situation in 1830 was hardly propitious for unification. Any groups arguing for the eventual emergence of an Italian state, even in the most theoretical terms, were liable to find themselves harassed or suppressed by the authorities. The conditions in which active political campaigns had to be conducted meant that little could be done to persuade wavering or neutral opinion. And without the semblance of an alternative political consensus, worthy apolitical opinion would inevitably find itself inclined towards the status quo.

Some of the most serious obstacles to change in Italy were structural rather than political or ideological. Economic development, except in Lombardy, had lagged behind that of northern Europe. Thus a large entrepreneurial and professional class, the force behind and target for so much liberal and nationalist propaganda in France, Germany and England, was lacking. Without pressure from this source, a coherent national movement was extraordinarily difficult to sustain. Literacy, too, was restricted. It is estimated that as late as 1871, 68.8 per cent of the population over six years of age were illiterate. The language of everyday life for most people was one of the many regional dialects rather than Italian. Indeed the proportion of Italian speakers in 1861 is put as low as 2.5 per cent. Italian had, of course, flourished as a literary language since the high Middle Ages. But its limited use beyond narrow élite circles was a severe constraint on the development of a popular movement.

More than anything else, it was the international situation which ensured that the 'Italian question' would remain on the European political agenda. The spectre of the French Revolution still haunted the political consciousness of Europeans. Both revolutionaries and reactionaries saw connections between events which might often have been occasioned by local and particular circumstances. Upheavals in Paris in 1830 and 1848, for example, sent shock waves through the continent, lending a larger significance to disturbances that might otherwise have simply fizzled out. Austria, in particular, found herself in an acutely vulnerable position. Her empire was a standing affront to liberal and nationalist opinion. She could not afford to be responsive to pressures in a particular quarter for fear of exciting clamorous demands elsewhere. In Italy her predicament was complicated by the fact that she could not present herself as an overt obstacle to indigenous economic development; and yet, as the pace of economic change quickened, demands would inevitably be made for political reform. A fiercely authoritarian stance, as Metternich recognized, ran the risk of precipitating a revolutionary challenge; a modest reformism would concede liberal reforms which, in the circumstances, would have revolutionary implications. It may well be that nothing could have saved the Austrian Empire. As the middle classes became more influential in Italy, so they would find arguments readily available to undermine the legitimacy of Austrian rule or dominance. The combination of deep attachment to a cultural tradition, coupled with awareness of the political possibilities spawned since 1789, was to prove irresistible.

These various factors contributed to the instability of the political situation in Italy in 1830. But much had to happen before there could be any real prospect of radical change. In the ideological sphere, in particular, the multitude of seething discontents had yet to coalesce into a political programme. Educated Italians, conscious of their national identity, were still not accustomed to think in terms of a prospective political identity. The position would be transformed as more and more groups came to see the achievement of an Italian state as a necessary condition for the advancement of their particular interests. This development, to be sure, was not without its own difficulties. As national passion reached a peak in 1860, expectations were pitched so high that the actual state established in 1861 could not fail to be a disappointment. Without the initial ideological momentum, however, little could have been achieved.

The thinker who did most to set the idea of a unitary state before the Italian public was Giuseppe Mazzini (1805–72). Mazzini had been inducted into the life of political activism and subversion in 1827 through the carbonarist movement. But he quickly became disillusioned with the secrecy, ritual and failure to articulate clear ideological objectives. In 1830 he was denounced to the authorities by a fellow carbonarist, Raimondo Doria. A brief period in prison afforded him an opportunity to take stock of his developing political ideas.

Mazzini was clear that the political transformation of Italy required (at least) the acquiescence of broad sections of the population. Yet such acquiescence would not be forthcoming if insurrectionary activity were left in the hands of small sects whose ultimate objectives might well be obscure even to some of their active members. Certainly insurrections would continue to be essential. And, given the nature of the activity, planning would have to be conducted in the strictest secrecy. But a necessary backdrop to a successful and co-ordinated insurrectionary campaign would be an elaborate propaganda exercise. Activists had to be clear about the longer-term goals they were pursuing. Whatever initial success might befall specific engagements would be evanescent if the passive population could not be persuaded to look upon the ideals of the revolutionary movement with sympathy.

A more broadly-based revolutionary strategy was thus a crucial desideratum for Mazzini. To this end, while exiled in Marseilles in 1831, he directed all his energy to the creation of a new movement, *La giovine Italia* (Young Italy), which would serve as a focus for the drive towards an Italian state. *La giovine Italia* combined the dual aims of educating the people politically and organizing popular insurrections. Mazzini was a tireless champion of a certain conception of Italy. Its mission was to emerge as a nation-state in an age in which the national principle had effectively undermined the legitimacy of outmoded political forms. Italy would be a free, independent and unitary republic, enabling its people to live together in a spirit of harmony and co-operation. But the status which beckoned would be achieved only if the Italian people were able to seize the initiative and fashion a new political identity for themselves through their own efforts.

Mazzini's practical achievements were limited. Insurrections planned for Savoy and Naples in 1833–4 were abortive; and various uprisings in the kingdom of Naples after 1837, culminating in the failure of the Bandiera brothers, were easily suppressed. To many sceptical observers it seemed that Mazzini had simply encouraged idealistic young men to embark upon foolhardy expeditions which would almost certainly cost their lives. But even failure has propaganda value. Mazzini had become the *bête noire* of the authorities. Though the insurrections he inspired might look pathetic in retrospect, they could not be disregarded. Governments had momentarily been overturned in Turin and Naples in 1820–1. And no government could be sure that a local spark would not ignite a wider conflagration. More important, though, Mazzini had forced Italian activists to think in terms of national political categories. Traditional loyalties to city or region had begun to seem anachronistic in the brave new world he evoked. Mazzini's tactics might have done little to shake the status quo. His propaganda, however, made a lasting impression across the political spectrum.

Mazzini was far from creating an ideological consensus. Even in radical circles, there was widespread disquiet about his identification of an Italian nation-state as the key to the regeneration of wider aspects of life. Carlo Cattaneo (1801–69), for example, editor of the influential Milanese journal *Il Politecnico* (1839–44), was unhappy with the mystical strain in Mazzini's thinking. Political reform was valued by Cattaneo as a means towards concrete improvements in society and the economy. He had made a name for himself as an economist, arguing vigorously for a general extension of free trade areas. When the issue of possible enlargement of the German *Zollverein* was being discussed, Cattaneo pressed for Lombard involvement, despite the reservations of nationalists. In the pages of *Il Politecnico* Cattaneo consistently championed the cause of modernization, in transport, industry, administration and the law. The lot of the ordinary Italian would be improved by applying the latest scientific ideas in these various spheres rather than by ambitious political reconstruction. Indeed, for Cattaneo, preoccupation with the national issue was something of a distraction, diverting attention away from the urgent task of raising the general educational level of the Italian people. Cattaneo would later play his part in the national movement; but before 1848 he was so far distant from nationalists such as Mazzini that he could vest his principal hopes for political change in the reform of the Habsburg empire along federal lines.

Italian thinkers influenced by socialist ideas were also suspicious of Mazzini. Giuseppe Ferrari (1811–76), who was to spend the last years of his political career as a deputy of the Italian Parliament, worked in France in the decade following 1838. Not only was he exposed to a wide range of ideas, but observation at close hand of the inner workings of French political and cultural life afforded him a novel perspective on Italian affairs. Where Mazzini stressed the special mission of the Italian people in the European political scene, charting a direction for other peoples to follow in their drive towards statehood, Ferrari saw, instead, the degeneration of Italian culture since the Renaissance. High Italian culture, in particular, had become stale and derivative, with leading ideas originating in the more vibrant cultures beyond the Alps. In politics her weakness was manifest. Since the French Revolution, political opinion in Italy had been dominated by French issues. Mazzini had certainly tried to arouse the Italian masses to work for their political salvation. But, writing in 1844, Ferrari was all too aware of the limitations of his approach. Ideological zeal alone would not create a successful revolution. The people needed to be persuaded that their real needs would be served in the scheme of things that revolution ushered in. It was not simply a question of responding to the cause of the nation but which national cause to respond to.

Both Cattaneo and Ferrari found that their differences with Mazzini would sharpen as political events unfolded. But their efforts in this early period were theoretical rather than practical. And the authorities were understandably more worried about the threat to public order posed by the Mazzinians.

Nor was concern about the activities of the Mazzinians confined to the authorities. Moderate opinion, sympathetic to the cause of reform, had begun to harden against Mazzini's insurrectionary strategy. Problems were perceived on two fronts. On the one hand, the despatch of small groups of insurgents to politically sensitive or vulnerable areas had so far proved to be ineffective. On the other hand, the sorts of doctrines preached by the Mazzinians gave no guarantee that concrete social, economic and constitutional reforms would necessarily follow in the wake of their triumph. Reliance on the untrammelled will of the people in Mazzini's programme seemed to many moderates to be both naïve and dangerous. The political lessons of 1793 were still uppermost in their minds. The risk of a repetition of the reign of terror was simply not worth running, no matter how worthy the cause. And, in any case, the prospect of a political upheaval involving far-reaching social changes would almost certainly precipitate a fierce and co-ordinated reaction.

An alternative national strategy began to emerge in the 1840s. Instead of looking to a movement motivated by pressure from below, a group of thinkers began to see more fruitful possibilities for political change in the conversion of one or more of the established ruling houses to the cause of reform. It would be misleading to see this group as a self-conscious school or party in the early 1840s. By the later 1850s, however, they would begin to dominate the national movement, at least in the north. As a group, they were deeply suspicious of populism in all its forms. Their interest in political reform was tempered always by a concern to maintain the social status quo. In the political sphere, too, their ambitions were strictly limited, extending (in most cases) no further than a modest constitutionalism. Yet even so moderate a stance had been interpreted as a revolutionary threat in the recent past. What made this group different was their close links with the liberal aristocracy, particularly in Piedmont. They could wield influence without having to have recourse to subversive measures.

Vincenzo Gioberti (1801–52) was perhaps the most influential of the 1840s moderates, and certainly the most bizarre from a modern point of view. A leading liberal Catholic, his *On the Moral and Civil Primacy of the Italians* (1843) created something of a political sensation. Yet its curious mixture of realism and utopianism makes heavy reading today. Like Mazzini, Gioberti was a passionate champion of political and cultural renewal in Italy. But he had no confidence in the Mazzinian formula of popular insurrections supported by ideological propaganda. Nor could he envisage political unity emerging from Italy's disparate regional cultures. The most likely means of achieving an independent Italy, free from foreign (especially French) influence, was, for Gioberti, a political confederation. And, given Italy's particular traditions and the rivalry between her separate states, leadership of such a confederacy would have to be given to the papacy. The pope, as the acknowledged spiritual and cultural leader of Italy, could serve as a figure-head. Crucial military support would come from Gioberti's own Piedmont, the 'warrior province'.

Much was omitted from Gioberti's account. There was no discussion of practical reforms; nor did Gioberti explain how the papacy could be expected to commit itself to a policy that might well involve war with Austria (a Catholic power). Indeed Gioberti had specifically set himself the task of creating a moderate consensus and was not concerned to confront divisive or con-troversial issues.

His tactic, at least in the short term, was strikingly successful. But what his more discerning readers focused upon was not so much the role of the papacy as that of Piedmont. Cesare Balbo (1789–1853), for example, saw Piedmontese military strength as the crucial factor in the Italian situation. But he was clear that Piedmont would not be able to fashion a united Italy without help from abroad. In *On the Hopes of Italy* (1844) he argued that unification of Italy would require a radical readjustment in the European balance of power. His hope was that Austria might be persuaded to accept losses in Italy in return for a strengthening of her position in the Balkans. Certainly changes on such a scale would not be achieved by fomenting popular unrest.

The constitutional monarchists, as a group, looked upon expressions of discontent from the lower classes with misgivings. Balbo's cousin, Massimo d'Azeglio (1798–1866), who was to be Prime Minister of Piedmont in the crucial years 1849–52, spent the September of 1845 investigating political unrest in the Romagna at first hand. D'Azeglio gained access to revolutionary groups; but he was sharply critical of their methods. Yet his account of his findings, *On the Recent Events in the Romagna* (1846), was by no means an unthinking defence of the status quo. D'Azeglio recognized that much was amiss with papal government in the Romagna. Indeed he saw misgovernment as one of the crucial factors inclining the ordinary people towards the Mazzinians. The lesson for the princes of Italy was clear. If they wanted to maintain their positions, they had to embark on an elaborate programme of reforms, involving constitutional concessions at national and local levels, overhaul of the various legal systems, encouragement of open discussion in the newspapers, together with wide-ranging economic and infrastructural improvements. But there was also a blunt lesson for the Mazzinians. Public opinion was simply not ready to accept the kinds of changes advanced by nationalist revolutionaries. The national cause would be furthered by patient efforts at persuasion rather than through precipitate insurrections. In the meantime, initiative should be left in the hands of the Piedmontese. Piedmont was the only Italian state with independent political options; she was accordingly best placed to foster the national movement without undermining the principle of constitutional monarchy.

The position of the moderates was thus complex. Though by upbringing and culture they might be readily identified as monarchists, they nevertheless had profound reservations about monarchical rule. They were opposed to autocracy in all its forms, whether exercised by the Austrians, the church or the Bourbons. Even Piedmont, which at least had the advantage of indepen- dence, was far from satisfying their constitutional requirements before 1848. As opponents of the settlement imposed on Italy in 1815, they could respond with guarded enthusiasm to the national movement. But they were reluctant to force the pace of political change for fear of upsetting the social status quo. Between the established order on the one side and the Mazzinians on the other, they clearly had to tread carefully. In the early 1840s they had, essentially, been responding to the misplaced initiative of the Mazzinians. In 1846, however, they found themselves thrust to the centre of the political stage by the most unlikely of developments.

The regime in the Papal States had long been regarded as the most obdurate and unenlightened in Italy. Yet the situation seemed to have been transformed overnight with the election of a new pope. Pius IX came to the papacy with a reputation for liberal sympathies, though little was known of the extent of his commitment to either political or religious reform. His first official act, however, raised the highest expectations. The grant of an amnesty to political prisoners (in itself a conventional gesture at the beginning of a pontificate) was greeted with rapturous enthusiasm. Demands were immediately made for broader reforms. Pius himself seems to have been somewhat intoxicated by the warmth of his reception. The concession of lay representa- tion on consultative committees, together with wider commit- ments to examine the civil and criminal law, press censorship and the economic infrastructure, confirmed the image of Pius as the liberal pope destined to lead the national movement. Gioberti's dream seemed to be on the verge of realization.

The authorities elsewhere in Italy regarded events in Rome with mounting anxiety. Such was the concern of the Austrians that an occupying force was sent to Ferrara, poised for further inter- vention should the need arise. Nothing, in the circumstances, could have been better calculated to lend a more general significance to sporadic outbursts of discontent throughout the peninsula. With a backdrop of economic crisis and severe food shortages to contend with, the various Italian states found themselves facing traditional problems of public order in a dangerously volatile ideological atmosphere. Disturbances in most of the larger urban centres, ranging from Milan, Turin and Genoa in the north, through Parma, Modena and Palermo, though they might have been sparked off by a variety of local issues, assumed a weightier aspect in relation to the wider national movement. Pressure for political concessions increased. The princes, in desperation, turned to the leaders of moderate opinion. Uneasy alliances were formed to stem the tide of events. Hastily drawn constitutions were conceded in the early months of 1848 in Naples, Piedmont, Rome and Tuscany. But, as would happen so often in Europe's modern revolutionary crises, the pace of change had gathered a momentum of its own.

Developments abroad ensured that Italy's local uprisings would be viewed in an international context. The February Revolution in Paris, together with news of serious disturbances in Vienna and Budapest, added a dimension to events which had certainly not been anticipated when demands were first raised for constitutional concessions. The resignation of Metternich in March assumed a symbolic significance. The end of an era seemed to be at hand. The Mazzinian dream of a popular war of national liberation now looked to be a realistic prospect. Certainly the stage was set for concerted action against Austria.

Events first came to a head in Milan in March. An initial boycott of tobacco (an Austrian state monopoly) led, almost spontaneously, to a more general insurrection. To the surprise of everyone concerned, not least the insurgents themselves, the Milanese managed to force a large and well-organized Austrian garrison under Radetzky out of Milan in the glorious *cinque giornate* of 18–22 March. But the Milanese were by no means clear on the policy that should be pursued thereafter. The city's patrician leaders, under the mayor, Casati, had initially allowed themselves to be swept along by popular pressure. After 20 March, however, military strategy was in the hands of a radical council of war, including Cattaneo. The moderate patricians began to fear that they had as much to lose from victory as defeat. They were resolutely opposed to republicanism, and their plans for the future extended no further than the freeing of Milan from Austrian control. Cattaneo and the radicals, by contrast, saw the Milanese campaign in the context of the wider quest for an Italian republic. In a delicate and dangerous situation, it was crucial that conflict between the two groups should not be pushed to breaking point.

Cattaneo recognized that the power and influence of the patricians within the city could not be effectively challenged. He accordingly agreed to defer discussion of ideological and constitutional issues until victory had been finally achieved. In effect, this left the patricians with a free hand to consolidate their position. They turned to Piedmont for support.

Piedmont found itself beset by conflicting pressures. The king, Carlo Alberto, viewed the prospect of a republican victory in Milan with alarm. He was reluctant to do anything that might further a republican campaign against Austria. But neither could he risk undermining the position of the Milanese moderates through his own inactivity. There was also the Piedmontese dynastic interest to consider. Piedmont was presented with a golden opportunity to put itself at the head of the national movement. There was intense pressure in Turin for intervention, including an influential article by Cavour published in the journal he edited with Balbo, *Il Risorgimento*, on the morning of 23 March. It became clear to Carlo Alberto that he could allow Milan neither to fall nor to succeed without his help. A major triumph for Milan against Austria, even if it did not entail republican consequences, would seriously threaten Piedmont's political hegemony in northern Italy. In the event, when Casati's request for military assistance was received, Carlo Alberto had little choice but to agree, despite his deep misgivings about the possible course of the revolution.

Piedmontese involvement proved to be disastrous to the Milanese cause. Delay and prevarication led to the military initiative being lost. Instead of pursuing the retreating Austrians resolutely, the Piedmontese army, under Carlo Alberto himself, was more intent upon consolidation than securing a striking victory. Indeed a decisive defeat for the Austrians in Italy might well have involved precisely those political repercussions that Carlo Alberto had been most anxious to avoid.

Carlo Alberto pursued his other principal target with rather more vigour. Victory for the radicals in Milan had always been the most serious threat to his own position. Once he had been invited to intervene militarily, however, it was a comparatively simple matter to exact an appropriate political price. The Milanese moderates, anxious to preserve social and economic stability, were content to accept immediate Piedmontese annexation of Lombardy. Opposition to such a move from the radicals might well have fatally divided the national movement. Only Cattaneo, who had never regarded the prospect of exchanging efficient Austrian domination of Milan for inefficient Piedmontese rule with any great enthusiasm, persisted in arguing for an autonomous Lombard strategy. Mazzini's presence in Milan finally proved to be decisive in radical circles. In his view, it was essential that ideological divisions between the different groups of nationalists should not undermine the drive for a unified Italian state. Piedmontese leadership was accepted for the duration of the struggle. A plebiscite of 12 May overwhelmingly supported annexation. The tragedy, however, was that a move designed to strengthen the national cause served in practice to undermine its vigour and coherence.

A similar pattern of events emerged in Venice. Popular clamour led to the release of the nationalist leader, Daniele Manin (1804–57), from prison. Unable to rely on their own forces, the Austrians chose to withdraw from Venice without forcing an armed struggle. But the Republic of St Mark, forthwith declared on 22 March, was only to enjoy a most precarious existence. Manin himself was anxious that Venice should not become overdependent on the vagaries of Piedmontese policy. Yet, as president, he had few options. Once mainland Venetia had opted for fusion with Piedmont, the city of Venice was left cruelly exposed. With no realistic prospect of help coming from abroad, Manin recognized that without Piedmontese military assistance the independence of Venice would be short-lived. On 3 July, under pressure from his own assembly, he accepted the inevitable.

The fortunes of both Milan and Venice were thus tied to Piedmont. But with its principal political objectives achieved – the defeat of the radicals in Milan and Venice and the confirmation of her dominant position in northern Italy – Piedmont had little incentive to pursue the Austrian war vigorously. Having failed to strike a decisive blow while the Austrian forces were engaged in difficult retreat, Carlo Alberto, whose strategic acumen was never a match for Radetzky, allowed time for the Austrians to regroup. Austria always had far more resources at its disposal than did Piedmont. It was simply a question of how firm its resolve was to hold on to its Italian possessions. Carlo Alberto's indecision effectively guaranteed Austria victory. Reinforcements duly arrived and the Piedmontese army was crushed at Custozza in July.

Given the ambiguity of Piedmontese policy, it could hardly be expected that Carlo Alberto would fight a resolute rearguard action. His principal concern was rather to limit the damage to his domestic interests. He hurriedly retreated to Milan in order to forestall the kind of popular unrest that could so easily spill over to Turin. But public opinion could not be easily quieted. Carlo Alberto had raised political expectations by putting himself at the head of the national movement. The return of Milan to Austria was thus a bitter disappointment. When international developments began to move markedly in Austria's favour, with the Great Powers determined to restore the status quo ante, Carlo Alberto bowed to pressure from the radicals in Piedmont, now exercising parliamentary power, to renew the war effort. His second military initiative was no more successful than the first. The Piedmontese army was defeated straightaway at Novara, in March 1849. Not only was Carlo Alberto's personal political credit exhausted but the fate of his dynasty hung in the balance. To salvage something he promptly resigned, leaving his son, Victor Emmanuel II, to make what he could of an impossible situation. Radetzky, in fact, behaved with some tact. The Austrians did not insist upon onerous peace conditions, for fear of exciting further disturbances. The Piedmontese constitution survived, on the tacit understanding that Victor Emmanuel would strive to suppress democratic and nationalist adventures. Piedmont seemed set to return to its earlier political stance.

The revolutions in northern Italy were thus stuttering to an inglorious end. Only Venice continued to resist. Its position, however, was desperate. Suffering from the multiple ravages of Austrian bombardment, food shortages and cholera, it could only delay the inevitable. A fundamental shift in the international position was all that could have saved it. But with the failure of revolution in Hungary, any hope that Austria might be embroiled in larger difficulties elsewhere vanished. Venice finally surrendered in August 1849.

Nor were developments elsewhere in Italy any more encouraging. In the Papal States Pius IX had been anxious to restore order and to calm the wild expectations which had accompanied the inauguration of his pontificate. Yet he had found himself committed to diplomatic support of Piedmont in the campaign against Austria. Pius was still seen by many as a natural leader of an independent Italy and had seemed to confer his blessing on the national cause. But such a course was fraught with danger for the papacy. It was one thing to mobilize troops in order to put pressure on Austria, quite another to commit the Papal States to war against a Catholic power. In the event, Pius withdrew, putting the interests of the church before the ambitions of the nationalists.

But Pius's problems were not at an end. His domestic situation had become almost untenable. Pellegrino Rossi, a liberal, was appointed Minister of the Interior specifically to impose the sorts of restrictions on freedoms of action and expression which would have been bitterly resented if they had come from an implacable cleric. But the policy backfired disastrously. Rossi was assassinated in November 1848, leaving Pius little option but to flee Rome.

The Republic which followed was a foretaste of what many radicals dreamt of for a united Italy. Power was initially in the hands of a triumvirate led by Mazzini. Progressive social policies were pursued and universal suffrage declared in December. But the Roman Republic was completely isolated. Unsuccessful efforts were made to form a democratic alliance with Venice. In the meantime, however, Austrian, French and Bourbon troops were massing. The Republic fought a heroic defensive action, organized by Garibaldi, but, with no help forthcoming from any of the other Great Powers, finally succumbed in July 1849.

In Naples and Sicily, too, republican hopes were dashed as forces of order managed to regain the initiative. Liberals and democrats would always have been forced to proceed cautiously in the face of the turbulence of the Sicilian peasants and the generally reactionary stance of the *lazzaroni*, the notorious urban poor, in Naples. Ferdinand II, having been forced initially to abandon Sicily, could afford to bide his time as the strategic situation throughout Italy began to favour the princes. The radicals cannot be said to have helped their own cause. Isolated from the other Italian centres and lacking any prospect of international support, it was essential that they at least co-ordinated tactics in Naples and Palermo. Instead they sought to pursue their particular causes, enabling Ferdinand to pick them off separately. By April 1849 Bourbon rule had been restored throughout the Kingdom of the Two Sicilies.

In the immediate aftermath of the failure of the nationalist revolutions, nothing seemed to have been achieved. All that had survived from the early months of 1848 was a constitution for Piedmont, restrictive in its provisions, leaving ample powers of political initiative in the hands of the king. Yet certain lessons had been learnt. Insurrection as a tactic had been shown to be almost wholly worthless without extensive co-ordination of policies across a wide range of political fronts. Nor could kings and popes be trusted to pursue nationalist goals if these should seem to clash with established dynastic interests.

What we see after 1848 is a new tone of realism. Where discussion of Italy's future had so often been couched in abstract or utopian terms, it was now felt that attention should be focused on more immediate concerns. After all, little was to be gained from endless consideration of the ideal form of an Italian state, whether unitary or federalist, republican or monarchical, if the deep divisions which such discussions revealed were to weaken the conduct of a national campaign. The revolutions in different parts of Italy had foundered in the face of intractable practical problems. And very many of these problems would be impossible to resolve at the theoretical level. The regions of Italy simply had different economic and cultural interests, as did the liberal aristocracy, the professional and entrepreneurial classes, the artisans and the peasants.

New regimes in Milan, Rome, Venice, Naples and Palermo had proved to be evanescent. Talk had been of Italy but regional and class rivalries reasserted themselves. Hostility to Austria or the papacy or the Bourbons quickly gave place to more traditional resentments: Palermo against Naples, Milan against Turin, the north against the south. But if disappointments were acute, the inference to be drawn seemed clear. Rhetoric and pious expectations would never overcome the profound divisions between the various subcultures within Italy, nor would theorists succeed in fashioning a common political programme without widespread popular support. What was lacking was a focus of political power which could manipulate propaganda in order to achieve practical objectives. Mazzini, to his credit, had long argued that ideological disagreements would have to be set aside in the national cause and had vigorously endorsed Carlo Alberto's leadership in the war against Austria. But in 1849 it seemed that Piedmont had betrayed

Italy. And no other Italian state had sufficient independence to assume her mantle.

Recriminations, especially among the radicals, were intense. Among the first to offer an analysis of the failure of revolution was Cattaneo. His *The Insurrection of Milan in 1848*, written while in exile in Switzerland, has remained a classic to this day. He had always been a reluctant revolutionary. And the events of 1848–9 generally confirmed his earlier reservations about precipitate action. What should have been a revolution in the name of liberty was transformed, for both the patricians of Milan and the Mazzinians, into the pursuit of independence for its own sake. Yet without liberty, the sacrifices incurred in political struggle would be futile. The interests of the Italian people would only be advanced, in Cattaneo's view, if the achievement of independence from foreign rule brought domestic liberty in its train. Above all, however, Cattaneo stressed the need to acquire detailed knowledge of a host of economic and political questions. Nothing could be expected from the masses until their level of civic and scientific awareness had been raised to a higher plane. The task ahead was thus essentially educational.

Cattaneo remained critical of Mazzini throughout the 1850s. He could neither accept the value of Mazzini's insurrectionary methods, nor his final goal of a unitary state. Political unity on Mazzinian terms would only constitute a thin veneer over a variegated mosaic of distinct cultures and economies. Italy certainly had an identity when considered in relation to foreign powers, but only a federal state would properly reflect the reality of her domestic conditions.

Mazzini came under pressure, too, from radicals influenced by socialist ideas. Ferrari, in *Philosophy of the Revolution* (1851), stressed the inadequacy of purely political solutions to Italy's dilemmas. The French Revolution of 1789 had caused giant strides forward to be made, but it had stopped short of eradicating the foundations of the *ancien régime*. What was required before a new order could be established was a determined assault on religion and property as the crucial props of a hierarchical society. Mazzini's preoccupation with the nation simply glossed over the larger social, cultural and economic implications of revolution. Yet without fundamental structural changes, political innovation would be merely cosmetic.

The 1848 revolutions had been vitiated, in Ferrari's view, by a failure to develop radical social programmes which would be attuned to the needs of the masses. Mazzini himself had always tried to avoid confronting social questions directly for fear of fostering class divisions within the national movement. For Ferrari, however, it was only by attending to the social needs of ordinary people that political problems would ever be solved.

Nor was Ferrari happy with the political form favoured by Mazzini. In *The Republican Federation* (1851) he argued that a unitary state could be imposed upon Italy's diverse traditions only at immense political cost. A federal republic, on the other hand, would be responsive to the needs of the people, without undermining a deeper Italian identity. Most important of all, however, Ferrari could see little chance of a radical revolution succeeding in Italy without parallel revolutionary upheavals occurring elsewhere in Europe. And, no matter how painful it might be to Italian national pride, revolutionary initiative on such a scale could only come from France.

Among the radicals, then, the post-mortem on 1848 exacerbated differences of view which had always been evident. Groups were split on the most fundamental questions. Cattaneo and Ferrari were sharply critical of Mazzini's conception of both the nation and the state; Mazzini despised the materialism of radical and socialist positions; Cattaneo could not accept Ferrari's arguments on redistribution of wealth; and there was no settled view on the vexed question of the relation of the Italian revolution to the European balance of power.

Problems among the moderates were more practical and pressing. Piedmont, the focus of moderate aspirations in the 1840s, had proved herself to be wanting. Yet her constitution and independence still singled her out as the one state that could lend political, economic and military weight to the national cause. Much needed to happen, however, before Piedmont would feel able to launch further initiatives. In the first place, the precarious gains of 1848 were under threat. Victor Emmanuel and the clerical right were intent upon emasculating the Piedmontese Parliament. That constitutional government survived in Piedmont owed a great deal to the skill and tact of d'Azeglio, Prime Minister from 1849 to 1852. Here was a man of impeccable nationalist (albeit moderate) credentials, who nevertheless enjoyed the confidence of the king. He was able to support the king in his stand against the democrats without compromising the principle of constitutional monarchy too far. But at the same time he could push the king further than he wanted to go, isolating the clerical right with the passage of the Siccardi Laws (1850). This ended a variety of ecclesiastical privileges and irreversibly shifted the balance between state and church.

D'Azeglio lacked the temperament and technical expertise to tackle Piedmont's deeper problems. Economy and society in Piedmont in 1850 still reflected the practices and values of an earlier age, lagging behind not only Paris and London but Milan as well. In the longer term, political independence alone would not be enough to secure her dominance of northern Italy. The events of 1848 had shown how rapidly the situation in the peninsula could be transformed. Piedmont would have to embark on a wide-ranging programme of reform if she wanted to retain her freedom of manoeuvre in the future, extending beyond politics and the law to finance, administration, industry and commerce.

Cavour (1810–61) was the principal architect of Piedmont's modernization. He was brought into the government by d'Azeglio in 1850 as Minister for Trade and Agriculture but quickly made himself a key figure in wider areas of policy through sheer force of intellect and will. He was deeply read in the most recent English and French writers on economics and politics. His technical mastery, combined with thrusting ambition, made him a difficult but at the same time indispensable colleague. He very soon assumed the ministry of finance, initiating a programme of economic liberalization. His first experience of economic policy-making augured well for the future. As an outspoken champion of *laissez-faire* economics, he might have been tempted to pursue a doctrinaire programme. But he managed to temper his pursuit of what was theoretically desirable with clear recognition of what was practically possible.

Cavour's rise to political power had been rapid. Yet he was by no means satisfied with the extent of his ministerial dominance. In 1852 he managed to conclude an agreement with the leader of the moderate democrats, Urbano Rattazzi, behind d'Azeglio's back. Cavour's *connubio* (literally 'marriage') with Rattazzi was the beginning of a style of parliamentary politics which was to persist throughout the liberal regime and arguably beyond. He had isolated both the monarchic right and the Mazzinian left at a stroke, leaving himself in control of moderate parliamentary opinion of all shades, able to pursue a variety of political options of his own without fear of parliamentary misadventure.

Cavour had always recognized that modernization on a large scale was a precarious undertaking. He had to negotiate the twin perils of revolution and reaction at home, while ensuring that his policies were sufficiently well received abroad to enable him to raise the kinds of loans he would need in the foreseeable future. With the *connubio*, however, he had given himself a parliamentary foundation that would assure him maximum discretion, ready to forge ahead or exercise restraint as occasion demanded.

From 1852 until his death in 1861, Cavour was to dominate the politics of Piedmont and Italy. Under his premiership, Piedmont began to look like a modern state. He persisted with the pragmatic liberalization of the economy which he had begun under d'Azeglio. A national bank was established, facilitating the raising of private investment capital. But Cavour also saw a dynamic role for the state in shaping Piedmont's economic development. He embarked upon a series of public works, involving railways, canals and elaborate irrigation projects. Reforms on such a scale were far beyond Piedmont's financial resources. Yet Cavour was anxious not to lose any time. He was content to go to the capital markets of London and Paris for funds, committing himself unreservedly to a very specific vision, both liberal and capitalist, of Piedmont's future. When he was forced to attend to the heated debate about Italy's political future in 1860, his own earlier policies had effectively foreclosed all but a narrow range of options.

In the early 1850s, however, Cavour was little concerned with the wider Italian question. He had set himself the task of advancing the immediate Piedmontese interest. If he had larger ambitions, they extended no further than effective control of a northern Italy freed from foreign rule.

Yet it was no longer possible to look exclusively at Piedmont's interest. The political élite in Turin had shared some of the enthusiasm of 1848, even if they had reservations about the direction an Italian revolution might take. Nor was Piedmontese political culture as narrow as it had been in 1840. Not only had the wars against Austria taught people to take a broader view, but

Piedmont had been a natural home for many of the activists forced
into exile after 1849. Those with Mazzinian sympathies would find
themselves living at the margins of Piedmontese society. Others,
however, of more moderate and flexible views, were enabled to
play responsible roles in politics, journalism, the law and
university teaching. Many of the political and cultural leaders of
united Italy, including Crispi, de Sanctis, Minghetti and the
Spaventa brothers, forged crucial ties in their years of exile.

Public opinion in Turin was thus cosmopolitan and volatile.
Cavour could rely on a secure majority in Parliament. But he was
aware that he would seriously weaken his position if he allowed
himself to get out of touch with informed and responsible opinion.
The heady expectations of 1848 could erupt again. And if they did,
Cavour was clear in his mind that he would swim with the political
tide. Taking a wider European view, he could see liberal and
nationalist ideas becoming dominant everywhere. His main
concern throughout the 1850s was to ensure that a sensible
reformism was not swamped by the wilder ambitions of democrats
and socialists.

It was in the international arena that Cavour displayed his most
characteristic skills. He would entertain a variety of options, some
of which might have appeared to be contradictory to colleagues
had they been brought into his confidence. He always waited for
the right concatenation of circumstances before pursuing a
particular course of action decisively. Like Gioberti and Balbo
before him, he recognized that political developments in Italy
would have profound implications for the European balance of
power. And instead of waiting to see how the Great Powers might
respond to upheavals in Italy, he chose to prepare the diplomatic
ground in order to bring about dramatic changes.

Cavour had seen more surely than others not only that the
Italian domestic situation was volatile but also that the traditional
alignments of the European states were shifting. France had
always been central to his thinking. While Ferrari and the radicals
had despaired at the prospect of a French-led wave of European
revolutions after Louis Napoleon's *coup d'état* of 1851, Cavour
could see the possibility of exploiting a nationally assertive France
in a more general anti-Austrian strategy.

But it would be misleading to suggest that he had a considered
policy from the outset of his premiership. He had seen a drift of

events and was simply prepared to take advantage of opportunities as they arose. The Crimean War (1853–6), for example,
marked a final breach of the alliance of autocratic states that had
effectively secured the status quo in Europe. Cavour himself could
initially see little point in involving Piedmont in what appeared to
be essentially a quarrel between Austria and Russia. But when
pushed by Victor Emmanuel to send a Piedmontese contingent to
fight alongside Britain and France, paradoxically in the Austrian
cause, Cavour was quick to seize a golden diplomatic opportunity.
He was busy behind the scenes at the Congress of Paris (1856),
especially among the British and French delegations, insisting on
the international implications of the Italian situation. And if he did
not come away from the peace conference with any tangible gains,
he had at least secured an uncertain ally in France and a degree of
sympathy (tinged with considerable mistrust of his immediate
intentions) among the British.

It was clear, however, that any radical realignment of powers in
Italy would very likely involve Piedmont in war with Austria.
Cavour could not risk a conventional trial of strength with a major
power. But he could persuade Britain and France that Piedmont
constituted an essential buffer between themselves and a
potentially dominant continental state. Cavour focused his
diplomatic efforts upon France. A secret meeting with Napoleon
III at Plombières committed France to support Piedmont in the
event of war with Austria. What is especially instructive about the
agreement is the clear limits that were set to Piedmont's territorial
ambitions. Piedmont was set to dominate northern Italy, but
independent kingdoms would be established in central and
southern Italy, involving a reduction in territories controlled by
the church. France would be compensated by the cession of Nice
and Savoy from Piedmont. Far from putting himself at the head of
a national campaign, Cavour was intent upon maximizing
Piedmontese advantage in the event of further nationalist
uprisings. The fact that he was prepared to see Italian territories
pass into the hands of a powerful neighbour was to sour
permanently his relations with some of the committed nationalists,
particularly Garibaldi, who could never be reconciled to Cavour's
calculating treatment of his home town of Nice.

Yet Cavour could not neglect domestic opinion. In 1857 his hand
was signally strengthened by the formation of the Italian National

Society under the leadership of Pallavicino, Manin and La Farina. The Italian National Society was never simply Cavour's instrument. The leaders were genuine nationalists, and Pallavicino in particular viewed Cavour with considerable suspicion. As realists, however, they had each come to see that the unification of Italy would only be possible under Piedmont's banner. The group was a bridge between Cavour and the wider nationalist movement. Branches extending throughout northern and central Italy enabled a new cohesion to be brought to the national campaign. And though La Farina tended to exaggerate the extent to which he had been taken into Cavour's confidence, the Society certainly performed a crucial role in fomenting popular demonstrations and insurrections in favour of Piedmont in 1859–60.

Cavour had thus prepared his position assiduously. Yet he still had to wait upon events. He could not present himself too transparently as the aggressor in a war against Austria, for fear of antagonizing Britain and precipitating international efforts to keep the peace. Nor, having provoked Austria into issuing an ultimatum in April 1859, could he rely on continued French military support in all circumstances. Indeed events began to move faster than he had anticipated. French and Piedmontese military victories against Austria were accompanied by 'spontaneous' insurrections in central Italy (organized in fact by the Italian National Society). Napoleon III, alarmed at the turn developments had taken, sought an independent peace with Austria, leaving Victor Emmanuel (against Cavour's advice) little option but to accept terms which fell far short of those agreed at Plombières. Cavour resigned, deeply disappointed that his schemes had been thwarted.

He was not to lose the initiative for long. Public opinion in Tuscany and Emilia, orchestrated by the Italian National Society, continued to press for union with Piedmont. Here was a dilemma for Napoleon III. As a declared champion of Italian nationalism, he could not publicly oppose expressions of popular sentiment, but neither was he happy with what appeared to be growing Piedmontese territorial ambitions. Cavour returned to office in January 1860, confident that he could secure Napoleon III's agreement to Piedmontese gains in central Italy in return for the cession of Savoy and Nice to France. Always a shrewd manipulator of public opinion, Cavour used popular plebiscites as a means of forcing Louis Napoleon's consent to what amounted to a Piedmontese *fait accompli*. The Italian National Society had served him well.

Cavour had shown himself able to take advantage of the most unlikely circumstances. In the spring of 1860, however, he was faced with a development which very nearly undermined his whole strategy. Garibaldi (1807–82) and the radicals, concerned that Cavour had no real intention of unifying the peninsula, exploited a small rising in Palermo in order to force his hand. The plan was for Garibaldi to sail to Sicily with a band of irregular volunteers (the legendary 'Thousand'). Everything would be done in the name of Victor Emmanuel and Italy, in the hope that popular enthusiasm (and fear of unrest) would commit Piedmont to extend the military campaign to the south.

Neither Victor Emmanuel nor Cavour supported the venture. Cavour, indeed, did everything in his power to ensure that it would fail. He could not confront Garibaldi openly because his own position in Piedmont was dependent upon the support of the moderate nationalists. But neither could he allow a Garibaldian campaign to generate a radical momentum which might prove difficult to resist. Cavour used all his unscrupulous arts to try to undermine Garibaldi's position. At the outset, he made sure that Garibaldi was supplied with archaic (and often faulty) arms. He even gave instructions that the expedition should be intercepted by the Piedmontese navy if it should use Cagliari as a port of call. Despite Cavour's best endeavours, Garibaldi went from strength to strength. A master of guerrilla tactics, he defeated the regular Bourbon army in a decisive battle at Calatafimi in May. By June he was dictator of Sicily.

Cavour was now facing one of the most acute dilemmas of his career. Not only was he compelled to think in Italian rather than Piedmontese terms, but the prospect of victory for Garibaldi might very well undermine the kind of economic future that had been central in his vision of northern Italy. Nor would the usual political wiles be effective against Garibaldi. His international reputation and personal integrity were proof against the sorts of tactics Cavour had deployed so successfully in his earlier Piedmontese career.

But Cavour's nerve held. His agents had been unable either to compromise Garibaldi in Sicily or to delay seriously his landing on the mainland. But as Garibaldi embarked upon his triumphant march to Naples, Cavour prepared to act. He was certain that it would be worth risking civil war in order to prevent Garibaldi from reaching Rome. The Piedmontese army would have to confront Garibaldi's volunteers. Yet the Papal States remained a diplomatic impasse. Cavour used the Italian National Society to foment disorders which he planned to use as a pretext for gaining a right of passage for his troops. His real object, however, was to stop Garibaldi in his tracks.

Once the Piedmontese army, with Victor Emmanuel at its head, had been brought into play, it was inevitable that Garibaldi would concede. He had always acted in the name of the king. Having devoted his life to the cause of Italian unity, he would not, at the last, risk sacrificing everything by waging a ruinous and unwinnable civil war. He was aware that much that he had striven for would be hopelessly caricatured by Cavour and the Piedmontese politicians. But the political battle had already been lost. The Piedmontese Parliament had opted for annexation of the south after a popular plebiscite. All that remained for Garibaldi was to offer the kingdom he had liberated to Victor Emmanuel.

The state established in 1861 is always seen as the culmination of a series of developments stretching back to the first stirrings of nationalist sentiment in the late eighteenth century. Yet from the very outset it was regarded as a hollow achievement. For Garibaldi, in particular, it was a deep disappointment that a final military effort was not made to bring the whole of the peninsula under Italian control. Rome and Venice remained in the hands of the papacy and Austria respectively. And they did not become a part of the Italian state until the balance of European power had shifted again. Nor was Italian military or diplomatic initiative crucial in the completion of the state. Prussian expansion obliged Austria to accept the cession of Venice to Italy in 1866, while the Franco-Prussian War of 1870 forced the withdrawal of French troops from Rome, leaving Italian troops free to take an almost defenceless city. It remained a source of deep shame to later nationalists that Italians had played such a minor role in the last stages of unification. Indeed some of the more strident groups, including the early fascists, contended that the process had never been completed, arguing for a renewed drive to bring all Italian speakers under the Italian flag.

Disillusion with the state went deeper than the question of frontiers. The various nationalist theorists had always seen political unification as the first step in a larger process of economic, social and cultural renewal. Yet the preoccupation with the state by no means reflects a national political consensus. Groups which could agree on little else had grown accustomed to regarding the emergence of an Italian state as the key to peace and prosperity in the peninsula. The deep divisions which had been evident in the immediate aftermath of the failures of 1848–9, however, still persisted. Arguments still raged, especially in radical circles, about whether an Italian state should be unitary or federal in form, republican or monarchical in constitution. In the event, such cohesion as existed in demands for unification in the hectic years after 1857 reflected an acceptance that constitutional issues should be treated as secondary to the freeing of Italy from foreign rule rather than a genuine political consensus. This, in itself, represented a significant political victory for Cavour and the Piedmontese moderates. Piedmont had been enabled to present itself as the state most likely to translate nationalist aspirations into political reality; but unification on these terms amounted to the acceptance of a Piedmontese state writ large, with the wider benefits which (it had always been assumed) would follow in the wake of political independence postponed for consideration in an indefinite future.

What unification amounted to, then, was a conservative (or, in Gramsci's term, 'passive') revolution, designed to accomplish far-reaching political changes while preserving the social status quo. In the prevailing national and international contexts, it may well have been all that could have been achieved. But it left united Italy with a host of political dilemmas which the liberal regime was never to resolve satisfactorily. Unification had been the work of a narrow political élite which was deeply suspicious of popular social movements. Cavour, indeed, had only entertained the idea of unifying the whole peninsula when it became clear that unification might otherwise be achieved on more radical terms. He and the moderates had worked indefatigably to ensure that the radical social programmes which had accompanied so much nationalist propaganda would not be put into practice.

Radicals could thus feel, with some justification, that Cavour had robbed them of their revolution. Mazzini and Garibaldi, having devoted the best part of a lifetime to unification, could not look upon the new Italian state other than with bitterness. Many of their followers and close associates, such as Crispi and Depretis, were able to make their peace with the regime, but on terms which effectively deprived united Italy of a regular opposition party. Those who persisted in agitating for the aspirations of 1848 found themselves pushed to the margins of political life, unable to exercise any influence upon policy because of their 'subversive' views.

The liberal leaders persisted in regarding the democrats of 1848 as a potentially revolutionary threat. Yet they were faced with problems enough at the other end of the political spectrum. Unification had been achieved in the face of fierce opposition from the church. Not only had Pius IX argued against liberalism and nationalism on doctrinal grounds, but he could also not accept the loss of his temporal powers. Problems were exacerbated after 1870 when Rome was finally added to the Italian state. Pius refused to recognize the state. He withdrew to the Vatican, urging Catholics not to involve themselves actively in political life. But the impact of this injunction on the liberal élite was slight. Most of the leading figures were either anti-clerical or indifferent to the church, and even those with religious sympathies (such as Ricasoli and Minghetti) recognized the need for far-reaching reform of the church. In the longer term, however, serious damage was done to the reception of the state in the country at large. The church had always remained closer to the ordinary people than had the political élite. Its active hostility to the state (formally ended only in 1929) effectively prevented the emergence of a broad-based conservative party which might have given the regime much-needed stability. Instead political life was conducted on the narrowest of foundations, with leaders feeling themselves unable to respond positively to threats from left or right.

Just how detached political culture was from the wider life of the country is evident from the constitution of 1861. Instead of devising a new constitution for a new state, the Piedmontese *statuto* of 1848 was extended to the rest of the peninsula. Piedmontese law and administrative structures were imposed, irrespective of the difficulties that might be encountered in extending the institutions of a relatively modern state to regions accustomed to vastly different practices. So insensitive to regional (or even Italian) sensibilities were the Piedmontese élite that the first king of Italy continued to be called Victor Emmanuel II. And the franchise itself, calculated as it was on a tax and literacy qualification, significantly overrepresented the advanced north. The 2 per cent of the population entitled to vote might have actually meant in practice only 300,000 people voting. The new political system was intensely personal, easily controlled by the moderates who had gathered around Cavour.

Parliamentary life thus continued very much as it had in Piedmont. Cavour himself died within a few months of the establishment of the Italian state. But though his technical and parliamentary command was sorely missed, political practices continued much as before. Though the Chamber of Deputies was divided into two broad groups, the Historical Right and the Historical Left, it should not be supposed that an orthodox party system was in operation. The Chamber was essentially dominated by factions whose leaders supported the government in return for political favours. The system was widely regarded as corrupt, but nothing could be done to change it. When the right fell from office in 1876, the so-called 'parliamentary revolution' heralded not a new-style party system but a further refinement of old habits. Depretis, the dominant figure from 1876 to 1887, raised parliamentary management to a fine art. The system of *trasformismo*, exploiting the personal and constituency interests of leaders of factions, sucked all 'right thinking' deputies into the government's ambit, leaving no clear distinction between opposition to the government and opposition to the regime. Parliamentary government amounted to something very like parliamentary dictatorship, with accountability reduced to a sham.

Nor were political leaders any more responsive to the wider impact of their policies. The regime had had to endure widespread civil unrest in the south in the early years (1861–5). Though the insurgents were officially described as brigands, the infant state was in fact locked in what amounted to civil war. The government was anxious to treat the problem simply as a question of law and order. But, as had often been the case in the past, endemic lawlessness in the south had been compounded by ideological disaffection, demobilized Bourbon troops and intransigent clerics exacerbating an already delicate situation.

The brutality of the Italian army in quelling the unrest did much to sour relations between north and south for generations to come. It was only in the 1870s, however, that official reports began to suggest that difficulties in the south might actually have followed from the imposition of Piedmontese laws, policies and practices. The removal of trade barriers had devastated southern industry. But the widening of the economic gap between north and south was no more than one aspect of a much larger problem. Southern culture could not assimilate Piedmontese legal practices. Northern intellectuals were doubtless sincere in wanting to see an end to the remnants of feudalism in the south. Equality before the law, however, could mean little to a peasant who could neither read nor speak Italian. In practice the rural poor became totally dependent on a local landowning class in their adjustment to a new and strange scheme of things. The very individuals against whom they might want to seek legal redress were thus cast in the role of their protectors.

It must be said that national political leaders had no real incentive to pursue social reform in the south. While they could rely on the political support of the great landowners, they were content to leave well alone. Practices which had vanished from the north a century before, involving the personal dependence of the peasantry upon a landed élite, were thus perpetuated. Nor has the so-called 'southern problem' been resolved to this day.

Suspicion of popular expressions of discontent persisted throughout the liberal era. The development of capitalism in Italy brought in its train new problems which would tax the flexibility of the political class. By the 1880s, for example, we see burgeoning trades union and socialist organizations, especially in the north. Indeed the first socialist deputy was elected in 1882, after the extension of the franchise to 7 per cent of the population. Artisans and agricultural and industrial workers were trying their political strength for the first time. And it was inevitable, given that they lacked parliamentary support, that they would express their demands in a new style. An enlightened political class, accustomed to the practice of *trasformismo*, might have been expected to accommodate at least the more innocuous of the practical demands of these newly enfranchised groups. Instead the response of successive governments was fiercely authoritarian. Crispi, in particular, Prime Minister in 1887–91 and 1893–6, used all the resources available to him to suppress socialism in all its guises.

In 1894 he dissolved the Socialist Party and its related organizations, even going so far as to purge the electoral lists in order to guard against adverse electoral reactions. The democrat of 1848 had become the champion of an authoritarian state.

The problems of the Italian state in the 1890s can be traced back to the same source as those encountered in the 1860s. A narrow élite had originally imposed political terms on a collection of widely diverse cultures and economies. Successive leaders had, in fact, recognized the fragility of the regime. But instead of seeking to bridge the gulf between the political élite and the wider society, policy and practice had served further to isolate the political class. The most urgent task facing the leaders of the new state had always been the creation of a genuine national political culture. Among moderates, d'Azeglio had early recognized that a unified state which failed to reflect the natural sentiments of the people would be a worthless thing. Yet his was a voice in the wilderness. The conventional wisdom was that a vulnerable state would have to be resolute in its suppression of civil unrest. This authoritarian attitude, however, deepened the afflictions of the regime. In the longer term, with the emergence of ideological movements not amenable to parliamentary control, it was to prove its undoing.

Further reading

The best single source for the period is Denis Mack Smith (ed.), *The Making of Italy, 1796–1870* (New York and London, 1968), which contains substantial extracts from crucial documents, together with perceptive introductory comments from the editor.

Further documents on the *Risorgimento* can be found in Derek Beales, *The Risorgimento and the Unification of Italy* (London, 1971).

Two recent general studies of Italy in the nineteenth century are Harry Hearder, *Italy in the Age of the Risorgimento, 1790–1870* (London, 1983) and Stuart Woolf, *A History of Italy, 1700–1860* (London, 1979), which is especially helpful on social and economic developments.

Someone wishing to set the events of the *Risorgimento* in the wider sweep of Italian history should see Giuliano Procacci, *History of the Italian People* (London, 1968) and Christopher Duggan, *A Concise History of Italy* (Cambridge, 1994). Beginners might like to start with the short but balanced accounts in John Gooch, *The Unification of Italy* (London, 1986) and Lucy Riall, *The Italian Risorgimento: State, Society and National Unification* (London, 1994). F. Coppa, *The Origins of the Italian Wars of Independence* (London, 1992) is also useful.

For general treatments of the period after 1861 students should see Martin Clark, *Modern Italy, 1871–1982* (London, 1984); Christopher Seton-Watson, *Italy from Liberalism to Fascism* (London, 1967); and Denis Mack Smith, *Italy: a Modern History* (Ann Arbor, 1969).

For detailed treatment of the period in Italian see the relevant volumes in Giorgio Candeloro's monumental, *Storia dell'Italia moderna* (Milan, 1956–86, 11 vols).

Among more specialized works, Denis Mack Smith's studies of the *Risorgimento* are outstanding. See his *Cavour and Garibaldi 1860: A Study in Political Conflict* (Cambridge, 1954); *Victor Emmanuel, Cavour and the Risorgimento* (Oxford, 1971); and *Cavour* (London, 1985). Those specifically interested in the larger problems of the south should also consult his *A History of Sicily: Modern Sicily after 1713* (London, 1969).

On specific issues see John A. Davis, *Conflict and Control: Law and Order in Nineteenth-Century Italy* (London, 1988), which provides a suggestive perspective on many of the central problems of united Italy, and Raymond Grew, *A Sterner Plan for Italian Unity: the Italian National Society in the Risorgimento* (Princeton, NJ, 1963).

On particular theorists and political activists see: Paul Ginsborg, *Daniele Manin and the Venetian Revolution* (Cambridge, 1979); W. K. Hancock, *Ricasoli and the Risorgimento in Tuscany* (London, 1926); Clara M. Lovett, *Carlo Cattaneo and the Politics of the Risorgimento* (The Hague, 1972), *Giuseppe Ferrari and the Italian Revolution* (Chapel Hill, NC, 1979) and *The Democratic Movement in Italy, 1830–1876* (Cambridge, MA, 1982), which surveys the careers of 146 prominent figures; R. Marshall, *Massimo d'Azeglio: an Artist in Politics* (London, 1966); Jasper Ridley, *Garibaldi* (London, 1974); Gaetano Salvemini, *Mazzini* (London, 1956); Harry Heardes, *Cavour* (London, 1994).

Students will find Frank J. Coppa *et al.* (eds), *Dictionary of Modern Italian History* (Westport, CT, 1985) a useful introductory source for obscure details and figures.

4

Germany: independence and unification with power

BRUCE WALLER

Anyone examining the map of Europe in 1830 would be unable to locate Germany. There was the German Confederation, the *Bund*, which was almost, but not quite, the same thing. The German part of Schleswig, which later belonged to the empire, was not a member. That is perhaps a minor point. But East and West Prussia as well as Posen were also beyond the pale. Though Posen had a mixed population of Poles and Germans, it was part of Prussia and therefore entered the empire; it is now with Poland. Bohemia and Moravia – then part of Austria – were inside the *Bund*. They are now the Czech part of Czechoslovakia. Luxemburg was also a member. Nine years later it lost its French speaking half to Belgium and the German speaking half remained within the Confederation. But is Luxemburg really a part of Germany? The Confederation was not Germany. The language boundary did not define its frontiers either. Alsace was solidly German-speaking, as was north-eastern Lorraine; so were seven-tenths of Switzerland. About one quarter of the Austrians were German speakers. But were they also Germans? The nobility of the Russian Baltic provinces were pure German as was their culture. Going by the standards of the day it would not be unfair to regard these areas as German too. Indeed in eastern Europe it was impossible to draw geographical lines between different linguistic cultures. There was many a city dominated by Germans and Yiddish-speaking Jews deep inside the Polish countryside. Here too each social group was sometimes a separate linguistic nation. In other words, in the east the lines of German nationhood were feathered, geographically and socially. In the west the language frontier was sharp and relatively stable over several generations. It ran in a more or less straight line south from just east of Liège to the north-eastern tip of Lake Geneva.

In 1830 there was no political definition of Germany. The linguistic gauge does not help either. Nor did those living in what was to become the German Empire have much notion of what Germany was. Hardly anyone would have believed that what was to emerge in forty-one years was the true Germany. Most of the inhabitants of what would be the empire hardly looked beyond the bounds of their own locality, or principality at best in 1830. To say that their outlook was provincial would be to attribute to most of them excessive vision. For the sake of simplicity this chapter will be confined, arbitrarily perhaps, to the area of the empire of 1871.

Most Germans in 1830 lived in the country, seven out of ten in villages. They were peasants or country artisans, and their life pattern had barely changed over the centuries. But the peasants were beginning to rotate crops and so to abandon the three field system. The process of serf emancipation had started some twenty years earlier and progressed in stages. Former common land was being divided and ploughed. The peasants' obligations to their lord had dwindled to a minimum, but so had the responsibility of the lord to them. Some former serfs, those who had been fairly well-placed under the previous semi-feudal set-up, were becoming independent farmers. Most were turning into landless labourers. The acute observer could see that these changes would eventually profoundly alter rural society. But in 1830 it did seem as if little had changed in a hundred years, and that German peasants would continue to plough and to harvest just as their fathers had done.

There were hardly any big cities. Berlin, Hamburg and Vienna had over 100,000 people, the rest had fewer. Essen had about 6,000, Düsseldorf three times as many. Most towns were small and isolated; many were still shielded by medieval walls. English travellers found them quaint and old-fashioned; they were. Led by Prussia, the German governments were hard at work dismantling restrictions on trade and manufacture. But there was little visible impact. Every aspect of town life was very much under the control of the guilds, which were not merely economic institutions but also powerful agents of social control. Even in wealthy and bustling city-republics such as Frankfurt guild control was all-pervasive. Citizens with voting rights could not change their profession without municipal approval. Competition was a dirty word. If this was true in enlightened bourgeois cities, one can imagine the extent of traditional corporate control in less favoured places. Transportation and travel were arduous. Roads were stony or muddy and interrupted by turnpikes. Goods were carried at walking-pace. Agreements in 1823 freed commerce on the Elbe and Weser from customs impediments and a similar, and more effective one, in 1831 facilitated communication on the Rhine. This was a first step, but no more than that. Movement from one place to another of goods or people was still an adventure.

People were divided not into classes determined directly or indirectly by financial factors, but rather into estates or corporations determined by birth. Most Germans accepted their lot in a fairly static society and took pride in their work, which in any case was done at home. There was no division between private life and employment. For artisans there was no retreat from their masters. On or off the job they stayed together. Primary education was widespread. About 85 per cent of the population could read and write, that is, they could sign their names in the parish marriage registers. This is how historians derive statistics on literacy. Secondary and tertiary education had been reformed, and so small numbers of well-educated individuals were beginning to emerge. It is important to note that the somnolence and narrowness everywhere apparent in Germany went hand in hand with a high work morale and relatively advanced standards of education at all levels.

The individual princes ruled not despotically but firmly, and with the help of enlightened bureaucrats whose attention to legal niceties was already becoming risible to some and insufferable to others. In the south and west several states had constitutions. But even where there was none the princes and their fussy bureaucrats adhered – more or less – to the law. The rulers' power was not absolute. They were naturally keen to preserve what rights they had and so were reluctant to change. But their large number led to a certain amount of rivalry. Each needed not only a town and country palace, but also a theatre or opera house and a university. This had long been the case. Strangely, provincialism and strong government furthered more than it hindered the cultural life of the nation. And the growth of a German national culture eroded both provincial and princely authority.

Two decades earlier Madam de Staël had characterized the Germans as philosophical, musical, fussy and impractical – gentle cranks, in other words. In 1830 there was apparently no reason to think otherwise.

A glance at imperial Germany in 1890 reveals a startlingly different picture. A languid people without identifiable frontiers, lacking influence and wealth as well as international standing had become the military, political and intellectual leaders of Europe. The population had almost doubled, going from just under 30 million to about 50 million. The predominance of the rural economy had been almost entirely overcome. Agriculture had been revolutionized. Output per man and acre was much improved. New methods were employed, as were new machines and the results of agricultural chemistry. But agriculture was not prosperous. Most of the previous, noble landowners had been replaced by middle-class men. Many of the descendants of former serfs had moved in droves first to the nearest town and then increasingly to the growing industrial agglomerations, especially the Ruhr, and in the 1880s abroad to the USA. Others remained as landless labourers on the verge of destitution. A few had established themselves as relatively prosperous farmers. Clearly, centuries of stagnation had been followed by sixty years of unexpected and hectic change. The anchor of tradition had been lost, leaving adrift virtually all who depended on agriculture. Remarkable as this revolution was, an even more astonishing metamorphosis took place in the towns. There were many more towns and large cities. Berlin was at 1.5 million, and seventeen other towns had more than 100,000 people. Düsseldorf had grown eight times over to about 150,000, and Essen sixteen times over to about 100,000. Here too the force of tradition – represented by the guilds and their virtually total control of town life – had been shattered. Estates, or corporations, had yielded to classes: the complex pre-industrial society based on simple technology was replaced by an apparently more simple society stratified according to income and based on complex technology. Not only were workplace and home separated; the towns themselves were segregated. Instead of high and low living together, they inhabited different parts of the town. We can see here already signs of the alienation which has become such a problem today. Not unconnected with the advancement of cold logic in relationships between men was the countervailing trend towards the sentimentalization of marriage. In 1830 marriage and children were 'facts of life' or, put another way, tended to be treated as assets to be acquired and deployed sensibly. Sixty years later people married more often for love, and children were objects of affection.

Products, methods of production and business organization were new and constantly in flux. A sign of the change was the levelling of the town walls. Medieval impediments to communication were paved over so as to facilitate the flow of people, goods and also ideas. On their ancient foundations curving avenues were constructed, like the *Ringstrasse* in Vienna which grandly paid ironic homage to modernity. The country was tied with a dense railway network. Travel and wire communication across the frontier was easy as well. Germans were increasingly becoming cosmopolitans. The arts and sciences flourished, and Germany's educational institutions led the world.

How can we explain this rapid and complete transformation? It was certainly far from inevitable and not foreseen at all from the outset. Four elements among many were of outstanding importance and need examination.

First of all there was the political side of the story. One thing we must get clear from the start: in the first half of our period there was no unswerving and firm determination to achieve unification and added power. There was much bickering and pettiness all round and little notion of direction. Even Prussian policy suffered from a surfeit of amiability concerning large issues and so had little sense of mission until this was thrust on it by Bismarck in 1862.

Within ten years of the Congress of Vienna twenty-nine of the forty-one member states in the *Bund* had constitutions of one kind or another. Of these the four large south German states of Bavaria, Baden, Württemberg and Hessen-Darmstadt were certainly the most important. Then, after the disturbances of 1830, either improved or new constitutions were adopted, mainly in central Germany, notably in Brunswick, Saxony, Hanover and Electoral Hessen. But they were not (almost) universally enacted until after 1848. The constitutions of this period were fairly conservative. They provided a balance between the government and monarch. In theory each element was equally strong; in practice the monarch usually had the upper hand. Conservative as this arrangement was, it did draw educated people into public affairs. Open discussion of political issues began – first in the south-west, but after 1848 there were platforms for public debate everywhere. This was one thing which prised Germans out of their provincial or municipal shells and so destroyed the old political set-up. But we must not attribute too much significance to the growth of constitutionalism, liberalism and a general public spirit. Public opinion reflected in the demand for constitutional and liberal reform was not quite so modern in outlook as we may think. Many early liberals merely desired the right of consultation for the wealthy and educated. This was not a very far-reaching political demand.

As for the economy, they wanted the retention of guild control. Wherever these groups were influential, as in the city-republics of Frankfurt or Hamburg, they acted more on traditional than on modern lines; after 1815 their first concern was to return to eighteenth-century habits. Much liberal reform came rather from the enlightened bureaucracy, staffed with well-to-do professionals and aristocrats who were conscientious rather than self-serving and had a keen sense for the real interests of their own individual states. They forced an ample portion of liberal measures on a resisting business class, which in the first part of the century at least keenly resented this intervention. Their negative attitude did not change until the industrial revolution began to take giant strides, after mid-century. By limiting the scope for arbitrary monarchical behaviour in countless ways the rule of law was buttressed, for the meddling bureaucrats did not act capriciously but rather on general guidelines. By hacking away at layers of traditional restraints such as those of the guilds, and by facilitating the change-over in the large agricultural sector from a late feudal structure to a more modern and freer society, bureaucrats performed an essential task. It was not generally appreciated but it did more substantially to modernize Germany than the parliamentary and extra-parliamentary activity of government opponents. The widespread German belief that good administration meant more than representative institutions had thus a firm foundation in reality and is not necessarily a sign of political otherworldliness.

The change from eighteenth-century absolutism to bureaucratic and firm government with liberal inclinations was revolutionary.

It was wrought from above and in many ways against the wishes of those who were the ultimate beneficiaries. It did not become clear to liberals until the 1860s, and in some cases the 1870s, that most of what they wanted had been accomplished by the individual states and not by their effort. That weakened their position *vis-à-vis* the state and helps explain the reluctance of the liberals to press hard for parliamentary government – a form of government which has not only a Parliament with extensive powers, but one to which the government is responsible. One could and did argue that a sound government should not be too much at the mercy of parliamentary windbags. After unification the whole of the German legal system was standardized on fairly liberal principles, culminating in the inauguration of the civil code in 1900. With this the ethos of restrained liberalism permeated society. The transformation from the vestigial feudalism of 1830 had, with the aid of enlightened bureaucrats, been completed; from 1871 on they were assisted by the imperial Parliament.

Turning to foreign policy, that is, the history of the relations between German states, the pattern of reasonably uniform advancement following a Prussian lead is not so clear. First of all, before Bismarck Prussian policy was self-effacing. There was only one possible exception. That was the short (approximately eighteen months) period in 1849 and 1850 when Frederick William IV and Radowitz, his chief adviser, tried to unite Germany behind Prussia. But this was merely an episode, the humiliating outcome of which is more characteristic than its ambitious conception. Secondly, the other German states which later became part of the empire followed a reasonable but necessarily provincial policy throughout. That meant that they were an impediment to unification. They made virtually no positive contribution, and it is easy to see why they did not and indeed could not have done so.

As for Prussia before Bismarck became Prime Minister the picture was similar. In this period he had already realized that Prussia could capitalize on its own inherent strength by conceding something to the powerful and popular constitutional-liberal and national movement. By yielding in some ways he could gain, and influence an ally. This was the secret to his success. It was not a question of saddling a spirited horse and riding it hard his own way as many books would have it. The war against Denmark in union with Austria in 1864 and the war against Austria in 1866 were the Machiavellian start. But these wars were immediately followed by the Constitution of the North German Confederation in 1867, which by uniting most of Germany went a long way towards satisfying the nationalists, and by offering constitutional and moderately liberal institutions without crushing Prussian dominance appealed to liberals. What the Parliament of the North German Confederation could not do was set up and bring down a government. And historians have dwelt on this admittedly important point rather too much. The fact is that it had very extensive powers and used them vigorously, in the spirit of liberalism. By no stretch of the imagination was it the lap-dog of the government. One might mention in passing that the Parliament had a mandate based on universal and secret manhood suffrage. This was inaugurated at the time when a parallel British electoral reform was a good deal more cautious.

The war of 1870 pitting Prussia and her allies against imperial France resulted in equal measure from the calculations and ambitions of the two foreign ministries concerned. It could have gone either way, but the odds were for a Prussian victory. Bismarck knew this, Napoleon and his advisers did not. Both sides gambled. It is to Bismarck's credit that after having won the war he refused to chance another. His nervous and erratic foreign policy after victory in Sedan in 1870 was peaceful in purpose. On the domestic scene he tried to achieve a balance between the old and the new. Looking at the 1870s and 1880s as a whole, and putting aside for a moment the fact that the 1870s seemed more liberal than the 1880s, the trend in domestic legislation was clearly from conservatism towards liberalism. Bismarck wisely did not seek to prevent this, but merely to guide and slow it in such a way as to create an equilibrium on the home scene between rival groups so that he could hold the balance. Since he was at the centre he could exercise disproportionate influence by encouraging one side or the other as the shifting exigencies of politics seemed to require. Perhaps as a legacy from the period leading to unification Bismarck's methods in both the domestic and foreign fields were not as peaceful as his ends. Both at home and abroad he sought to obtain a balance of tension between his opponents so that they would cancel each other out. Though he worked for peace, it was an armed and precarious peace in Europe and a tense equilibrium at home. In the circumstances he felt that an imaginative use of sabre-rattling would be effective. Others disagreed.

Historians rightly concentrate on the unification movement and the policy of Bismarck, who was surely one of the great political figures in modern times. Unification is a tangible event of primary significance, but it did not necessarily make Germany and Germans what they were in 1890. The simultaneous process of rapid modernization in almost all German states throughout the century, and the concerted effort after 1867 were less conspicuous but more important. Unification alone would not have made Germany Europe's leading power in 1890 unless there had been a vast change in the structure of society and the attitude of Germans as they existed in 1830.

The second element in the explanation of the rise in German standing and power is the army, the military establishment. It hardly needs stressing that this was mainly a Prussian matter. It is not that Prussians were the only good soldiers in Germany – something which, given the heterogeneous make-up of it and Prussia, would be hard to believe. But Prussian guidelines were influential throughout Germany.

It is common to attribute German success in war to Prussian 'militarism'. But the word defiantly eludes definition. The standing army was certainly not large, but it and the trained reserves added together were. The army was also prestigious and served by the best families. It is true too that military virtues ranked high in Prussian society. But one may legitimately ask to what extent the situation in Prussia *substantially* differed from that in Britain, for example. Service with the colours was voluntary on this side of the channel. Prussia had a conscript army which was a little larger than the British. After 1871 the imperial German force was much larger. But a man in uniform was as attractive in Manchester as in Magdeburg. And if we look at the century as a whole, British regiments probably saw more action than did Prussian units. And throughout our period Britain spent consistently more on defence both per capita and absolutely. One should be careful not to overstate the contrast between a peaceful Britain and a warlike Prussia. Of the five Prussian kings in our period, only William II, enthroned in 1888, was warlike. Frederick William III, king for forty-three years to 1840, inaugurated the terse and brisk military rhetoric, but otherwise he was a peaceful, even fearful, man. His successor, Frederick William IV, king till 1861, was a romantic without military ambition. William I, who reigned until 1888, was an exceptionally good soldier. His military judgement was sound, but he too was peaceful and cautious, though he also had a strong sense of pride and so preferred to fight rather than to accept unnecessary indignity. But he was not a warrior. Whoever reads the published correspondence of Queen Victoria and William I may be excused for thinking that Victoria was Prussian and William English, for the queen's language was often strong and occasionally violent whereas the king's was detached and matter of fact. Frederick III, king for ninety-nine days in 1888, was also inordinately proud but would probably not have been belligerent. His son, William II, half English and half Prussian, was unfortunately both belligerent and foolish. He was definitely not typical. In fact the political Left in Germany lived probably more in the spirit of Frederick than all but one of his successors.

Just as the kings before 1888 were unwilling warriors, so was the Prussian army in spirit. There were, however, exceptions. Moltke was occasionally keen to break loose, and his successor as head of the German general staff from 1888, Waldersee, looked for adventure. But on the whole the Prussian nobility which ran the army was fairly cautious in our period, and it is probably true that the French army had more fighting spirit than the Prussians.

The general circumspection of the kings and the nobility had the advantage that decisions tended to be rational. Where the 'up and at 'em' attitude prevailed, as it did on occasion during the Franco-Prussian war, it led to very heavy losses. But the right decisions were usually made.

The army was ostensibly based on universal conscription – in fact less than half the able-bodied men served – and involved a period in the active army and a longer one in the reserves. This meant that on the outbreak of war the Prussians had a large and fairly well-trained back-up for the field army. This as much as quality is what brought victory in 1870. There were other things as well: training was good; mobilization was prepared carefully in detail; expert use was made of roads and the railway; the officer corps was turned increasingly into a professional body. In 1830 most officers had been amateurs; in 1890 they were professional soldiers. Prussian officers were surely no military wizards, but they had the edge in professionalism over their opposite numbers in other countries. We have an illustration of this in the surprise felt by the Germans at the illiteracy of some of the captured French officers in 1870.

Where Prussia was clearly in an entirely different league from the others was at the top of the army – the general staff. It was composed of well-trained and sophisticated professionals who took their work seriously. Just as the top civil servants were recruited from the universities, almost all of the general staff officers were graduates of the three-year war academy. Very few came from the line. The zenith of the general staff coincides with Moltke's term of office, that is, from 1857 to 1888. Every schoolboy knows of his towering military genius. What is not so well known is his ability as a poet, painter and economist. He was far more than a mere expert. What most people failed to appreciate was that the sureness of his judgement depended on the universality of his gifts and breadth of education. Amateurs preceded him and narrow professionals, such as Schlieffen, followed. The combination of Moltke at the general staff and Roon at the Ministry of War (1859–73) during the crucial period of the 1860s was fortunate for Prussia. In the early 1860s the general staff was subordinate to the War Minister and otherwise had little influence. When Roon drew up his army reorganization plan, mentioned below, he did not consult Moltke. As an intellectual supposedly out of touch with reality, Moltke was also not consulted during the Danish war until the army ran into trouble. After this his ability was quickly recognized. Moltke had the requisite military knowledge and Roon the force of personality to back him.

In the dispute over its future the army might have suffered a serious set-back which could well have so damaged its effectiveness as to make victory in 1866 much more troublesome and triumph in 1871 perhaps unlikely. During the Franco-Austrian war, in 1859, the Prussian army had mobilized, and numerous defects in it had come to light. Moltke and Roon determined to remedy them, and did so with remarkable success. But there was protracted conflict with Parliament over whether conscripts should serve two or three years with the regular army before going to the reserves. Parliament wanted only two years, which it thought had sufficed in the past. The king, William I, believed that three were needed. Two years probably would have been adequate for defensive purposes; for any kind of active foreign policy, however, three were really advisable. But what was also at stake in the famous army conflict, apart from military effectiveness, was the political allegiance of the army. The longer a soldier wore the king's coat, the more likely he was to serve him well. To put it another way, in a domestic crisis the king of Prussia, or any other European country, hoped to use a professional army, but Parliament banked on an amateur one. The king was on the verge of yielding when Roon persuaded him to call in Bismarck for one more try. We know that Bismarck came to save the principle of three-year service; he got his way and William was subsequently proved right to accept his advice. Without his arrival at the critical time the Prussian army may never have been able to gain a reputation for invincibility.

As important as the shrewdness of key decisions and the professionalization of the officer corps, and especially the general staff, was the degree of discipline and seriousness of mind prevalent at all levels. This was only partly a carry-over from feudal subservience. It was also the result of thorough training and good schooling generally. That this was the case is demonstrated by the fact that discipline and earnestness increased as the feudal past subsided. The same trend can be seen in all great European armies of the day. In our period the Germans were a little ahead. But if we look forward to 1914, there was discernibly less difference in the discipline of German, British or French troops. German discipline was not a function of subservience; it was a sign of modernity.

The victories of the Prussian army were not gained principally by excellent weaponry. German technological superiority was a sign of the period only after 1870. In 1866 the Austrians probably had better cannon and in 1870–1 the French had better small arms. Where the Prussians excelled in both cases was in the ability to get their troops in the right place at the right time. An American general inelegantly put it this way: it was the knack of getting there 'fustest with the mostest'. This was of course the task of faceless staff officers.

One further factor needs mentioning: the Prussian army, and that of her allies, was properly used by the civilian authorities. It went into action when it really mattered, not otherwise. It fought against rebels in 1848 and 1849 so as to complete the defeat of the revolution, and at the same time it was deployed cautiously against the Danes. But it was not used in 1850 against Austria. Then, rather than risk war and possible defeat when challenged at Olmütz, Frederick William IV chose humiliation. There were other times in the 1850s when the Prussian army let slip some opportunities for adventure. The imperial German army was also not called out between 1871 and 1890. This sort of restraint was not shown by Austria and France, which both dissipated their resources in pointless or unimportant trials of strength. The French and Austrian armies thus saw more action than the Prussian army, but were not stronger because of it.

We turn now to the economic element in the modernization of Germany and in its rise to prominence. What appeared as a fairly backward area in 1830 underwent rapid transformation in the following sixty years. The growth of heavy industry and the birth of high technology business were the two most prominent aspects of this expansion, but were not the whole story. The upsurge in agricultural output was not only impressive, it also made industrialization possible. The population was growing before industrialization started, but until about mid-century agricultural output managed to swell just enough to accommodate this expanding population. Before 1848 poverty was very widespread but people could somehow manage. After mid-century the numbers in farming stabilized, but production expanded more rapidly than the population and so allowed industrialization to go ahead. Nevertheless the agricultural sector remained so massively important that investment in it was larger than in industry and commerce till the early 1870s. As already mentioned, this expansion was facilitated by the introduction of crop rotation and by the ploughing of common lands; this was part of the outcome of freeing the serfs. English and even American machinery was also used. A German development was agricultural chemistry. From about 1840 onwards, Justus Liebig was working tirelessly in the laboratory and as a popularizer for the cause of increased production. He made the use of fertilizer into a science. He, more than any other single man, demystified farming and turned it in a scientific direction. It was here that the German educational system paid off: where theoretical skills, academic capacity, systematic work and attention to detail were required rather than practical experience and the ability to improvise, those with a German education were at a clear advantage. In addition to this the states were keen to disseminate the knowledge attained from abroad and from Germany's own laboratories. Agricultural schools and experimental stations were set up, farming associations encouraged. They actively distributed information through journals, exhibitions and popular shows. The Munich October festival was one example. All these activities led to impressive increases in production, and in fact until into the 1850s output per man in agriculture increased at a faster rate than in the factories.

The gains made in industry and commerce were all the more amazing for not being anticipated in those areas. But some of the reasons for progress are not hard to find. First, Germany was not as impoverished a country as it seemed. Once the profitability of investment in trade and industry was proved, by mid-century, money was forthcoming. The population was skilled, diligent and relatively educated. There were abundant resources of coal. It is no accident that all the great European industrial centres grew up near coal seams. In comparison to this, supposed differences in national attitudes or the impediments or inducements offered by various national institutions matter little. The German states were also sensitive to the possibilities and advantages of economic change. But the amount of direct support they gave can be exaggerated, especially in the initial stage of industrialization. What the states mainly did was create the framework for development rather than force its pace: they strove to release private initiative. For a start, the guilds were whittled down to size. The Prussian corporation regulations of 1843 were interpreted liberally. A general German commercial code was agreed in 1861, and before this the fragmented money system was simplified. More bank notes were also printed: between 1850 and 1870 the amount in circulation in Prussia quintupled. In the 1880s, of course, the empire did begin to intervene in a more determined way. But this was fairly late.

In some ways the pattern in manufacturing was similar to developments in agriculture. The first steps were in imitation of the English (and were partly an attempt at self-preservation). As late as the 1870s there was a stream of complaints from Britain about shady and shoddy German imitations of its manufactures. But once the obvious artisanal skills had been mastered, the

Germans could move ahead by taking advantage of their educational system. At all levels of the economy the use of school-based skills began to produce worthwhile results. This was one of the secrets of German development. So it is not surprising that Germany was quick to advance into the more technological areas of the economy, chemistry and electricity, for instance. They were also very good at making sophisticated machinery. The states were quick to realize that educational institutions focused on useful skills were needed.

The Customs Union, or *Zollverein*, must figure prominently in any discussion of the nineteenth-century economy, especially of the period from 1830 to 1890. The *Zollverein* was inaugurated in 1834 after a decade of troublesome preparation, but it was not finally complete till the forced entry of Bremen and Hamburg in 1888. This lengthy gestation is sobering to remember. The *Zollverein* and the railways were both started simultaneously and were of paramount importance in uniting a country which without them was little more than a collection of provinces. The parallel and rapid development of roads and waterways was less noticeable but equally important. Together they created an integrated transport system within a single economic unit. A hundred years ago Treitschke described the commencement of the *Zollverein* on 1 January 1834 in these terms:

> On all the highways of Central Germany heavily laden wagons surrounded by noisy and merry crowds waited in long queues at the customs houses. With the clock's final stroke of the old year the turnpikes rose: accompanied by cheers and the crack of whips the horses pulled ahead into the liberated land.

It was indeed a great occasion, although it would not have been so but for the vast improvement in transportation which took place in tandem.

The reason for the *Zollverein* was quite straightforward. After the collapse of the Holy Roman Empire, with its colossal number of virtually independent principalities, German territory was reorganized in two stages – first by Napoleon and then by the Congress of Vienna – in such a way as to absorb nine-tenths of the states. All of the larger emerging states had considerable new areas to integrate, and the problems faced by Prussia were not unique. But Prussian territory was spread across the map of Germany and so the *extent* of organizational difficulties was unique. The creation of an economic unit was patently important, and the Prussian tariff was transformed in 1818 for this purpose. The next obvious step was to try to create a net of trade agreements with neighbouring states so as to facilitate trade with the widely separated Prussian possessions. This was the origin of the *Zollverein*. It was an act of self-preservation and an effort at consolidation. The king, Frederick William III, looked no further than this, but the bureaucrat in charge, Minister of Finance Motz, hoped that this kind of economic policy could indeed serve a more ambitious political purpose; his ultimate goal was a national and constitutional state. As the *Zollverein* was gradually extended by means of persuasion, cajolery and reprisals, Metternich saw the eventual danger to Austria but he apparently believed that some sort of economic concession to Prussia was advisable as a quid pro quo for loyal political support in his effort to use the *Bund* as a bulldog of conservatism. Seeing how restive most members, especially bourgeois strongholds, were he may well have hoped that the Customs Union would become a vipers' nest. Metternich's successors in the 1850s were not so complacent and tried either to include Austria, or to get a rival group underway. The trouble was that Austrian economic interests differed from those of Germany proper. Austria was more or less self-sufficient and needed a high tariff wall. The other German states were becoming integrated into the wider European and world economy and so required rather lower tariffs. Prussia therefore had a good hand of cards and the subordinate official in charge of *Zollverein* matters, Rudolf von Delbrück, played it skilfully. By the early 1860s the area to become the German Empire was closely linked economically and developing very much more rapidly than Austria. Germans were thus brought together first of all in the interest of survival and then, after mid-century, for the purpose of prosperity.

It is obvious that the *Zollverein* was in the interests of its individual members which were striving hard to integrate new territory after 1815, that it brought Germans together and directed their attention to north-west Europe, and that it stimulated economic growth and the accumulation of wealth. The extent to which it contributed to a closer political union is less clear. Since economic unity preceded political unity it would seem as if the one led to the other. But did it? Most of the members of the *Zollverein* were wary of Prussian domination and as long as Austria was a significant German power they looked to Vienna for political leadership in the belief that with Austria and Prussia in balance they would have the maximum ground for manoeuvre. And in the war of 1866 most members of the Customs Union were on the Austrian side. Once Bismarck had won that contest it was easier for him to use the Union as an economic carrot and stick for political ends. After 1866 the other German states recognized the significant advantages of co-operation with Berlin and the troublesome drawbacks of refusal to do so. Once the empire was founded in 1871, the economic integration of the member states was therefore less onerous than the smaller scale efforts by each of the larger states earlier in the century to organize its new possessions and stimulate the economy.

Throughout the period from 1830 to the end of the 1870s the individual German governments had followed the Prussian lead in trying to stimulate the economy and encourage the progress of modern capitalism at the expense of vestigial feudalism. The governments' approach was increasingly *laissez-faire* as regards internal as well as foreign economic affairs. The long depression from 1873 led to a clear and rapid turn-about from 1879 on. Steadily increasing economic liberalism had probably been a powerful force for modernization and growth. Whether it would have worked during the downswing after 1873 is debatable. Bismarck certainly had his doubts. It is however reasonable that when the economy is troubled, the government should step in with positive measures. Most twentieth-century states believe firmly in economic regulation and intervention. Indeed the origins of this century's interventionism are to be found in the German turn-around in 1879. Germany was not the first country to impose higher tariffs, but the rapidity and thoroughness of the new departure were very influential.

Although the states' mounting liberalism before 1879 was good for trade and in general beneficial for industry, the more traditional branches of industry were very hard hit. Sectors such as textiles, and metal production and working, which were having to face powerful competition from countries with a head start were greatly relieved when the change came at the end of the 1870s.

Until the growth of a rail network gradually created a national market independent of local conditions, agriculture conformed to its own logic. When the English corn laws were abandoned in 1846 the large German grain farmers, mainly in the east, began exporting to Britain on a grand scale. They bought British consumer goods and machinery in exchange and so were free traders. Prosperity lasted until the early 1870s, when the American and Russian plains were opened up for the world market and could produce at lower prices. The creation at this time of a world market in grain was a supremely important event because it enabled local crop failures to be counteracted. From this point on it became possible to alleviate even fairly widespread famine. But this blessing had its price: the cost of food was lowered and standardized to such an extent that the countryside suffered. Henceforth German farmers, not only grain producers, also wanted protection. They gained this in 1879, and in the following decade received much more. Prices nevertheless were so low that many farmers could not cope. Free traders believed that they all deserved to go to the wall, but in a period when labourers were leaving the countryside in droves for the German industrial cities and even for the USA it was certainly better to aid farming so as to prevent its total collapse. Therefore, whereas the effect of the change in economic policy on trade and industry was debatable, it was surely a blessing for agriculture which, we must remember, had already undergone remarkable transformation.

The educational element remains to be discussed. Education in its broadest sense is the least obvious, because least tangible, of factors, but it might well be the most important. Education by itself can do little, but the process of restructuring the vestigial feudal society which was rapidly collapsing in the first half of the nineteenth century depended on an educated population. The spread of literacy to virtually every German household by the beginning of the century was not the essence of education but the necessary means by which it was imparted. The essence was, and is, the implanting of rational thought and behaviour patterns in individuals who at the beginning of the century were unaccustomed, and even opposed, to this. Rationality is not everything in life, and many people whose reason predominates are nevertheless not immune from even the weirdest flights of fancy. Be this as it may, the need to familiarize millions with the advantages of rationality was pressing if Germany were to have a chance first to catch up with the others and then to make its own way. In the creation of a sensible, alert and adaptable population the German states were uniquely successful in the nineteenth century. A rough, but illuminating, indication of this is the fact that the number of book titles published annually – 6,000 in 1830 and 15,000 in 1880 – was about three times the British production. As early as 1831 Victor Cousin had remarked that Prussia was the land of barracks and schools. As the century progressed many others could see the significance of German ascendancy in education. If we look for lessons in history, there is none more vital than the value of learning in a rapidly changing world.

In the eighteenth century most German states realized the need for education of sorts and adopted the principle of universal primary schooling. By 1800 basic literacy was widespread and higher education, although perfunctory, was avidly pursued. When Napoleon overwhelmed Germany several universities and many schools collapsed. After ignominious defeat at Auerstädt and Jena in 1806 and in Prussia's darkest hour, so to speak, William von Humboldt planned a complete recasting of education. It was partly based on the French model but was more advanced and ambitious. His view was that Prussia could regain through mental effort what had been lost on the battlefield. And the government backed him in this notion. What Humboldt wanted was a comprehensive three-tier educational system which would actually educate at all levels. This meant that even in the primary school the ability to think would be encouraged, as would appreciation of the individual's intrinsic worth. This was in the long run explosive stuff for a traditional government and its officials to support. But they did so, though unfortunately not quite to the extent that Humboldt had hoped. Especially after the conservative swing in 1819 doubts loomed large and so the quantitative aspect of learning was stressed at the expense of the qualitative. Still, the new Prussian departure was epochal; it was swiftly imitated throughout Germany.

Those in any age group who completed grammar school were perhaps just under 2 per cent in 1830 and a little more in 1890. Figures for university study were naturally a little lower, but the upward trend was there as well. Most Germans therefore were products of the *Volksschule*, the primary school, and a myriad of higher, largely practical, schools. The primary school was clearly very important. It reached virtually all boys and girls and for a gradually longer time span. At the beginning of our period literacy was at the same level as it was in Britain at its end, in 1890. In 1830 four out of five school age children were actually in school. Within forty years it was nineteen out of twenty. That means that by 1870 virtually every child went to school for eight years and came from a literate family. In the 1850s and 1860s the conservatives tried to keep the curriculum as limited as possible, fearing that any amount of the wrong kind of knowledge was bad. Afterwards, Adalbert Falk, the main author of the *Kulturkampf*, put more resources into the system, adding extra classes; until then most schools had but one class and the older children helped the younger ones. He also made the teaching programme tangibly useful. Here in the lowly *Volksschule* we can see the central problem for the conservatives, a problem which was visible at higher levels as well: they wanted practical education, believing that it was safer, but the encouragement thus given to rational thought and behaviour insidiously undermined the old order based on deference and unthinking obedience.

Scholars have emphasized rather too much the patriotic purpose of primary education, arguing that the teacher inculcated the fear of God and secular authority. This is true, especially in the period before the 1870s and after our period. But during the 1870s and 1880s education was more factual. One should remember however, not only the corrosive quality of logical thought, but also the fact that especially in the first half of the period under discussion the village school masters were often disaffected and not enamoured of the regime.

The humanistic grammar schools, *Gymnasia*, were the élite schools. They alone pointed to the universities, and so to the professions and government service. Until the 1860s all grammar schools taught Latin and Greek to a high standard. They were almost purely literary and had little scientific content. Once the industrial revolution was in full swing, *Gymnasia* with a more scientific curriculum began to spring up. But only those with a large amount of Latin led to the university, and so the contrasting *Realgymnasia* and the lesser breed of *Oberrealschulen* had lower standing.

The nineteenth century humanistic *Gymnasium* was conceived by Humboldt who wanted to show that the civilization of the ancient past was greater than what the French had on offer. He hoped that young German minds would be warmed and ripened by the sun of Hellas. After about 1819 and the ensuing general conservative swing the programme of study was kept as non-political as possible. But as the famous opening passage to Bismarck's memoirs testifies, boys did not fail to notice that the Greeks were republicans of sorts, and so carried with them into later life ideas which were uncongenial to the authorities. The German *Gymnasia* were not quite as unpolitical as is sometimes thought.

Since the *Gymnasium* was a fairly standard institution throughout Germany, it helped to create a national élite with a shared education and outlook where an excess of provincialism had existed. It is worth noting that all the great German minds in the previous century were educated in these schools, the chemists as well as the philosophers. In no way did this classical education hamper Germany's rapid scientific and economic development. After 1890 the more practical *Gymnasia* received extra attention from William II, who did his best to support them. They trained narrow experts more thoroughly, but these men were probably less well educated.

Humboldt had planned a well co-ordinated system in which the three main levels, primary, secondary and tertiary, educated individuals for self-realization. The universities were the crown of the whole. In fact the three pieces did not necessarily fit well together, but the university Humboldt created in Berlin in 1810 was a magnificent and bold achievement. Hitherto universities everywhere were much like schools; they taught quantities of material to be learned. Humboldt wanted them to teach how to think and work independently by linking teaching and research as never before. Students and dons had virtually complete freedom – there were no set programmes. They were to work together in the advancement, not the recapitulation, of knowledge. Humboldt believed that everything academically worthwhile was important and interrelated. One must therefore see the connection between the whole and the details. So it did not matter what or how one studied as long as one could add to the store of knowledge and see how it fitted into the overall picture.

The research orientation which involved asking questions and seeking answers revolutionized academic life, first in Germany and then in the rest of the civilized world. The German universities were perhaps in some ways aloof from the questions and troubles of the day. That is a frequently made point. But there were nevertheless numerous politically influential professors. And graduates had more social standing and therefore influence than, say, in England. They occupied the key positions in the bureaucracy and the professions. Not so many of them were in business or industry until towards the end of our period. The prestige of German universities depended on their accomplishments in research, and their influence was felt partly through their well-educated graduates. There were thousands of graduates, but the size of universities was very moderate. In the middle of our period, in 1871, Berlin, the largest German university, had just over 2,000 students and Heidelberg little more than 500.

Humboldt's university was originally arts-based, and when the University of Berlin was founded German science was in the doldrums. After mid-century however the sciences had outdistanced the arts. Henceforth the reputation of German universities rested on their scientific accomplishments. Parallel with these, more practical technological institutions were established. They were modelled on the French *Ecole Polytechnique*, founded in 1794, and in the first half of the century they offered artisanal training. As science advanced, their approach became more abstract, more mathematical and theoretical, and by about 1860 several of them, led by Karlsruhe, had become virtual technological universities. Again a foreign institution had shown the way: the Technological University in Zurich, founded in 1856. As new and useful establishments without secure funding (they depended on the generosity of industry) they lacked the lustre of the universities, but provided the skilled technicians to keep the wheels of industry spinning ever faster.

German technological education made little contribution to the early phase of industrialization, whose initiators had emerged from the *Volksschule*. But it enabled the more sophisticated areas to develop. So by 1890 German industry was already shifting its centre of gravity away from the simpler technologies.

The thorough transformation of German society by 1890 was the product to a very large extent of the *Volksschule*. Almost 100 years of something approaching universal literacy had an enormous cumulative effect. Since attitudes change slowly, indeed the resistance to change is formidable, the effects of widespread literacy take generations to trickle through the layers of society and so to erode the rock of superstition and ignorance. The great strides in secondary and tertiary technological education were beginning to take effect.

If we want to understand the Germany of 1890 in historical perspective it is not enough to examine the supreme achievements of Bismarck and Moltke, the diplomatic and military story. There is another equally important political aspect – the modernization of the institutions of the several German states. The Customs Union must also be seen in its wider economic context. Finally there was the work of the threadbare village teacher, the pompous Latin master, and the professor, part entrepreneur, part recluse. The picture that emerges is very different from the cliché of a militarized society, technologically sophisticated but completely in the grip of feudal barons.

Further reading

SURVEYS

W. Carr, *A History of Germany, 1815–1985* (London, 1987) – the best brief survey; G. Craig, *Germany, 1866–1945* (Oxford, 1978) – well-balanced traditional history superbly written; H. Holborn, *A History of Modern Germany*, Vol. II (1648–1840), Vol. III (1840–1945) (New York, 1964 and 1969) – clearly the best extended account; A Ramm, *Germany, 1789–1919* (London, 1967) – solid and full; J. Sheehan, *German History, 1770–1866* (Oxford, 1989).

T. Nipperdey, *Deutsche Geschichte 1800–1918*, 3 vols, (Munich, 1983, 1991, 1992); M. Stürmer, *Das ruhelose Reich: Deutschland 1866–1918* (Berlin, 1983) – two magnificent new accounts.

RECENT INTERPRETATIONS

D. Blackbourn and G. Eley, *The Peculiarities of German History: Bourgeois Society and Politics in Nineteenth-Century Germany* (Oxford, 1984) – claim that Germany was moderately liberal; H. U. Wehler, *The German Empire, 1871–1918* (Leamington Spa, 1985) – argues that the empire was foredoomed.

IMPORTANT STUDIES

E. Anderson, *The Social and Political Conflict in Prussia, 1858–1864* (Berkeley, CA, 1954) – still the best study in English on this crucial period; F. Eyck, *The Frankfurt Parliament, 1848–9* (London, 1968) – a comprehensive and positive treatment; T. Hamerow, *Restoration, Revolution,*

Reaction: Economics and Politics in Restoration Germany, 1815–1871 (Princeton, NJ, 1958); *The Social Foundations of German Unification, 1858–1871*, 2 vols (Princeton, NJ, 1969 and 1972) – deal impressively with the background of unification; F. Hertz, *The German Public Mind in the Nineteenth Century: a Social History of German Political Sentiments, Aspirations and Ideas* (London, 1975) – a history of ideas in a political setting; P. Pulzer, *The Rise of Political Anti-Semitism in Germany and Austria* (New York, 1964) – clear comparative treatment from 1870 to 1933; J. Sheehan, *German Liberalism in the Nineteenth Century* (Chicago, 1978) – about ideas, politics and society; J. Snell, *The Democratic Movement in Germany, 1789 to 1914* (Chapel Hill, 1976) – deals very broadly with the Left, stressing similarity with changes in the West; R. Stadelmann, *Social and Political History of the German 1848 Revolution* (Ohio University Press, 1975) – most useful book on 1848; W. Carr, *The Origins of the Wars of German Unification* (London, 1991).

BISMARCK

L. Gall, *Bismarck, the White Revolutionary*, 2 vols (London, 1986) – the most thoughtful but also the most demanding full biography; W. Medlicott, *Bismarck and Modern Germany* (London, 1965) – by far the best brief biography; O. Pflanze, *Bismarck and the Development of Germany*, 3 vols (Princeton, NJ, 1990) – masterly and detailed; B. Waller, *Bismarck* (Oxford, 1985) – a brief interpretation.

BISMARCK'S COLLABORATORS AND OPPONENTS

M. Anderson, *Windthorst: a Political Biography* (Oxford, 1981) – sound biography of Bismarck's craftiest opponent; E. Evans, *The German Center Party, 1870–1933* (Carbondale, 1981) – a careful study of Windthorst's party in the 'centre' of politics; W. Guttsman, *The German Social Democratic Party, 1875–1933: from Ghetto to Government* (London, 1981) – thematic approach to Bebel's party; W. Maehl, *August Bebel: Shadow Emperor of the German Workers* (Philadelphia, 1980) – on Bismarck's most extreme opponent; F. Stern, *Gold and Iron: Bismarck, Bleichroeder and the Building of the German Empire* (London, 1977) – shows how closely they worked together.

EDUCATION

J. Albisetti, *Secondary School Reform in Imperial Germany* (Princeton, NJ, 1983) – deals with the issues behind reform; K. Jarausch, *Students, Society and Politics in Imperial Germany: the Rise of Academic Illiberalism* (Princeton, NJ, 1982) – a compendium of student life; C. E. McClelland, *State, Society and University in Germany, 1700–1914* (London, 1980) – a comprehensive treatment of the university sector.

5

Explaining the Habsburg Empire, 1830–90

ALAN SKED

Taken as a whole, the years 1830–90 cover a number of eras: the age of Metternich; the 1848 revolutions; the decade of neo-absolutism; the constitutional experiments of the 1860s; and the age of dualism.[1] Naturally, there is a number of controversies concerning most of these periods, yet before examining them it will perhaps be best to explain how the Habsburg monarchy worked.

Basically, it was a family concern, a collection of estates on a huge, international scale, which taken together formed the largest state in Europe apart from Russia. Most of the territories were kingdoms or duchies, acquired through marriage or war. The main ones in 1830 were the Austrian, the Bohemian and the Hungarian lands, along with Lombardy-Venetia in Italy. The dynasty also possessed Galicia (part of the former kingdom of Poland), Dalmatia, and Istria; while junior branches of the family ruled in Parma, Modena and Tuscany. According to Sir Lewis Namier, the *raison d'être* of the family was merely to acquire new territories; 'Every piece of driftwood carried to their shore was to them a promising sprig, which might yet grow into a crown . . . Their instincts were purely proprietory; the one meaning of an Austrian state to them was that they possessed it.' The Habsburg Monarchy, therefore, was first and foremost a *Hausmacht*, whose function it was to provide a power base for whichever Habsburg emperor had inherited it. It was his duty to keep what territories he had inherited; to add to his patrimony when possible; and never to surrender any land without a fight – or at least compensation. As the Minister for the Interior, Alexander Bach, put it in 1854,

'Austria will never relinquish one of her provinces'.[2] He should have added, 'peacefully' or 'willingly'.

In this dynastic state, all subjects of whatever nationality owed their personal allegiance only to the Emperor. They were not to consider themselves Germans, Italians, Hungarians or Poles. Hence Francis I's famous remark, when informed of the patriotism of a particular poet: 'But is he a patriot for me?'[3] The dynasty in return was supposed to rule its peoples impartially. As Archduke Albert explained: 'In a polyglot Empire inhabited by many races and peoples the dynasty must not allow itself to be assigned exclusively to one of these. Just as a good mother, it must show equal love to all its children and remain foreign to none. In this lies the justification for its existence.' Ideally, the result should have been an Austrian Empire run by the Austrian Emperor all of whose subjects regarded themselves as 'Austrians', meaning Habsburg loyalists. Yet this never happened. Baron Andrian-Warburg, described Austria, as early as 1842, as

> a purely imaginary name, which signifies no self-contained people, no country, no nation, a conventional usage for a complex of distinct nationalities. There are Italians, Germans, Slavs, Hungarians, who together constitute the Austrian Empire, but there is no Austria, no Austrian, no Austrian nationality, nor has there ever been any, save for a strip of land around Vienna.[4]

Reality, therefore, remained a very pale shadow of the ideal. This was particularly the case bearing in mind that the dynasty did not treat the nationalities equally, and in any case failed to produce any inspired rulers throughout this whole period. As a result, nationalism grew stronger, although only the Italians chose to break with the dynasty altogether. Until that break occurred in 1859–66, the dynasty continued as far as possible to run the empire from Vienna. Opposition from local diets was overcome or ignored and the revolutions of 1848 were crushed. But defeat in the Italian War of 1859 ended purely dynastic rule. It was not until 1867, however, that the *Ausgleich* (compromise) with Hungary was agreed and the Dualist System established. The river Leitha divided the empire into a 'transleithanian' – Hungarian, and a 'cisleithanian' – Austrian, half. Yet despite the introduction of dualism, Franz Joseph retained a huge amount of power and remained easily the single most important person in the management of the monarchy's affairs.

Between 1830 and 1890 the monarchy had three Emperors: Francis I until 1835; Ferdinand I until 1848; and Franz Joseph from 1848. Francis I had ascended the throne in 1792 as Holy Roman Emperor with the title Francis II; however, in 1804 he adopted the title Emperor of Austria and in 1806 dissolved the Holy Roman Empire. Franz Joseph ruled until his death in 1916.

There is no evidence that any of these monarchs was unpopular. Republicanism certainly never became part of the Austrian political tradition and even during the revolutions of 1848 the imperial family never came under attack or even threat. True, there was a patrician republican tradition in Venice, but even Venice in 1848 voted to unite with the House of Savoy. Likewise, in Hungary, after the deposition of the Habsburgs there in 1849, Kossuth failed to declare a republic but offered the Crown of St Stephen to others. The real fear of the Habsburgs in 1848–9, therefore, was that they might be replaced as the ruling dynasty in Italy or Hungary or might even lose their imperial pre-eminence in Germany to the Hohenzollerns (which eventually happened) but they did not have to worry about republicanism. Indeed, this had never been the case. Francis I and his Empress had always taken their promenades in Vienna unaccompanied by bodyguards. He greeted local citizens in their dialect and held a public audience once a week to which they or the peasants from the surrounding area might come to discuss their problems. His successor, Ferdinand, tried his best to do the same. After the revolution, this tradition was modified, yet Franz Joseph's reputation grew as his reign went on, until in his old age he seemed the very personification of monarchy and of the old Europe. Moreover, the pageantry and ceremonial of the court were part and parcel of Viennese life. Monarchy, therefore, remained at the very heart of the empire, whose *raison d'être*, in fact, it really was.

The human beings who wore the imperial crown of Austria, on the other hand, were hardly impressive. Indeed, for all its political longevity, the House of Habsburg very rarely produced sovereigns of stature. In the nineteenth century it seemed particularly deficient in this respect.

Francis I was a narrow-minded, suspicious reactionary, whose life was devoted to resisting revolution and indeed change of any kind at all. He told the students of the university of Pavia *'Voglio sudditi devoti, non sapienti'* (I want devoted subjects, not wise ones).[5] He revived the secret police of Joseph II and every morning listened to choice extracts being read out of intercepted correspondence, including that of his family, courtiers and political servants. He resented any limit to his power and after 1815 wanted even to abolish the already emasculated diets which existed in many provinces. The following conversation is supposed to have taken place between him and a deputation from the Tyrol, which had been returned to Austria in 1815:

'So ye want a constitution do ye?'
'Yes Francis', answered the two commons with a firm voice, while the lords and prelates bowed.
'Now look ye', replied he, 'I don't care; I will give you a constitution, but let me tell you, the soldiers are mine, and if I want money, I shan't ask you twice; and as to your tongues, I would advise you not to let them go too far.'
    To which imperial impromptu the Tyrolese replied, 'If thou thinkest so, we are better without any.'
'I think so myself', concluded His Majesty.[6]

Metternich, in fact, was able to persuade the Emperor to allow diets throughout the empire. When, however, in 1817, he attempted to establish in Vienna a *Reichsrat*, or Imperial Council, including some representatives from these diets, Francis ignored the scheme. It was still in his desk drawer at the Hofburg when he died in 1835.

Kolowrat, Metternich's great rival in the imperial government, was no luckier when it came to recommending change. In 1831, when he attempted to back up the suggestions of the Governor of Bohemia, Count Chotek, that the position of the peasants should be improved, Francis replied that Chotek had 'become infected with liberal ideas' and should 'leave well alone'. Later that year, the Emperor told Kolowrat: 'Look here, now, the landlord-peasant relationship is a red-hot poker. You can't touch it without gettering blistered. Take care that you don't burn yourself.' Hence it was no surprise that on 9 December 1831, he could declare 'I am killing these proposals'.[7]

When he died in 1835 the passage in his will containing his advice to his heir and successor ran: 'Disturb nothing in the foundations of the edifice of the State. Govern and change nothing.' Ferdinand was also told, 'Repose in Prince Metternich, my truest servant and friend, that confidence which I have bestowed on him through the course of so many years'.[8] Metternich, for his part, was almost as reactionary as Francis.

Between 1835 and 1848 the monarchy was ruled by Ferdinand. This was a great misfortune since the new Emperor was mentally retarded. In the words of a distinguished Austrian historian, 'Like Julius Caesar he was an epileptic. Unlike Caesar he was a simpleton.' His appearance was quite shocking: 'An enlarged cranium of great size, flattened at the sides, with, above all, the forehead arching steeply out, a long, powerful nose, and strong, thick, drooping lips.' Tsar Nicholas I of Russia reported after first meeting him in 1835: 'Good God, but the reality surpassed all description!' Little wonder, that his wife, Maria Anna of Savoy, is always depicted as a saint.

Yet there was another side to Ferdinand. He was always known in Vienna as Ferdinand '*der Gütige*', or kind-hearted, and was never despised for his stupidity. If he is supposed to have said things like 'I am the Emperor and I want dumplings' or 'To govern is easy but to sign one's name is difficult', he was also one of the most popular monarchs ever.[9] This was partly because he was supposed not to be so stupid as he seemed. And indeed he could read, write and speak four languages. He was, in fact, the first sovereign of Hungary for about three hundred years to address the Hungarian diet in its native tongue. His popularity derived from stories which had him saying genuinely quite clever things. For example, he is supposed to have slapped the shoulder of the court conductor after a performance of Haydn's 'Emperor' Quartet, saying 'I know that one.' After Radetzky's victory in Italy he is reported to have said, 'It's just as well we paid his debts again.' During the revolution in Vienna in March 1848 he would not allow the troops to fire on the Viennese, saying, 'Am I the Emperor, or am I not?' On the eve of his abdication he is said to have told Franz Joseph, 'Even I should have been able to manage.' Finally, he is believed to have greeted the news of Austria's defeat in 1866 with the words 'Even I could have done better than this.'

Why was he allowed to accede to the throne? Metternich originally opposed the idea, but Francis was adamant that the succession should pass through his eldest son in the interest of legitimacy. None of his offspring in fact was particularly bright, especially the next in line to the throne, Archduke Francis Charles. However, his wife, Archduchess Sophie, an extremely powerful figure at court, never forgave Metternich for allowing Ferdinand to succeed. Consequently she did nothing to save the Chancellor in March 1848. Even after his return to Vienna in 1851, she held her ground, saying that Metternich should never have attempted to run a monarchy without a monarch. Metternich's wife, Princess Melanie, now extracted her revenge, exclaiming 'But Madame, who was there to replace him?' Sophie reportedly 'bit her tongue'.[10]

It is not clear how Metternich could have prevented Ferdinand succeeding in any case, given Francis's wishes. However, there can be little doubt that he hoped to exploit these wishes in order to run the monarchy himself. (Rumour had it that he had even forged Francis's will.) In all events, the imperial family intervened (in the shape of the Archduke John) to make sure that this did not happen. As a result, Metternich was forced to run matters in tandem with Kolowrat in conjunction with a State Conference, presided over by the Archduke Louis, the reactionary youngest brother of Francis I. With the outbreak of the 1848 revolutions, however, and the fall of Metternich, the need for a strong monarch became ever more apparent. Ferdinand's abdication was the obvious solution, and eventually this was arranged in December of that year. His nephew, the young Franz Joseph, ascended the throne and was to remain there until his death sixty-eight years later.

Franz Joseph's reign was to witness many changes, but through all of them the character of the monarch remained remarkably fixed. Trained in the school of absolutism and ascending the throne in the midst of a triumphant counter-revolution, he endured as a cold, detached autocrat, with just enough cynicism to enable him, in an opportunist fashion, to compromise with constitutionalism whenever necessary. His basic faith in autocracy, though, never wavered. 'Believe me', he told Field Marshal Conrad von Hötzendorff, 'the Monarchy cannot be governed constitutionally.'[11] Hence, despite promises made in his accession speech in favour of parliamentarianism, he soon hired Kübeck to undermine even Stadion's imposed constitution of 4 March 1849. By the end of 1851 he was an absolute monarch, having already, between the ages of 18 and 21, succeeded in cutting down to size the strong man of the counter-revolution, Prince Schwarzenberg. Absolutism always remained Franz Joseph's basic faith. But in the early 1860s he was forced, by military defeat and financial desperation, once more to accept constitutional innovations. Then in 1867 he eventually accepted the *Ausgleich*. However, he still retained control of defence and foreign policy and had a very large say in domestic affairs. He may even have viewed the *Ausgleich* as an emergency measure, something designed to keep the Magyars happy while he prepared a war of revenge with Prussia. He certainly tried to alter it in 1871 by offering a special status to Bohemia within the monarchy, once Bismarck's victory over France had finally excluded Austria from Germany. However, the opposition he encountered from both his Magyar and German subjects at the thought of sharing power with the Slav element within the monarchy caused him to withdraw the relevant ordinances. Thereafter Franz Joseph became a devoted adherent of the 1867 arrangements.

His autocratic style, on the other hand, was always apparent. When the German Liberals in Cisleithania opposed the occupation of Bosnia-Herzegovina in 1878, they found themselves excluded from office for almost twenty years. The Hungarians, for their part, were equally firmly dealt with after 1902 over the army question. On issues of foreign, defence and constitutional policy, Franz Joseph simply expected his subjects to do his bidding and never to question the imperial will. In this way whole nations which had played their part in saving the dynasty in 1848–9 could be ignored. Statesmen, too, could be disregarded once they had outlived their usefulness – even Taaffe and the elder Andrássy. Franz Joseph's ingratitude was legendary. He acted as a landlord whose bailiffs were there to keep the peasants quiescent, and who could be summarily dismissed either if trouble occurred or if the money stopped coming in to support their master's primary duty – the pursuit of dynastic ambition or, in other words, foreign policy. This then is how Franz Joseph ruled – for almost seventy years.

To rule their empire the Habsburgs relied on a number of instruments, particularly the imperial army, the Catholic church and the imperial bureaucracy. Until 1867, all three were vehicles of Germanization, for the ideal of all Habsburg rulers and statesmen, despite protestations of impartiality, was of a centralized, Germanized and Catholic monarchy capable of dominating central and eastern Europe. Even after the *Ausgleich*, the Germans were far and away the most important nationality within the monarchy. Thus, although they comprised only 24 per cent of its total population and only 36 per cent of that in Cisleithania, they still accounted for 76 per cent of the civil servants in the Cisleithanian central ministries in 1914, and 56 per cent of those of the joint ministries. In 1910, for example, they occupied no less than 81 per cent of the top six grades of the Imperial Finance Ministry and 65 per cent of those of the Foreign Ministry. In 1910, too, roughly 75 per cent of all officers were German and in Cisleithania, 85 per cent. In 1873, 66 per cent of Reichstag deputies were German, a figure which declined to 44 per cent in 1907 (after the introduction of universal suffrage in Cisleithania). Most Austrian cabinets were predominantly German also. Finally, Germans dominated finance and industry, so that there was never any real fear of their deserting to the Hohenzollerns. As Peter Katzenstein has written,

> Until 1918 empire-wide institutions like the bureaucracy and army continued to offer the German-Austrians opportunities for upward social mobility (especially at the centre of the empire) which they could hardly expect to find in Germany. Furthermore, the German character of these institutions provided symbolic and actual reassurance and strengthened the sentimental commitments of the Austrian-Germans to the empire.[12]

In a united Germany they would have had to compete with Prussians, Bavarians, Saxons and other German-speaking rivals, whereas inside the monarchy they could easily dominate the non-German-speaking Slavs and others. It is easy to see, therefore, why the *Ausgleich* was so resented by Austrian Germans and why the Badeni ordinances of 1897 (which, if implemented, would have made Czech equal with German in the administration of Bohemia and Moravia), caused so much uproar among the German-speaking population of Cisleithania that they had to be withdrawn. On the other hand, the Austrian-Germans genuinely looked upon their language as a unifying and educative force within the monarchy and perceived themselves as pursuing a civilizing mission towards the Slavs.

The Slavs, for their part, deeply resented German self-serving assumptions of cultural superiority. They did so all the more, since they – not the Germans – formed the majority of the inhabitants of Cisleithania, and indeed of the monarchy as a whole. Thus Palacky, the main Czech spokesman in 1848, rejected all calls for Bohemia to form part of a united Germany, in the hope that the establishment of a truly representative system within the monarchy itself would give the Slavs the upper hand there. In point of fact, he well knew that they had nowhere else to turn. For if the monarchy broke up, its Slav constituent parts would merely be absorbed by Russia or Prussia. This after all had been the fate of Poland. Hence his famous statement, that if the monarchy did not exist, it would be necessary in the interests of Europe and mankind to invent it. The result was that throughout the nineteenth century, the Slavs of the monarchy saw no, or little, alternative to dynastic loyalty.

The Magyars found themselves in the same position, save that in 1848 they managed to secure well-nigh independence from Vienna and then fought to protect what they had obtained. Even after their defeat in 1849 they still refused to accept any constitutional arrangements which did not recognize their ancient constitutional rights. The result was that Franz Joseph finally compromised with them and accepted the *Ausgleich* in 1867. Yet it was only his defeat first in Italy and then Germany which made him do so. It is difficult to believe that the Hungarians would otherwise have secured a separate deal. None the less, not all Magyars were satisfied with an arrangement which left defence and foreign policy firmly in the hands of the monarch and which allowed him great influence in other matters also. However, Deak, the Magyar leader in 1867, made it clear that the deal was the best one possible. He said: 'Once we were a large state, but can we stand on our own now, wedged between the Russians and the Germans? . . . we cannot survive without powerful support'–and by that he meant the Austro-Germans and the Habsburgs. The Magyars were thus in the same position as the Slavs. In A. J. P. Taylor's words, 'In the last resort the Habsburg Monarchy was not a device for enabling a number of nationalities to live together. It was an attempt to find a "Third Way" in Central Europe which should be neither German nor Russian.'[13] Habsburg dynastic leadership, therefore, however bad it may have seemed, always appeared better to both the Germans and the non-German-speaking peoples of the monarchy than the Romanov and Hohenzollern alternatives. The Italians alone had a better choice. Hence their decision in favour of the House of Savoy.

As already stated, in order to rule effectively, the Habsburgs relied on a number of instruments, particularly the Catholic church, the army and the bureaucracy. The church, naturally, had greatest contact with the masses and was thus kept under strict supervision. Joseph II had regulated its links with Rome, appointed its leaders and prescribed its ceremonial, a state of affairs which continued until the Concordat of 1855. This freed the church from state constraints and gave it control of education and marriage within the monarchy. Liberal government in Cisleithania after 1867, however, not to mention Franz Joseph's own reaction to the declaration of papal infallibility in 1870, brought about the abrogation of the Concordat in the same year. Later on there was also a *Kulturkampf* in Hungary (1892–5). Thus however Catholic the monarchy prided itself on being, state interests always came first. The Vienna Eucharist Congress of 1912, for example, was to witness less the glorification of Christ than the apotheosis of the dynasty. The church for its part accepted Habsburg policy with relatively good grace, in accordance with its traditional alliance with the dynasty against heretics and revolutionaries.

The close links between dynasty and church went back to the Holy Roman Empire and in particular to the role of the Habsburgs in the Counter-Reformation. More recently, the experience of the church regarding the French Revolution and Napoleon meant that it was hardly likely to criticize absolutist, Catholic government. The illusion that Pius IX in 1848 might lead a crusade against this had therefore turned out to be short-lived. The church in Austria for its part had lent unstinting support to the Habsburgs. Indeed, the Vienna Bishops' Conference of 1848–9 had issued the following appeal to the troops:

> Brave warriors of the army who defend the iron righteousness of law and order with a strong arm, let no one do you harm or injustice and be content with your pay. Be seduced by nobody, remain true to your oath of allegiance which you have sworn before Almighty God. Because death stands near you constantly, think of Eternity and God and His Reich. Have a

conscience as clean as your weapons so that when the enemy
bullet strikes your brave heart, it will immediately release a
hero's pure soul to Heaven.[14]

The army itself was considered, in the words of Archduke
Albert, to be 'the dumb instrument of the supreme commander'.[15]
In 1848–9 it saved the dynasty, although many of its Italian troops
deserted and the Hungarian regiments stationed in Hungary in
October 1848 fought for Kossuth. In 1859 and 1866, on the other
hand, the nationality problem within the army proved negligible.
Mythology notwithstanding, the Habsburg dynasty had no
diabolical system worked out whereby troops of one nationality
garrisoned the homelands of others. Rather, in a multi-national
empire which conscripted men from all its constituent parts,
troops of several nationalities would inevitably be found at
different garrison locations at any given time. Paradoxically, at
least if the evidence of the Italian troops in 1848–9 is considered,
the longer regiments remained located within their own home
areas, the more loyal they remained.[16]

To ensure unity, the language of command within the army was
German. This meant that all officers and troops were required to
know about eighty words or commands in German, if it was not
their native tongue. In fact the vast majority of officers were
Austrian-Germans (two-thirds in 1910, 85 per cent within
Cisleithania alone). On the other hand, the regimental language
of each regiment depended on the nationality of the troops
composing it. There might indeed be more than one such language
if the regiment contained more than 20 per cent of troops from
a minority nationality. After 1867, the language issue in the army
was used as a political tool by the Hungarians, not so much as an
intrinsic grievance, but as a means of exerting political pressure
on the dynasty. The real defects from which the army suffered
throughout the nineteenth century were under-funding and
technological backwardness.[17]

It might be thought that the aristocratic ethos of the army was
yet another means by which the dynasty could preserve its supra-
national character. Yet the aristocratic nature of the army quickly
disappeared after 1867 once reforms were instituted requiring
examinations for promotion. By 1890, most officers were either
bourgeois, petit-bourgeois or even proletarian in origin. A

German pamphlet published in Leipzig in 1890 complained that not an insignificant proportion of them hailed from the lower classes.[18] This was a factor which worried people like Archduke Franz Ferdinand, who feared that such officers would be susceptible to socialist propaganda. Yet the army was to remain remarkably loyal to the dynasty right until the dissolution of the empire.

The final instrument of dynastic loyalty was the imperial bureaucracy. This was the creation of Joseph II and always retained its character as the Germanizing agency *par excellence* of the dynasty. As such it came under bitter attack in the 1840s from the local diets and nobles who opposed the Metternich System. However, after 1848, along with the army, it became the mainstay of the dynasty. After 1867 the Hungarians created their own bureaucracy, but in Cisleithania the German character of the traditional bureaucracy survived. Count Badeni attempted to alter this in 1897 by making Czech the linguistic equal of German within the civil service in Bohemia and Moravia. The result, however, was a revolt by the German-speaking subjects of the Emperor, whereupon the relevant ordinances were withdrawn. The role played by the bureaucracy in providing jobs and pensions for middle- and lower-middle-class Germans within the monarchy therefore simply cannot be under-estimated – as indeed the figures previously quoted show. The aristocracy for its part, although well represented in the higher bureaucratic posts before 1848, withdrew steadily thereafter. A few remained, but for the most part it was the foreign service of the monarchy which they found better suited to their talents and social status.

The Habsburg Monarchy in the period 1830–90, therefore, was a state primarily run in the dynastic interest of the Habsburg family, whose main function was to preserve its accumulated territorial possessions and if possible to add to them. To facilitate this task it employed an army and bureaucracy both of which were dominated by Austrian-Germans. The Catholic church acted as a spiritual ally. The position of the Hungarians was regularized in 1867 by allowing them to run their own affairs and to dominate the non-Magyar peoples of the lands of St Stephen's Crown. With the exception of the Poles, the Slav and Romanian citizens of the monarchy, on the other hand, were treated as second-class citizens. They realized, however, that they had nowhere else to go and so the monarchy could survive.

It is now time to examine certain of the more controversial aspects of Habsburg history during the period 1830–90. In practice this means judging the career of Prince Metternich; analysing the 1848 revolutions; examining the record of the neo-absolutist period; explaining the disastrous foreign policy pursued between 1853 and 1866; and coming to some kind of conclusion regarding the degree of success achieved by the 1867 *Ausgleich*.

As far as Prince Metternich is concerned, a number of issues have to be confronted. To what extent did he control events within the empire? Did he wish to reform it in any way? In particular did he wish to federalize it and devolve power to provincial diets? Did he run a police state? To what extent was he responsible for the outbreak of revolution in 1848? How successful was his foreign policy? What role did he play in the diplomacy of the period 1830–48? Did anyone pay any attention to him after 1830?

Let us examine his foreign policy first. There can be little doubt that Metternich's greatest triumphs in this field were achieved before 1830. Thereafter he occupied a position increasingly on the sidelines. For example, the Belgian question was settled mainly by Lord Palmerston, and Vienna played a distinctly secondary role in the diplomacy of Greek independence and the Mehemet Ali crises which followed. Moreover, if Great Britain and Russia dominated these affairs, it was Great Britain and France which dominated the diplomacy of the Iberian Peninsula. Even in the diplomacy of the *Sonderbund* War in Switzerland in 1847, Metternich found himself completely unable to control events that were taking place on Austria's doorstep. Meanwhile, in Italy, Austria's control also began to loosen. Nor could Metternich any longer think of intervention there. Previous attempts had proved too expensive; the last one, indeed, had provoked a French counter-move; besides, the European and Italian reaction to Radetzky's attempt to reinforce the Austrian garrison in Ferrara in July 1847 had shown how unpopular any new interference was likely to prove. Hence all Metternich could do was to negotiate defensive alliances with the Italian duchies and await attack from the revolution outside. By 1848, therefore, he was far from dominating the diplomacy of Europe.

This was not his fault. Circumstances had changed dramatically since the period immediately after the Napoleonic wars. Great Britain, in particular, was no longer so co-operative; France had recovered from defeat; Nicholas I of Russia resented being lectured to; Austria herself was financially weak and unable to support her military obligations, while Prussia had grown in both military and economic strength. Indeed, Palmerston in 1830 had already written: 'Interested as England must be in the maintenance of the Balance of Power in Europe, there is no state to which she can look with juster confidence than to Prussia for co-operation in her endeavours to preserve the balance.' In 1848 Nicholas I of Russia wrote to Frederick William IV of Prussia: 'Dear Friend, be the deliverer of Germany!'[19] By 1848, therefore, Austria was no longer seen as the main defence of the established order in central Europe, and Metternich could really only hope to sustain Austrian influence by continuously warning against the threat of revolution that he perceived in every sign of progress.

His warnings, however, were liable to be taken seriously. After all, despite Austrian internal weaknesses, Metternich was the Chancellor of the leading power in Italy and of the presiding power in the German Confederation. He was also Europe's foremost conservative statesman, whose principles were so well known that the Continent was supposedly dominated by them. In short, he enjoyed great moral authority. Finally, despite reports of Austrian financial and military weakness, it was never really clear just how badly or how well the Austrian army could perform. War alone could tell that, and war was still something that all the powers wished to avoid. Metternich, therefore, simply could not be ignored. In fact, he remained the pre-eminent, if not the predominant figure, in European diplomacy right until 1848.

From his own point of view, moreover, it is difficult to fault him. Clearly, he was never going to be able to dominate Europe without the help of others. Alone he could only expect to influence German and Italian affairs. Spain, Portugal, Holland, Belgium and Greece, on the other hand, were in the British and French spheres of influence. In Poland and the Near East, Russian interests would prevail. This situation Metternich understood and accepted. He worried, however, that the British and French would promote liberalism and revolution, and that the Russians would undermine the stability and territorial integrity of the Ottoman Empire.

After the Münchengraetz Agreements of 1833 and the Straits Convention of 1841 he could feel reassured about Russia. Tsar Nicholas I appeared quite content to preserve the Ottoman Empire. Metternich was also fortunate in that no liberal alliance of any permanence arose between Britain and France. Instead, disputes between these powers over Belgium, Spain, Tahiti and North Africa meant that Europe was spared the fate of being rigidly divided into two ideological camps. Metternich as a result could retain his role in European diplomacy as the major spokesman for the conservative powers, which remained more united than their liberal opponents.

Traditional criticism of Metternich, however, has centred less on his abilities as a diplomat, than on his role as Europe's would-be Chief of Police. In short he is blamed for opposing nationalism and liberalism in Italy, Germany and within the Habsburg monarchy itself. To some extent this criticism is anachronistic. His job after all was to preserve the integrity of the Habsburg monarchy, not to divide it into nation states. Moreover, the monarchs who had defeated Napoleon had hardly done so in the name of liberalism, republicanism or democracy. From their – and Metternich's – point of view, it was exactly those countries toying with constitutions which ended up with full-scale revolts. Hence it was France, Great Britain, Spain and Portugal along with parts of Italy and Germany, which seemed most at threat from revolution. Metternich, for his part, could boast that no revolutions at all took place within the Habsburg monarchy. There peace and harmony could reign between 1815 and 1848 simply because no concessions to liberalism had ever been contemplated. The outbreak of revolution in 1848, on the other hand, has convinced most historians that this defence will not pass muster.

The standard view of the textbooks is that Metternich was bound to fail precisely because he refused to contemplate change. In Henry Kissinger's words, 'Perhaps Metternich's policy should be measured not by its ultimate failure, but by the length of time it staved off inevitable disaster.'[20] Such a view however can only be adopted if one is convinced, first, that Metternich never did contemplate change; secondly, that there were forces of change which could have been accommodated; and third, that the revolutions of 1848 were the direct result of his failure to accommodate these forces. One must also be able to prove, of course, that Metternich was in a position to direct the domestic policy of the Habsburg Monarchy.

It is not in fact easy to decide exactly how much power Metternich exercised in these domestic affairs. As has been seen, Francis I ignored his memoranda of 1817 concerning the creation of a *Reichsrat*. Even in diplomatic matters the Emperor was very suspicious. Talleyrand – exemplifying this – at the Congress of Vienna, had reported to Louis XVIII, 'Your Majesty will judge of the confidence placed by the Emperor of Austria in his minister, when you hear that this morning he sent the Comte de Sickingen to me, to ask whether what had been reported to him by M. de Metternich respecting yesterday's conference, was true.' By the end of his reign, however, Francis had come to depend on Metternich and in 1831 had told him, 'Without you I don't know how to undertake anything.'[21] His will certainly made this dependence explicit, yet after 1835 Metternich's room for manoeuvre was once again limited, thanks to the intervention of Archduke John and the establishment of the *Staatskonferenz*. Metternich was now forced to share power with Kolowrat and to submit everything to the lethargic and reactionary Archduke Louis.

According to at least one historian, the result of these arrangements was that Kolowrat became the leading figure in the administration of the Habsburg monarchy.[22] Yet this is implausible. Metternich still managed foreign affairs; he still took the lead regarding Hungary and Lombardy-Venetia; and, along with the servile imperial Police Director, Count Sedlnitzky, still controlled the censorship. Kolowrat, on the other hand, controlled imperial finances and was therefore in a position to curb the Chancellor's ability to manoeuvre in foreign affairs, particularly by controlling the army budget. In fact, Metternich made the best of the situation, telling his colleague Clam, 'From now on we are united, one for all and all for one . . . the mere existence of this Council [i.e. the *Staatskonferenz*] will tranquilize the masses, who have a tendency to trust representative deliberations.' Earlier he had told him: 'We cannot sack Kolowrat – he would only come back as a ghost.'[23] However, given the rivalry between the two men, and the notorious inability of Archduke Louis to reach a decision over anything, the monarchy was now set for a period of stagnation. In Metternich's favourite phrase, it would be 'administered, not governed'.

Without the intervention of the imperial family in 1835, Metternich would certainly have changed the way in which the monarchy was run. However, this would have involved more co-ordination at the centre by the creation of executive ministries, not by any concessions to constitutionalism. His reform plans, in fact, had always been designed to establish bureaucratic efficiency, not federalism or devolution. At heart Metternich was a Josephinist, who wished to impose upon the monarchy a uniform system of administration run by a German civil service. But he was a Josephinist with a difference, and that difference was that he was prepared to tolerate the existence of emasculated provincial diets in order to delude the provincial nobles that they still had some part to play in local affairs. It should be stressed, however, that he never had any plan to increase the powers of these diets in any meaningful way.

The evidence for this is clear, indeed, overwhelming: for a start, his 1817 proposals were essentially designed to give the monarchy a coherent system of strong, central government, not to enlarge the rights of local diets so as to make them akin to the Hungarian one.[24] As Andics has put it, 'One of the fundamental aims of . . . Metternich's proposals was in reality to take away from Hungary her ancient rights and her, albeit very limited, independence; not, however, to endow other people with *similar* rights.' Hence his attempt to curb the power of the Hungarian diet and to control county assemblies in Hungary with appointed pro-government administrators. In his own words, 'If it is impossible to govern Hungary without a constitution based on the Diet, we are faced with the unavoidable task of so manipulating this constitution, that it will become possible to govern Hungary in the regular fashion.'[25]

In Lombardy-Venetia, too, all proposals for constitutional reform were ignored. Metternich persuaded himself, instead, that he knew everything that was going on there from the frequent reports sent to him after 1826 by his special envoys in Milan. The last of these, Count Ficquelmont, however, had the temerity to inform him that he was completely out of touch. He even had the gall to suggest a modest, indeed cosmetic, strengthening of the viceroy's position in Milan and Venice. Metternich, however, was adamantly opposed to such a scheme, which he feared would be taken for weakness on the government's part. He told Ficquelmont:

'Only by centralizing the action of the various branches of authority is it possible to establish its unity and hence its force. Power distributed is no longer power.' To concede any extra authority to Lombardy-Venetia would be 'dangerous' – 'the same thing would be immediately demanded by other parts of the Empire.' Hence Metternich's admonishment, 'Here is what is needed: that what we order on this side of the Alps should be carried out on the other; that people there should not seek to weaken our directives but to put them into effect exactly as advised.'[26]

Metternich's feelings towards Galicia, finally, are also worth bearing in mind. His reaction to the events of 1846 there – when Galician peasants slaughtered Polish nobles involved in an attempted revolution – was to suggest that 'the promotion of the German element' might obviate trouble in the future. He explained: 'One race of people can only be transformed into another with the help of time – and under altogether peculiar circumstances. The promotion of the German element must be sought through its continued presence and influence by means of the help immediately available, that is through its civilization in the truest sense of the word. The means to this end lie in increasing the sales of feudal estates to Germans, in encouraging the growth of the German city population, in promoting and spreading the use of German in schools and in other ways.'[27] This, then, was how Metternich thought of rewarding the Emperor's loyal Poles. In short, he was a believer in an empire administered from the centre and based on German political and cultural leadership. If he toyed with the idea of dividing Galicia into two separate administrative units, this was a plan designed not to grant greater autonomy to these units, but to help rationalize the overall structure of administration and to make the local Poles and Ruthenes more content with the basic system of centralized government.

As is well known, however, Metternich never actually got around to doing anything about administrative reform after 1835. Partly this was on account of political constraints; but character also played its part. Somehow, he simply never found the energy to push for administrative change. (He had, after all, apparently allowed Francis I to dally over his 1817 proposals until 1835.) This lack of vigour was sometimes ascribed to a 'feminine' streak in Metternich's character and it is curious how the English writer

Hazlitt once described something very much like Metternich's personality type in an essay entitled 'On effeminacy of character':

The idea of the trouble, the precautions, the negotiations necessary to obviate disagreeable consequences oppresses them to death, is an exertion too great for their enervated imaginations. They are not like Master Bernadine in *Measure for Measure*, who would not 'get up to be hanged' – they would not get up to avoid being hanged.[28]

Metternich fitted this character-type perfectly, particularly with regard to political concessions. Here he fell into precisely the kind of mental trap which Hazlitt had described. For when there was no opposition, Metternich saw no need to initiate any changes. When there *was* opposition, change was excluded as a sign of political weakness. The result was that nothing ever happened. It was the future British Foreign Secretary and Prime Minister, Lord Salisbury, who was to say: 'Whatever happens will be for the worse and therefore it is in our interests that as little should happen as possible',[29] but Metternich operated on the same principle for most of his career after 1815.

He always believed, however, that he was in touch with public opinion, which he could both monitor and – to a certain degree – control through the secret police. The traditional view, that Metternich's Austria was a police state, however, is a great exaggeration, not to say a myth. According to nearly all the memoir accounts of the period, people could read practically anything they wanted and booksellers could sell (but not display) even works published abroad which attacked the government. Foreign periodicals were also smuggled into the country in huge numbers (particularly the critical *Grenzboten*) and no one found in possession of banned literature suffered any penalty. Instead the censorship was used as a means of moderately controlling the press and the book trade within the empire in the interests of dynastic loyalty, religious good taste, and government policy. There was little radical opposition to the government anyway and such as did exist could express its views in the diets, the foreign press and private reading clubs. In Hungary and Italy the situation was, admittedly, worse, but the government simply did not have the means to act in a totalitarian fashion to eliminate dissent, even had the will been there. (The police force was exceedingly small.)

Instead it tried merely to manipulate opinion, close diets if they were too obstructive, or (as in the case of Lombardy-Venetia in 1848) impose martial law if rioting got out of hand. There were very few political prisoners, no evidence of torture and the interception of the mails amounted only to about 1–2 per cent of letters posted.[30] What, then, did lead to revolution in 1848?

The traditional view of the causes of the 1848 revolutions within the monarchy is that irresistible forces of liberalism and nationalism were pent up by Metternich like steam in a hermetically-sealed boiler (Palmerston's simile) until inevitably an explosion occurred. (In the case of Lombardy-Venetia, something like this may indeed have actually happened.) The trouble with this standard account, however, is that these great irresistible forces are hard to find before 1848. This version of the outbreak of the revolutions, therefore, may yet have to be replaced with another one, which will describe them as a sort of accident.

Let us consider for a moment a few awkward facts. First, there were no outbreaks of revolution within the monarchy between 1815 and 1848. Indeed, when Polish exiles attempted to stir one up in Galicia in 1846, the peasantry slaughtered their would-be supporters. In Italy in 1820, 1831 and later, Metternich was actually petitioned to annexe more Italian territory to bring some order to Italian affairs. Austrian rule in Lombardy-Venetia, it turns out, was both the most efficient and most enlightened in the whole of the Italian Peninsula.[31] In Hungary, meanwhile, even in 1847, the liberals failed to dominate the diet; while in Vienna, even after the fall of Louis Philippe in France, there were no calls for a republic. Members of the imperial family were able to ride about in their carriages to the applause of all, even after the fall of Metternich. Nor was there any question of the establishment of a revolutionary government. Metternich was succeeded not by any democrats, liberals, or republicans, but simply by his former colleagues – Kolowrat, Ficquelmont, Pillersdorf and Wessenberg, all of them loyal Habsburg bureaucrats. It is not even clear whether the majority of people wanted much change. Professor Rath's analysis of the petitions of the time concluded:

Considered from a present day perspective the demands of the Viennese radicals expressed in these petitions were surprisingly moderate . . . Included are the usual entreaties for freedom of the press, speech and religion; but such typical 'liberal' demands as freedom from search and the right of public assembly are missing. The hesitant appeals for provincial assemblies and a united diet, with members chosen by traditional Austrian, not democratic methods and with the limited prerogatives of approving taxes and the budget and sharing in the legislation, are certainly a far cry from the demands of modern liberals.[32]

Where then was the great liberal-nationalist tide which would sweep away the Metternich system?

Probably it did not exist, save perhaps in Lombardy-Venetia. There the nobility had been alienated from Habsburg rule and looked to the House of Savoy to restore its prestige and job opportunities. Its main grievance was that Italian nobles were unable to compete with German or even Hungarian ones in the service (civil, judicial, diplomatic, or military) of the Habsburg state. The peasants for their part had been influenced by a priesthood under the delusion that the reforming pope, Pius IX, would lead a military crusade against Catholic Austria. The middle classes felt excluded from the law courts and excessively taxed. Finally, the intellectuals had come under the influence of writers such as Mazzini, Gioberti and d'Azeglio and were in favour of expelling the foreigner. How solid resistance to Austrian rule actually was, however, is unclear, since the alternatives were also unclear. Piedmont, for example, until 1848 had been a reactionary and priest-ridden state, allied to the Habsburgs. All previous popes had likewise ruled over corrupt, authoritarian and extremely inefficient regimes. Under these circumstances, it was difficult to foresee what would replace Austrian rule in Lombardy-Venetia. Thus, although the Austrians faced apparently widespread hostility initially, a few months of Piedmontese administration in Lombardy alienated large sections of the population from Charles Albert of Savoy. Radetzky's own efforts to win over the peasantry and poorer sections of the people, on the other hand, were also to meet with failure.[33]

Knowing how representative or unrepresentative the revolutionaries of 1848 really were is a key problem for historians of the period. What did the peasantry in Italy or Hungary really think about events? Did it make any difference to them which dynasty or nobility controlled the affairs of state? Most of the Italian deserters from the Austrian army took to the hills or went home; they did not sign up with Charles Albert. Were they, therefore, anti-Austrian, or simply tired of being cannon-fodder? Certainly, it was the fear that Radetzky was beginning a new recruitment campaign that turned the peasantry against him in 1849–50. Even in the case of Lombardy-Venetia, therefore, it is difficult to know how irresistible the tide of liberalism and nationalism really was. In the end, of course, it was military force which blocked it.

Elsewhere in the monarchy, there were few signs of radicalism before 1848. The diets of Hungary, Lower Austria and, to a lesser extent, Bohemia, had become critical of the government, but a few well-timed concessions would almost certainly have served to restore public confidence. Once again, the question of how representative the opponents of the government actually were is both crucial and difficult to answer. The rioters in 1848 were mainly students, egged on by unemployed workers who had economic grievances but little in the way of a political programme, and no hostility at all to the imperial family. Nor does there seem to have been a radical middle class at hand straining to seize power. Most of those who acquired a vote in 1848 do not seem to have bothered to use it. The Reichstag proved almost irrelevant to the course of events and certainly never attempted to emulate the role of the National Assembly in France in 1789 or in 1848. Given that during the crucial months of March to October, the Emperor was an idiot and his ministers mostly unknowns, it is almost incredible that it failed even to try to seize the initiative. When revolution occurred again in Vienna in October 1848, the Reichstag was in the hands of the parliamentary Right and Centre.

Let us return again to the causes of the revolutions. There were powerful nationalist currents at work, especially in Italy and Hungary. In the latter kingdom, however, conservative forces still retained the upper hand. In Italy, given the alienation of the nobility and the existence of an alternative dynasty, the government's room for manoeuvre was narrower. Even there, however, by 1848 its influence had not disappeared entirely. Metternich, on the other hand, was determined to resist the slightest concession. In the rest of the monarchy, there were growing economic problems. Harvest failures in 1846 and 1847, accelerating inflation throughout the 1840s, plus the rising unemployment resulting from industrial change meant that by 1848 a large proportion of the population was experiencing severe hardship. By 1848 the police were reporting all sorts of human misery, from starvation to cholera. Yet the government was unable to do anything. It had no means to make good the harvests; it could not afford to reduce taxes (which in themselves were probably not excessive by European standards); and in any case it faced a crisis of confidence in its currency, due to balance of payments difficulties and a large national debt. With the fall of Louis Philippe and the possibility of war with republican France, there was a run on the banks. What occurred in March 1848, therefore, was a diplomatic, political and financial crisis, all rolled into one. The measure which everyone hoped would resolve the situation was the sacking of Metternich. This would allow moderate reforms, lessen the possibility of war, save the currency (memories of the state bankruptcy of 1811 were still fresh) and perhaps lead to reductions in state expenditure. In any case Metternich had been around for so long, that everyone was bored with him. The trouble was that before his resignation could be secured or even agreed on, a crisis of public order occurred as well. A student mob which was attempting to deliver a petition to the court was fired on by a detachment of troops causing loss of life. This led to rioting, which the limited police forces available in the capital could not control. In the ensuing panic the imperial family let Metternich go. They also promised some sort of constitution and ruled out the option of declaring martial law and putting down the riot with troops. Some witnesses believed that a couple of battalions could have done the job, but the Emperor would not hear of it, and the Archdukes, like Kolowrat, were only too glad to rid themselves of Metternich at last. Yet his resignation was the signal for the outbreak of revolution throughout the empire. Authority had been dismissed along with him and thus his resignation brought about the revolutions, not vice versa. It is difficult to resist the temptation of saying that the revolutions came about, less because of a tidal wave of liberalism within the monarchy than because the dynasty lost its nerve. Once recovered, the revolutions were crushed.

Just as the causes of the revolutions should be interpreted less in terms of profound social and political forces than has been usual, so too should one beware of seeing the revolutions themselves in purely social and ideological terms. In the final analysis, they ended up as dynastic struggles, which were won on the battlefield, rather than on the barricades. This was because the Lombard nobility, and later the Venetians, offered Lombardy and Venetia to Charles Albert of Piedmont. This in turn meant dynastic war, for promising concessions was one thing, but losing a kingdom quite another. No Habsburg would ever peacefully agree to that.

The Italian question soon impinged on Hungarian affairs. For the Hungarians had quickly extorted concessions from Vienna which allowed them to run their own affairs. In particular they secured control over defence and finance, and hoped even to conduct a separate foreign policy. Before long they persuaded themselves that, if the dynasty lost the war in Italy and the German provinces were merged within a united Germany, the Habsburgs would have to look to Budapest for a home. The Hungarian government, therefore, by mid-summer 1848, was refusing to send troop reinforcements to Italy; was refusing to pay for the Croatian troops fighting there; was refusing to pay part of the former imperial debt; and was generally acting as if Hungary was not part of the monarchy. Once Radetzky had defeated Charles Albert, therefore, Vienna decided to put the Hungarians in their place. Having failed to secure concessions from Budapest, the imperial government backed Jellačić's attack from Croatia. The astonished Hungarians, who had wanted nothing less than a Hungarian Habsburg Empire, now found themselves treated as rebels, having been attacked with the blessing of their king. In fact, most of them still professed loyalty to him even as they resisted his invasion army. It was not until April 1849 that Kossuth eventually deposed the dynasty. In Hungary, too, therefore, the dynastic factor turned out to be the most important one.

With the final victory in Hungary, the dynasty could turn its attention to Germany. There the King of Prussia was attempting to unite the German princes behind his leadership of the Erfurt Union. Once again, therefore, the Habsburgs faced a dynastic challenge. They had held the German crown for centuries before 1806, and since 1815 had held the presidency of the German *Bund*. They were not now about to concede the leadership of Germany to the Hohenzollerns. Once again, it looked as if the issue would be resolved by war and, indeed, a small skirmish did take place in

1850. However, the king of Prussia submitted to Austrian demands at Olmütz and dissolved the Erfurt Union. After a conference of the German princes at Dresden, the German *Bund* was restored.

How then had the Habsburgs managed to survive? In many of the textbooks, the explanation is put forward that once the peasantry had been emancipated from compulsory labour service (*robot*) to their landlords, the population lost interest in the revolutions. This explanation, however, is beside the point. For a start, there is no evidence that the peasantry before 1848 was revolutionary. Even during the year itself, the part played by peasants was very minor. The revolutions were made by the political classes – students, aristocrats, intellectuals, townsfolk. Thereafter, events were decided by the clash of large professional armies. The peasants were largely irrelevant. True, the *robot* was abolished by the Austrian Reichstag in September 1848, but the law was not actually implemented until 1853 and, as will be seen, made little difference to the economy. In Hungary, in 1848, peasant grievances were left largely unattended. The truth is that military, not social, factors defeated the revolutions.

In Italy, after the fall of Venice and Radetzky's retreat from Milan, the critical mistakes were made by Charles Albert. First, he moved too slowly allowing his enemy to find refuge in the Quadrilateral; his own army meanwhile was under-equipped in terms of horses, tents and maps; he himself proved a poor general; crucially, he allowed Radetzky to be reinforced, while he himself spurned all aid either from republican France or from guerrilla irregulars, who were also suspected of republicanism. Radetzky, for his part, was able to keep his non-Italian troops together, and out-generalled the Italians after he had been reinforced. The latter, in any case, had become too confident, foolishly rejecting peace overtures from Vienna, which would have offered home rule to Lombardy-Venetia as a whole, or even independence to Lombardy. In March 1849 Radetzky once again defeated Charles Albert who, against British and French advice, had renewed the war. This time the campaign lasted only a week.

In Hungary, the Habsburgs also won, thanks to military causes. Here the crucial factor was not the intervention of Russia in May 1849 – the Tsarist army missed nearly all the fighting – but the disadvantage Hungary suffered from having to build up an army and an armaments industry almost from scratch. Given such a disadvantage the achievements of her leaders were more or less miraculous, but they could never be permanent, especially in the light of the country's total diplomatic isolation. Hungary's only real hope was that Austria would be defeated in Italy and would then come to terms. But this was a hope which Radetzky destroyed.[34]

In the light of her basic military dilemma – how to raise and equip an army – Hungary's other problems were merely secondary. The alienation of the nationalities did not help. Yet the lack of any compromise with Croatia was the fault of Jellačić, not Kossuth, and for most of the war the nationalities were kept in check. In the end, the Austrians found a capable general, Haynau, and their military and industrial superiority secured their victory. Görgey's surrender to Paskievich (who led the Russian forces) was interpreted therefore as a deliberate insult aimed at humiliating the army which had truly won the war. As such, it was to produce an extraordinary degree of bitterness against both the defeated Hungarians and the Russians who began to patronise them.

What then were the results of the revolutions? If their causes now seem less profound than once thought, their consequences now too seem less important. By 1852, the monarchy had returned to absolutism without any pretence of constitutionalism. Josephinism had returned with a vengeance. The empire was now run by the army and the bureaucracy and even the cosmetic diets had been swept away. This was Franz Joseph's ideal and he would have stuck with this system had not defeat in war in 1859 and 1866 forced him to experiment with constitutions. The revolutions, therefore, had merely presented a new emperor with the opportunity to tighten up the old system. Schwarzenberg, it is true, between 1848 and 1851 had attempted to retain at least a façade of constitutionalism but he had been easily outmanoeuvred. He also failed in his bid to create a 'Reich of seventy millions' by merging the entire monarchy with the states of the German *Bund* and integrating it into the *Zollverein* (Customs Union). The Dresden Conference rejected both proposals and endorsed a return to the pre-1848 status quo. So Franz Joseph in the 1850s found himself in the position dreamt of by his grandfather Francis I – the truly absolute ruler of the empire of 1815.

Economically, the revolutions represented no real turning point either. The latest work by economic historians indicates that neither the abolition of the *robot* nor of the customs border with Hungary made any appreciable difference to the monarchy's economy. Nor did these developments lay the foundations for take-off into sustained economic growth. According to the latest research, that had already begun in the 1830s and would continue fairly steadily throughout the history of the monarchy.[35]

On the other hand, the revolutions could not simply be forgotten. If they had failed to achieve anything but the purification of absolutism, they had none the less revealed glimpses of an alternative future for central Europe. The issues of German and Italian unification, of Hungarian self-government, of nationalism within the monarchy, would not simply disappear. They remained, instead, on the political agenda. With a degree of wisdom, the dynasty might still have been able to settle matters to its permanent advantage. With diplomatic skill, it might even have been able to secure a lasting triumph of absolutism. Yet, as things turned out, blind faith in continued military success, combined with a refusal to compromise in domestic affairs brought about the loss of its position in both Italy and Germany within the space of twenty years.

Why did this happen? To begin with, there was hubris. The victory of the counter-revolution convinced the young Franz Joseph that the monarchy could stand up to Russia in 1854. He even toyed with the idea of a new alliance with the West. This was madness: the break with Russia over the Danubian principalities served merely to isolate Austria in its future struggles with France and Prussia. Paul W. Schroeder has argued that Britain could have saved Austria from the results of this policy, but the argument is unconvincing.[36] The break with Russia was indeed the first of two unilateral decisions on the part of the monarchy which led to disaster. The second was the decision in 1859 to send an ultimatum to Piedmont. In both cases, Vienna assumed that Prussian backing would be immediately forthcoming, which it was not. Prussia simply did not see that it had any interest in defending Austrian policy in the Balkans or in Italy against one or other of its powerful neighbours. Besides, Austria made no attempt to offer inducements. It merely assumed that Prussia had a duty to back it as the leading German power.

Austria, in fact, was already pursuing the same anachronistic policy with regard to Germany that it had always pursued in Italy. That is to say, it met all demands for change with a refusal. Yet Prussia was extremely conscious of its own changed position. For it was now the leading German economic power and the one relied upon to commit most troops to any federal defence against an attack by France. As a result, Prussia expected to be rewarded in German affairs for supporting Austria elsewhere. A memorandum of the Prussian Foreign Ministry stated the position quite baldly in 1860: 'It is well to be clear that it is Austria who needs help . . . If . . . Austria asks us to regard an attack on the Mincio [Venetia] as an act of war, then we would have to explain the reasons which prevent us from complying with this request if our aspirations in Germany are not taken into account.' Yet Austria would not share the formal leadership of Germany with Prussia. In the words of the Austrian Foreign Ministry: 'such a thing . . . would have a disastrous effect internally for the Habsburg Monarchy and cause it to lose face throughout Europe.'[37] The result was that Austria could only wait upon events. Having nothing to offer, it could take no initiatives.

With the advent of Bismarck such a posture became pathetic. Rechberg's policy over Schleswig-Holstein was one of seeking co-operation for the sake of co-operation, which, given Bismarck's manoeuvrings became ridiculous. Bismarck also thwarted Franz Joseph's attempt to regain the German crown through the Fürstentag (meeting of princes) in 1863. When war looked unavoidable, the Austrian response was again astonishing – the secret treaty with France of July 1866. By this Austria agreed to surrender Venetia, whether it won the war with Prussia or not, the hope being to compensate itself by taking Silesia and other Prussian territory. And this was in return, not for French aid, but simply for French neutrality. As in 1859, however, the Austrian army was defeated. Austria lost the leadership of both Germany and Italy; having refused to make any domestic or diplomatic concessions, it had been forced to rely on a badly led and underfunded army.

Only military defeat and financial desperation led to the constitutional experiments of the 1860s, the final outcome of which was the Dual Monarchy. This lasted until 1918, and has been the subject of much controversy. Many historians have argued that, through the *Ausgleich* (Compromise), the Hungarians took control of the empire, a view which is resisted by the historians of Hungary. Certainly, the Magyars received special treatment: control of their domestic affairs and great influence over foreign policy and imperial finance. Yet Franz Joseph retained control of the armed forces, made foreign and defence policy, and had a preliminary veto over Hungarian domestic legislation. On the other hand, he never intervened to prevent the Hungarians suppressing the civil rights of their nationalities, and made concessions to them over the army issue. These concessions were fairly limited in nature, but the fact that they were made at all and that the Slav and Romanian populations were kept under control gave the impression to the Germans of Cisleithania that Hungary had acquired a dominant position within the monarchy. They, in contrast, were unable to control their Czechs. In fact, the running battle between the Czechs and Germans in the western 'half' of the monarchy, meant that Franz Joseph could easily retain the political initiative there. Thus, having dismissed the German liberals after their opposition in 1878 to the occupation of Bosnia-Herzegovina, he installed his boyhood friend, Count Taaffe, as Prime Minister. Taaffe undertook electoral reform in Bohemia, created a separate Czech university in Prague, and made Czech equal with German as a language of external administration in the Bohemian lands. These concessions, however, still failed to satisfy the Czechs, who resented the position of German as the sole language of internal administration and who knew that the majority of civil servant posts still went to Germans. The result was that both national groups remained discontented with the *Ausgleich*. But the Czechs, for all their grievances, enjoyed a much better position in Cisleithania than their Slav and Romanian counterparts in Hungary, whose schools were closed down and whose freedom of political expression was ruthlessly curbed by the Hungarian government's policy of Magyarization. Yet, as has been noted, Franz Joseph simply ignored the grievances of the nationalities in Hungary. Hence the feeling among the Germans of the monarchy that the Magyars were really in charge.

Today, two key questions concerning the Dual Monarchy are debated by historians: to what extent did the Hungarians influence its foreign policy and to what extent did they exploit it economically? The career of Count Gyula Andrássy, who became

Prime Minister of Hungary in 1867 and then Foreign Minister of the monarchy between 1871 and 1879, is sometimes held to demonstrate how the Hungarians succeeded in establishing an anti-Russian basis for the monarchy's foreign policy after 1867. For it was Andrássy who, during the Franco-Prussian War of 1870–1, ensured that the monarchy would not intervene on the side of France, and who as Foreign Minister in 1878 was prepared to declare war on Russia. In short, his policy was one of abandoning all hope of regaining the leadership of Germany in favour of an anti-Russian alliance with Bismarck and a forward policy in the Balkans. By 1879, therefore, he had not only signed the Dual Alliance with Berlin (and on terms more favourable to Austria than Germany), but had seen the Congress of Berlin both dismantle the large Bulgaria of the San Stefano treaty and allow Austria-Hungary to occupy Bosnia-Herzegovina and the Sanjak of Novibazar.

All of this did indeed fit in with Hungarian notions of foreign policy which since 1848–9 had been pro-German and anti-Russian. Indeed, the survival of the German Empire was taken to guarantee the survival of the *Ausgleich*. For if Austria were to succeed in recapturing the leadership of Germany, Hungary would no longer enjoy such an important position within the monarchy. On the other hand, it is easy to overrate the real influence exercised by Andrássy or Hungarians in general after 1867. For a start, it was clear that the Balkans were bound to become the main arena for Habsburg foreign policy ambitions whether a Hungarian was foreign minister or not. As for Andrássy, while there is little doubt that the part he played in 1870–1 was indeed a crucial one, the probability is that Austria-Hungary would not have entered anyway. The French had collapsed too rapidly and Austrian public opinion saw no reason to rescue a power which had declared war on fellow Germans. Even Franz Joseph, who was in favour of intervention, saw the difficulties involved. Nor did the circumstances arise which might have afforded a reasonable excuse to intervene later. As for 1878, it should be noted that Andrássy was unable to muster the support necessary to force a war on Russia. Both Franz Joseph and the Austrians were opposed to the idea. He also upset the monarch by failing to get the Congress of Berlin to agree to the outright annexation of Bosnia-Herzegovina. Indeed, he even wrote a letter to the sultan suggesting that it might be returned to him one day. Thus, while it is true to say that Andrássy laid down the foundations for Austrian foreign policy after 1867, it is misleading to say that he dominated foreign policy to such an extent that it was run in Hungarian interests ever afterwards. When Kálmán Tisza and Kálnoky in 1888 (with Andrássy's support) once again attempted to have war declared on Russia, they also failed. Finally, it should not be forgotten that in July 1914 it was Istvan Tisza, the Hungarian premier, who was opposed to war with Serbia over the Sarajevo assassinations, but who felt he had to give way. Hence it is difficult to conclude that Hungary after 1867 dominated the monarchy's foreign policy.[38]

As far as economics is concerned, the main argument in support of the claim that Hungary exploited the monarchy was put forward at the time by German Austrians, who pointed out that Hungary's *quota* (the percentage of revenue paid to the joint exchequer, which was fixed by negotiation every ten years) amounted to only about 30 per cent, a share which seemed disproportionately small. Today the main critic of Hungary's economic role within the monarchy after 1867 is John Komlos, the American economic historian, who has written that 'the Austria economy . . . could have done as well without its Hungarian partner'.[39] According to Komlos, Hungary exploited Austria, rather than vice versa, as Hungarian nationalists and Marxist historians (before the 1960s) used to claim. His argument is that Austria provided Hungary not merely with a reliable market for her agricultural products, but with an indispensable source of skilled labour and capital. Indeed, from the 1870s, he argues, Hungary raised so much capital in Austria that she positively retarded industrial development and prolonged the depression of 1873 there. In Hungary itself, on the other hand, the symptoms of the Great Depression were essentially absent.

Hungarian historians take a different view. According to Peter Hanák, the *Ausgleich* greatly contributed to the economic prosperity of both halves of the monarchy. As for capital movements:

Hungary provided a secure market for both the direct and indirect export of Austrian capital, and this was not merely a consequence of common statehood or the guarantees of interest for railway construction, but was also the result of the tight *link* between the banking systems and commerce of the two countries. Austrian capital placed in Hungary during this period amounted to some 3 billion crowns, which proved to be a fruitful investment for *both* parties.[40]

Hanák's general arguments, though not all of his statistics, have been supported by the Canadian economic historian, Scott M. Eddie. Yet Eddie accuses Hanák of having failed to mention Hungary's 'arguably greatest contribution to overall prosperity in the monarchy', namely her agricultural exports abroad. According to Eddie,

> Without Hungarian agricultural exports outside of the Monarchy, Austria could not have financed her massive imports, particularly of fibres and textiles, on which much of her industrial activity was based. While common knowledge among historians of this period, a look at figures for net exports and net imports makes this contention strikingly clear . . . Hungary's agricultural net exports not only covered the entire net export of the Monarchy in those categories, they covered Austria's import surplus as well. This, therefore, has to be a prime candidate for Hungary's principal contribution to the Monarchy as well.[41]

Despite Komolos's view, therefore, it would seem that the Compromise was an economic success.

By 1890, none the less, there was a great deal of pessimism to be found over the monarchy's prospects for survival. The loss of Italian and German leadership, the nationality problem, Balkan troubles, social and economic change, the suicide of the Crown Prince in 1889, were all factors which gave rise to doubt. Yet the monarchy was not in decline: the economy was growing steadily and would continue to do so; the nationalities still supported the dynasty; the Balkans would soon be 'put on ice'; and economic and social change would be accommodated. Franz Joseph, for all his faults as a ruler, represented a reassuring continuity; and there was still time to reform the political and constitutional structures of Dualism. The First World War was still in the future; its outbreak was not inevitable; neither was the fall of the Habsburg Empire. The period 1830–90, therefore, should not be seen merely as some sort of signpost to disaster.

Notes

1. For more detailed analysis of the differing interpretations of these periods, see A. Sked, *The Decline and Fall of the Habsburg Empire, 1815–1918* (London, 1989).
2. L. Namier, *Vanished Supremacies* (Harmondsworth, 1962), pp. 139f; Ernst II, Herzog von Sachsen-Coburg-Gotha, *Aus meinem Leben und meiner Zeit*, Vol. 2 (Berlin, 1888), p. 178.
3. apocryphal.
4. B. Hamann, 'Die Habsburger und die Deutsche Frage im 19. und 20. Jahrhundert', in H. Lutz and H. Rumpler (eds), *Österreich und die deutsche Frage im 19. und 20. Jahrhundert* (Munich, 1982), p. 222; B. Sutter, 'Die politische und rechtliche Stellung der Deutschen in Österreich 1848 bis 1918', in A. Wandruszka and P. Urbanitsch (eds), *Die Habsburgermonarchie 1848–1918*, Vol. III, i, *Die Völker des Reiches* (Vienna, 1980), p. 164.
5. H. Rumbold, *The Austrian Court in the Nineteenth Century* (London, 1909), p. 115.
6. C. Sealsfield (Postl), *Austria as It Really Is or Sketches of Continental Courts by an Eye-Witness* (London, 1828), p. 124.
7. J. Blum, *Noble Landowners and Agriculture in Austria, 1815–1848* (Baltimore, MD, 1948), p. 222.
8. R. Metternich and A. de Klinkowström (eds), *Memoirs of Prince Metternich*, Vol. 5 (London, 1882), pp. 473f.
9. On Ferdinand, see H. L. Mikoletzky, 'Bild und Gegenbild Kaiser Ferdinands I von Österreich: Ein Versuch', *Archiv für österreichische Geschichte*, vol. 125 (1966), pp. 173–95.
10. H. du Coudray, *Metternich* (London, 1935), p. 387.
11. R. W. Seton-Watson, 'The Emperor Franz Joseph', *History*, vol. 17 (1932), p. 121.
12. P. J. Katzenstein, *Disjointed Partners: Austria and Germany since 1815* (London, 1976), pp. 113f.
13. G. Vermes, *István Tisza: the Liberal Vision and Conservative Statecraft of a Magyar Nationalist* (New York, 1985), p. 23; A. J. P. Taylor, *Europe: Grandeur and Decline* (Harmondsworth, 1967), p. 132.
14. A. Sked, *The Survival of the Habsburg Empire: Radetzky, the Imperial Army and the Class War, 1848* (London, 1979), pp. 32f.
15. F. Walter, 'Von Windischgrätz über Welden zu Haynau: Regierung und Armee-Oberkommando in Ungarn 1849–50', in F. Walter and H. Steinacker, *Die Nationalitätenfrage im alten Ungarn und die Südostpolitik Wiens* (Munich, 1959), p. 68.
16. A. Sked, op. cit., pp. 51f, 56f.
17. See G. E. Rothenberg, *The Army of Francis Joseph* (West Lafayette, 1976).
18. *Offene Worte über die österreichisch-ungarische Armee in ihrem Verhältnis zum deutschen Reichsheer. Auf Grund eigener Beobachtungen von A. von E.*

19. L. J. Baack, *Christian Bernstorff and Prussia: Diplomacy and Reform Conservatism, 1818–1832* (New Brunswick, 1980), p. 183; W. B. Lincoln, *Nicholas I, Emperor and Autocrat of All the Russias* (London, 1978), pp. 285f.

20. H. Kissinger, *A World Restored: Metternich, Castlereagh and the Problems of Peace, 1812–22* (London, 1957), p. 174.

21. Duc de Broglie (ed.), *Memoirs of the Prince de Talleyrand*, Vol. 3 (London, 1891), p. 22; Metternich and Klinkowström, op. cit., p. 117.

22. E. Radvany, *Metternich's Projects for Reform in Austria* (The Hague, 1971), p. 110.

23. C. de Grunwald, *Metternich* (London, 1953), p. 255.

24. See A. Sked, 'Metternich and the federalist myth', in A. Sked and C. Cook (eds), *Crisis and Controversy, Essays in honour of A. J. P. Taylor* (London, 1976), pp. 1–22.

25. E. Andics, *Metternich und die Frage Ungarns* (Budapest, 1973), pp. 32, 116.

26. A. Sked, 'The Metternich system', in A. Sked (ed.), *Europe's Balance of Power, 1815–1848* (London, 1979), p. 111.

27. B. Sutter, op. cit., pp. 161f.

28. W. Hazlitt, *Table Talk* (London, 1967), pp. 248–55.

29. C. J. Lowe, *Salisbury and the Mediterranean, 1886–1896* (London, 1965), p. 1.

30. For further details, see A. Sked, *Decline and Fall of the Habsburg Empire*, pp. 44–53.

31. A. Sked, *Survival of the Habsburg Empire*, p. 91.

32. R. J. Rath, *The Viennese Revolution of 1848* (Austin, Tex., 1957), p. 35.

33. A. Sked, *Survival of the Habsburg Empire*, part III.

34. On Hungary in 1848–9, see I. Deák, *The Lawful Revolution, Louis Kossuth and the Hungarians, 1848–49* (New York, 1979).

35. See D. F. Good, *The Economic Rise of the Habsburg Empire, 1750–1914* (Berkeley, 1984).

36. P. W. Schroeder, *Austria, Great Britain and the Crimean War, the Destruction of the European Concert* (London, 1972).

37. Franco Valsecchi, 'European diplomacy and the expedition of the Thousand: the conservative powers', in M. Gilbert (ed.), *A Century of Conflict, Essays for A. J. P. Taylor* (London, 1966), p. 60.

38. For further details, see A. Sked, *Decline and Fall of the Habsburg Empire*, pp. 239–51.

39. J. Komlos, *The Habsburg Monarchy as a Customs Union, Economic Development in Austria-Hungary in the Nineteenth Century* (Princeton, NJ, 1983), p. 218.

40. P. Hanák, 'Hungary's contribution to the monarchy', in G. Ranki (ed.), *Hungarian History–World History* (Bloomington, 1984), p. 166.

41. S. M. Eddie, 'On Hungary's economic contribution to the monarchy', in G. Ranki (ed.) op. cit., p. 195.

Further reading

For narrative accounts of Habsburg history in the period 1830–90, consult: Barbara Jelavich, *Modern Austria, Empire and Republic, 1800–1986* (Cambridge, 1987); Robert A. Kann, *A History of the Habsburg Empire, 1526–1918* (London, 1974); C. A. Macartney, *The Habsburg Empire, 1790–1918* (London, 1968); E. Pamleny (ed.), *A History of Hungary* (London, and Wellingborough, 1975); A. J. P. Taylor, *The Habsburg Monarchy, 1809–1918, a History of the Austrian Empire and Austria-Hungary* (London, 1968). Of these, Macartney's work is the most detailed, Taylor's the most brilliant.

Also of interest, although confusing to read and now very dated, is Oscar Jaszi, *The Dissolution of the Habsburg Monarchy* (London, 1961).

For an up-to-date and controversial review of the period as a whole, see Alan Sked, *The Decline and Fall of the Habsburg Empire, 1815–1918* (London and New York, 1989).

On economic affairs, consult: David F. Good, *The Economic Rise of the Habsburg Empire, 1750–1914* (Berkeley, 1984); Thomas Francis Huertas, *Economic Growth and Economic Policy in a Multinational Setting: the Habsburg Monarchy, 1841–1865* (Chicago, 1977); John Komlos, *The Habsburg Monarchy as a Customs Union, Economic Development in Austria-Hungary in the Nineteenth Century* (Princeton, NJ, 1983); John Komlos (ed.), *Economic Development in the Habsburg Empire in the Nineteenth Century: Essays* (Boulder, 1983).

On foreign policy see: F. R. Bridge, *The Habsburg Monarchy among the Great Powers, 1815–1918* (Leamington Spa, 1990); István Diószegi, *Hungarians in the Ballhausplatz: Studies on the Austro-Hungarian Common Foreign Policy* (Budapest, 1983); Barbara Jelavich, *The Habsburg Empire in European Affairs, 1814–1918* (New York, 1975); Alan Sked (ed.), *Europe's Balance of Power, 1815–1848* (London, 1979).

Military affairs are superbly covered in Gunther E. Rothenberg, *The Army of Francis Joseph* (West Lafayette, 1976); the intellectual background to events is in William Johnson, *The Austrian Mind: an Intellectual and Social History, 1848–1938* (London, 1976).

Finally, students ought to be aware of Peter Katzenstein's study of the Austro-German connection in the period, *Disjointed Partners, Austria and Germany since 1815* (Berkeley, 1976).

On more particular topics, key books include the following. On Metternich, see G. de Bertier de Sauvigny, *Metternich and his Times* (London, 1962) and E. Radvany, *Metternich's Projects for Reform in Austria* (The Hague, 1971).

On 1848, see István Deák, *The Lawful Revolution, Louis Kossuth and the Hungarians, 1848–49* (New York, 1979); R. John Rath, *The Viennese Revolution of 1848* (Austin, 1957); Alan Sked, *The Survival of the Habsburg Empire: Radetzky, the Imperial Army and the Class War, 1848* (London, 1979).

On the period from 1848–66, see William A. Jenks, *Francis Joseph and* the Italians, 1849–59 (Charlottesville, NY, 1978) and Paul W. Schroeder, *Austria, Great Britain and the Crimean War. The Destruction of the European Concert* (Ithaca and London, 1972).

For the period 1866–90, see Janos Decsy, *Prime Minister Gyula Andrassy's Influence on Habsburg Foreign Policy during the Franco-Prussian War, 1870–1871* (New York, 1979) and Joseph Redlich, *Emperor Francis Joseph of Austria* (Hamden, 1965).

Key articles may be found in *The Austrian History Yearbook* and in the various collections edited by Bela Kiraly in the *East European Monographs* series distributed by Columbia University Press, the sub-series of which, entitled *War and Society in East-Central Europe*, is extremely important.

The main controversies, however, are covered in Alan Sked, *Decline and Fall of the Habsburg Empire*, op. cit.

6

Russia: tsarism and the West

EDWARD ACTON

The question of Russia's relationship with Europe has long been vexed and emotive. For some, the Russians are the barbarians at the gates, Asian intruders at a western feast. Converted to Christianity through Byzantium, they never had the benefit of Roman law and Catholic culture. Succumbing to the Tartar invasion of the thirteenth century, for two hundred years they were virtually cut off from western commercial and intellectual currents. They barely felt the impact of either the Renaissance or the Reformation. They remained largely immune to the Enlightenment and their autocratic political system was unaffected by the constitutional development triggered by 1789 and 1848. The revolution of 1917 set Russia on a path which again diverged sharply from the West. The three-quarters of a century of Communist rule which followed forged a society, a system, a culture fundamentally at odds with that of contemporary western Europe.

For others, Russia forms an integral part of Europe. The Russians are one of the family of white Caucasian nations living to the west of the Urals. They share with the west of the continent a common Christian heritage which in the world perspective is of far greater significance than denominational differences. For all Russia's periods of intellectual isolation, the culture of Pushkin and Lermontov, Tolstoy, Dostoyevsky and Turgenev, Pasternak and Solzhenytsin is unmistakably European. Though uneven and fluctuating, Russia's commercial links as well as her military and diplomatic entanglements with her western neighbours have played a vital role in her development. It defies common sense to treat as anything other than European a state and a people of the

East European Plain whose fate has been so intimately bound up with that of the rest of the continent.

The difficulties in the way of arriving at any consensus on the subject are manifold. Part of the problem lies in the ill-defined concept 'European'. What is common to Spain, Norway and Sicily, Warsaw, Athens and Belgrade? Even if consideration is restricted to the Great Powers of the modern era, much depends on whether the term denotes a civilization centred on Paris and London, or on Berlin and Vienna. And different light is thrown on the question according to the criteria – economic, political, social or cultural – taken to be central. Moreover, any comparison over time is confronted by the inherent difficulty of comparing two complex entities each undergoing constant change. Yet the question of Russia's kinship is one that will not go away. It has long been a major concern of Russia's own intellectual élite, and differing answers to it have coloured and continue to colour the way in which Russia is seen from outside. Moreover, provided it is recognized that the relationship has passed through continuous ebb and flow, Russia seeming at one moment to be moving more in line with western developments, and at another sharply diverging, the comparison provides a fruitful agenda for analysis.

Of few periods is this more true than the middle decades of the nineteenth century. Was Russia being caught up in the dramatic changes overcoming the continent and shedding her distinctive features? Or were the differences between her and her western neighbours actually deepening? Radicals and conservatives of the period argued passionately over the evidence. Soviet historians, anxious to assert the universal significance of the revolution of 1917, have stressed the common ground between the two. Western historians have been divided over the question. Some have been impressed by the convergence between late tsarist Russia and western European societies in the century before World War I, and have regarded 1917 as an historical aberration. Others, more impressed by the deep roots of the Russian revolution, have been inclined to regard tsarist society as a world of its own. Yet others have seen the last decades of tsarism in terms of a structural crisis which foreshadowed those characteristic of contemporary underdeveloped countries.

What, then, was the common ground between Russia and the West in the reign of Nicholas I, who succeeded his brother

Alexander I in 1825 and ruled until 1855? Like her major continental rivals, Russia was ruled by a monarch claiming divine sanction. Like his Habsburg and Hohenzollern counterparts, the incumbent Romanov was personally responsible for questions of war and peace and his primary concern was with foreign policy, international diplomacy and the prestige and status of his realm. The Romanovs were bound by close family ties to the royal houses of the West. Both Alexander and Nicholas took German princesses for brides, and indeed by their time the Romanovs had precious little native Russian blood in their veins. In Russia the church was more directly subordinated to the state than in the West. But there was nothing unique in the church furnishing the ideological sanction and rhetoric of the regime, nor in the regime using its secular power to uphold the dominance of the official church. Nicholas's Minister of Education, Uvarov, self-consciously sought to shore up the ideological ramparts of the monarchy with the doctrine of so-called 'official nationality', celebrating the peculiarly Russian national virtues of autocracy and orthodoxy.

The culture and life-style of Russia's largely noble élite was by Nicholas's time a variation on a European theme. A small number of the most privileged young Russians continued to pursue the eighteenth-century tradition of travelling to the West for higher education. Of greater significance were the six universities, modelled on western patterns and initially staffed in large part by western scholars, established by the end of Alexander I's reign. The universities generated the core of a reading public hungry for western-style literature, history and philosophy. Polite society had not fully abandoned the eighteenth-century preference for French over Russian, but at the same time a native literature expressed in secularized Russian was taking shape. The history of Karamzin, the poetry of Pushkin, the fiction of Gogol reflected the growing maturity of a distinctively Russian yet unmistakably European high culture. As in most European countries, this élite was responding to the powerful cosmopolitan cultural currents emanating primarily from France, Germany and Britain while simultaneously becoming increasingly conscious of its own national identity. By the 1830s Russia's relationship to and place in Europe was among the most vigorously debated of the 'cursed questions' concerning Russia's future which preoccupied the small coteries of Russian intellectuals. It was characteristic that both the 'Slavophiles', who stressed what was distinctive in Russia, and the 'Westerners', who looked to development along western lines, drew much of their intellectual armoury from the Enlightenment, the philosophic idealism and the romantic nationalism of the West.

The problems confronting the tsar had much in common with those of his western counterparts. Like his brother-monarchs from Prussia to Naples, he was beginning to experience pressure for limitations upon his autocratic power. Nicholas's reign opened in December 1825 with a quixotic challenge from a group of officers seeking to impose constitutional limitations upon the Crown. Although the 'Decembrists' were easily quelled, and the following three decades saw no comparable organized challenge, Nicholas remained acutely suspicious of the slightest criticism of his regime. And, despite vigorous censorship both of western-imported literature and of native public comment, the current of social and political criticism gathered momentum. The demand for civil liberties, political participation and above all the abolition of serfdom were covertly pressed in public lectures and the 'thick journals' of Moscow and St Petersburg. The more radical idealists looked beyond liberal goals of constitutional government and security under the law and eagerly seized upon the ideals of the early French socialists. In 1849 the regime moved to disband an amorphous but far-flung network of radical discussion circles made up predominantly of civil servants, junior officers, teachers and students – dubbed 'the Petrashevtsy' after a flamboyant leading figure.

Like his western confrères, Nicholas was confronted by increasing national aspirations among the more advanced minorities subject to his rule. The tsar's empire was made up of a complex mosaic of different national and ethnic groups. He sought to bend them to his will with the aid of active proselytizing by the established church and the promotion of Russian culture and language. He found himself able, with considerable effort, to consolidate his authority over the more primitive peoples in the empire, and indeed to expand his realm to the south and east. But there were ominous rumblings in the Ukraine and White Russia. In 1831, six years after he ascended the throne, Nicholas faced a full-scale rebellion by the most nationally conscious of the minorities, the Poles. It required large-scale mobilization of Russian forces to crush the rising.

The presence of a restive Polish minority was a problem the tsar shared with the monarchies of Prussia and Austria, and was but one thread in the network of international relations which bound Russia to the West. Russia's crucial role in the defeat of the Napoleonic armies had provided Alexander I with a leading position at the peace of Vienna. He had provided the inspiration behind the Holy Alliance founded in 1815 to combat attacks upon both the domestic and international status quo on the continent. He had lent active support to conservative regimes during the 1820s, and the help he gave the Habsburg monarchy constituted the cornerstone of European diplomacy for the following four decades. This was borne out as domestic tension in western and central Europe mounted during the 1840s. In 1849 it was with assistance from Russian forces that Habsburg rule over Hungary was restored, and St Petersburg's conservative influence was a significant factor in dashing the aspirations of liberals and radicals in Germany.

Yet, for all the common ground between Russia and the other Great Powers, the first half of the nineteenth century saw the gap between the two steadily widen. At the outset of Nicholas's reign, tsarism had been one absolute monarchy among many. By the end of it, a measure of public participation in government policy-making had spread eastward across much of the continent. The Prussian monarchy had been compelled to accept a representative assembly and in Austria the period of neo-absolutism and constitutional experiment had begun. The franchise, the budgetary and legislative powers of these assemblies might be limited, but a forum for public discussion had been created, and the context for a more articulate, institutionalized civil society established. In Russia there was still no national consultative assembly of any kind. The tsar's personal will remained the sole source of legislation and in Nicholas's last years active steps were taken to discourage even the most informal airing of social and political issues. Censorship was intensified, the university curriculum narrowed to exclude the teaching of subjects regarded as potentially seditious, such as philosophy, and every effort was made to forestall the emergence of unofficial, independent organizations.

That Russian absolutism outlived its western counterparts owed less to any qualities peculiar to the tsar's regime than to the acute economic and political weakness of the social groups which might have established effective checks upon it. At the base of the Russian social pyramid, as elsewhere, was the great mass of the rural population. By the end of the reign, rather over half of the peasantry was bound to state land and subject to heavy taxation. It was the object of a series of piecemeal reforms undertaken by Nicholas's Minister of State Domains, Kiselev. The impact of these reforms, designed to improved the peasants' conditions, curb the arbitrary authority exercised by state officials, and raise peasants' productivity, was limited. But the concern shown them was in marked contrast to the state's treatment of the 22 million peasants owned by members of the nobility. Whereas central Europe had seen the abolition of serfdom during the course of Nicholas's reign, no such relief had met the Russian peasants. Even before the revolutions of 1848 had precipitated emancipation in Austria and completed the process in Prussia and elsewhere, the legal condition of Russian peasants was markedly inferior to that of the peasants of central Europe. During the eighteenth century, even though some feature of western serfdom had been eroded, the system had been extended over newly incorporated areas of the Russian Empire and intensified. Providing for the nobility with payments in labour, rent or kind, while eking out a living on land set aside for their use, the private serfs were beyond the reach of the state. They were subject to the whim of their noble masters, who had the power to trade them, to inflict corporal punishment, to exile them to Siberia, or commit them to the army. And serfs were explicitly denied the right of appeal over the heads of their masters.

Moreover, the institutional arrangements of the Russian peasantry set them apart from their western equivalents. Peasant affairs over most of the empire were organized through the village commune. It was the commune, run by the village elders under the supervision of the rural police, which apportioned taxation payments to the state and rent and labour dues to the landowner, administered justice, and furnished conscripts for the army. To ensure that each household was in a position to meet its obligations, the practice had spread whereby the commune periodically redistributed strips of land among the households. The result was both to inhibit consolidation, experimentation and accumulation and to foster a collectivist mentality in which concepts of private landownership played no part. The distinctive culture and ethos of the peasantry was further guaranteed by their tenuous contact with the world outside the village. The most important channel was the church, but the 'black' clergy of the parish were ill-educated themselves, differing only in degree from their generally illiterate parishioners. Inarticulate, atomized in tens of thousands of scattered villages, peasant protest was restricted to endemic but generally isolated and short-lived violent protest, primarily against private landlords.

The serf status of 80 per cent of the population conditioned the relationship between the landed nobility and the autocracy. As in the West, the nobility constituted the most privileged social stratum. They had long escaped legal compulsion to serve the tsar, though many continued to spend several years in either the army or the civil administration, and promotion through the Table of Ranks established by Peter the Great remained the route to ennoblement for commoners. They provided the tsar's immediate entourage, and dominated the senior posts in both civil and military service. They enjoyed a range of legal privileges enshrined in Catherine II's Charter to the Nobility (1785), they were exempt from taxation, and they enjoyed the sole right of serf-owning. Yet their organized political impact was slight. Political consciousness among provincial noblemen was undeveloped. The regional diversity and highly stratified distribution of wealth among the nobility inhibited a strong sense of corporate interest. The practice of dividing estates among several heirs worked against the establishment of noble families with strong local ties comparable to those in Britain, Prussia, or pre-revolutionary France and the provincial assemblies established by Catherine II were ill-attended. The close correlation between major land-ownership and senior posts in the tsar's service blunted the leadership that might have been expected from the most prominent families. In any case, the combination of tax exemption and dependence on government forces to keep the serf in place limited the motivation for a noble challenge to the autocracy. The tsar could not flout the interests of the nobility, as the assassination of Nicholas's father Paul I in 1801 had gruesomely demonstrated. But the monarchy had little to fear from a Russian 'Fronde'.

If the landed nobility was ill-equipped to challenge the auto-cracy, Russia's urban classes were in no position to do so. By Nicholas's death the relative weakness of Russia's urban middle class was becoming one of the most distinctive features of her social structure, while the miniscule industrial labour force bore no comparison with that of France or Prussia, let alone Britain. The serf-based economy had since the early eighteenth century developed very much more slowly than those of its Great Power rivals. Serfdom impeded mobility and enterprise, and agricultural methods remained primitive. In most regions of the empire yields remained far below those of Germany and France. The limited rural market, further handicapped by vast distances and poor communications, severely inhibited the development of commerce and manufacture.

The economy was not, however, stagnant. The military-oriented industries founded on forced labour early in the eighteenth century gradually gave way to more diversified manufacture based on hired labour (generally serfs still sending payments back to their villages). Domestic demand slowly rose as increasing numbers of peasants entered handicraft production and petty commerce, in response to the demand by government and nobility for cash payments. Foreign trade responded to the opportunities opened up by a growing market for Russian grain. By the beginning of the nineteenth century the urban population had, according to the most generous estimate, reached 8 per cent, and it crept up to some 10 or 11 per cent by the end of Nicholas's reign. But this limited urban growth was not accompanied by the emergence of a dynamic and articulate bourgeoisie comparable to those making increasing impact in the West. Many of the most wealthy merchants and industrialists were to be found in the capital. Yet these potential leaders of Russia's 'third estate' were made acutely conscious of their dependence on government favour and contracts. They were unable even to persuade the government to help them break the stranglehold on foreign trade enjoyed by foreign companies. A high proportion of the merchants in the textile-dominated Moscow region belonged to the inward-looking tradition of the schismatic Old Believers. As the ranks of the merchant guilds swelled in the early nineteenth century, many of the newcomers were petty entrepreneurs from the peasantry still closely tied to the village. So, numerically small and culturally backward, Russia's middle class was but a shadow of its counterparts to the west.

It is against this background, then, that the survival of untramelled autocracy in Russia is to be understood. Far from possessing unique qualities of coherence and dynamism, Nicholas's regime was exercised through a legal system and administrative machine that was much less sophisticated than those of the West. This is not to deny that in both respects Nicholas's reign saw significant developments. In the 1830s the most distinguished minister of the early nineteenth century, Speransky, completed a massive *Complete Collection of Laws of the Russian Empire*. Although little was done to reform the cumbersome and almost universally maligned judicial system, Speransky's work provided at least a starting point for the creation of a legal profession and for increasing both popular and official respect for the letter of the law. Significant changes also overcame Russia's civil service in the course of the reign. The total number of officials almost trebled in the first half of the century, while the ratio of officials to total population almost doubled. Moreover, in the central ministries, the level of literacy and training rose appreciably as an extended period of formal education became a necessary condition for a successful civil service career. At the centre, too, the previous pattern of frequent interchange between military and civilian posts gave way to one of much more professional specialization.

When attention is switched from the central to the provincial civil service, however, the relatively low level of training, specialization and numbers stands out in sharp relief. At Nicholas's death just over half the provincial civil servants had no more than elementary education. Moreover, the limited resources at the tsar's disposal ensured that expenditure on the administration did not keep pace with its growth. Pay at the lower levels was so inadequate that it was assumed that public servants would take advantage of their fragment of public power to augment their income. The overall increase in the size of the bureaucracy looks much less impressive in the light of western trends where the ratio of civil servants to population stood three or four times higher than in Russia. And the central ministries expressed intense frustration at their inability to control provincial officials effectively, to elicit meaningful reports, ensure the implementation of policy, stem the flow of unproductive paper-work and overcome deep-rooted corruption. The notorious police of Nicholas's 'Third Section' were the latest in a long line of officials outside the regular hierarchy charged with overseeing the tsar's servants. Yet initiatives from the centre continually disappeared into the sands of provincial inertia, maladministration and poverty.

It is not surprising, therefore, that the range of activities undertaken by the state failed to match that of its western counterparts. The role of the state in fostering economic development was very modest. Nicholas's Finance Minister, Kankrin (1823–44), was adamantly opposed to industrialization. He adhered to a highly restrictive fiscal policy and while he was willing to shore up indebted members of the nobility he proved extremely reluctant to provide state loans for investment in industry. In a number of fields Nicholas's reign did witness considerable socio-economic progress: the laying of the first railway lines, centred upon Moscow; a slow fall in the death rate and slight rise in GNP per head; greater attention to technical and commercial education; and an overall increase in the number of students in every thousand of the population from one to six. But the rate of change bore no comparison to the dynamic changes overcoming her Great Power rivals. In virtually every sphere – in mass literacy, in health provision, in communications – the disparity was rapidly growing.

During the last years of Nicholas's reign, Russia's relative political, social and economic backwardness was brought home in the most indisputable fashion: military defeat. The tsar underestimated the concern felt by Britain, France and her traditional ally Austria over Russia's growing influence in the Balkans. In western eyes, the steady decline of Turkish power raised the spectre of Russia gaining control over Constantinople. In 1853 war broke out between Turkey and Russia over the tsar's insistence upon his right to protect the sultan's orthodox subjects. Britain and France came to Turkey's aid, and Russia paid the price of relative backwardness. She proved unable to defeat the western powers despite the fact that they were operating from distant bases. The administration of the war effort was bedevilled by corruption and incompetence, wretched communications hampered efforts at every turn, the training and weaponry of the army proved hopelessly anachronistic, and the wooden sailing vessels were annihilated by the steam-powered warships of the enemy. Despite the massive proportion of the budget lavished on the military, Russia was humiliated on her own doorstep. The diplomatic repercussions of Russia's defeat and alienation from Austria were to change the face of central Europe. The domestic repercussions were to initiate the most dramatic period of change and reform the empire had hitherto undergone.

The centrepiece of the 'Great Reforms' of Alexander II's reign (1855–81) was the abolition of serfdom. Alexander's predecessors had often contemplated this step. The moral case against serfdom had been widely accepted during Nicholas's reign. So too had the belief that serfdom constituted a major source of instability in the empire. Nicholas himself had been persuaded that in the long run emancipation was the only cure for the chronic incidence of peasant rebellion against noble landlords, which had risen gradually throughout the first half of the century. Moreover, the view had steadily gained currency, both within the administration and in the 'thick journals', that serfdom was a major restraint on economic development, cramping the mobility, the productivity, and the potential market of the peasantry. The Crimean War provided the catalyst. The notion that Russia's military might enabled her to afford chronic peasant unrest and growing economic backwardness became untenable. Peasant disturbances had significantly disrupted the war effort in the course of 1855, and the connection between economic development and military power had been made all too plain on the battlefields of the Crimea and in the desperate straits of the Treasury. Furthermore, the case for following the western example of reducing the costly standing army by building a reserve of trained men became incontrovertible. Yet as long as serfdom remained, so did the objection that it was not safe to return hundreds of thousands of trained ex-serfs to the countryside.

Powerful though the pressure for emancipation had become, five years elapsed between the Peace of Paris in 1856 and the Emancipation Edict of February 1861. For one thing, noble resistance remained strong. Only a minority were persuaded of the economic advantages of freely hired labour and were willing to forgo their traditional rights over their peasants. Conservative senior officials sagely agreed with Alexander that emancipation was desirable and must come eventually, but regretfully shook their heads at the insoluble problems involved. The critical question was the distribution of land. There was a deeply held belief among the peasantry that the land should rightfully belong to those who worked it. The nobles, on the other hand, regarded all the land worked by their peasants as part of their own property. The logical outcome of one view was that, along with their personal freedom, the peasantry would at the very least be granted the allotments which they were currently using for their own subsistence. The logical outcome of the other position, by contrast, was landless emancipation.

The objections to either strategy were seemingly insuperable. To deprive the peasantry of land appeared a recipe both for disastrous economic disruption and massive peasant resistance. To deprive the nobility, the mainstay of the regime, of a substantial proportion of their property as well as their free labour was unthinkable. So intractable did the problem appear that for the first two years of his reign Alexander himself oscillated uneasily between support for the efforts of officials in the Ministry of the Interior committed to emancipation, and acceptance of the warnings of the secret committee established to consider the issue. Only by the autumn of 1857 had the Ministry of the Interior evolved the outlines of a solution which the tsar was persuaded to back. The guiding principle adopted was that on emancipation the peasants were to retain use of an area of land more or less equivalent to their current allotments, but that they were to pay for it through redemption dues spread over a period of forty-nine years. These payments were to be made to the state, which in turn would compensate the nobility.

Once the government was publicly committed to a reform along these lines, it was borne in upon the nobility that to reverse the decision would be to run the risk of large-scale peasant rebellion. Their energies were directed instead towards ensuring that the detailed terms were as favourable to them as possible. The government, conscious that no reform could be effected without noble acquiescence, had been compelled to enter into dialogue with them. The nobility took advantage of the provincial committees established for the purpose and the general loosening of the framework of public life to press their claims. Moreover, the implications of emancipation affected areas of social life far beyond the immediate seigneurial relationship. Proposals for a whole range of reforms were publicly debated and quickly gathered momentum.

Administratively, the most innovative reform of the emancipation era was the introduction of a new structure for local government. An important impetus for this reform was pressure from the provincial nobility. In part they were concerned to compensate for the loss of influence over local affairs suffered by their estate through emancipation. But they were also seizing the opportunity to express their frustration with the caprice and inadequacy of provincial administration. At the same time, the slackening of censorship after the Crimean War had given voice to a more socially diverse public opinion, which concentrated attention on local government reform. Even without pressure from outside the government, senior officials in St Petersburg and governors in the provinces were themselves moving in the same direction. They had long been exasperated by the incompetence of the local bureaucracy.

The financial difficulties in which the government found itself after the Crimean War ruled out a straightforward extension of the existing administration to take on new duties. Instead, a solution was sought through the establishment, outside the regular bureaucracy, of elective councils with responsibilities for some aspects of local government. A statute of 1864 duly established the *zemstvos*, elective bodies at provincial and district level. They were empowered to improve a range of local facilities from transport, credit, and insurance to education and health care, and were granted limited tax-raising powers to help fund these activities. A small permanent board was to oversee the teachers, medical workers, veterinary surgeons and other specialists whom the more dynamic *zemstvos* soon began to employ. True, the chairmen of *zemstvo* assemblies were to be state appointees and the franchise, while providing minority representation for urban and peasant proprietors, ensured the domination of wealthier members of the nobility. Moreover, in practice the regime would freely intervene to limit the scope of *zemstvo* activity and the freedom of speech within *zemstvo* assemblies. Nevertheless, the *zemstvos*, and their rather less effective urban equivalents, the city dumas created under a statute of 1870, constituted a remarkable innovation. The autocracy had established administrative institutions which enjoyed a measure of autonomy and derived their authority and legitimacy in part from elections. The framework had been created for a very substantial increase in the range of public services, and for a significant measure of public participation in the running of these agencies.

Of comparable significance was a series of statutes approved in 1864 effecting far-reaching reform of the legal system. Explicitly modelled on advanced western practice, the reform sought to refound Russian justice on entirely new principles. The law was to be overseen by an independent judiciary which would be separate from the administrative bureaucracy and whose members could not be removed except for misconduct. Juries were to adjudicate serious criminal cases, elected justices of the peace were to hear minor criminal and civil cases, and trials were henceforth to be held in public. At the same time the appeals procedure was streamlined, court practice was refined, and the crudest forms of punishment were abolished. The new system took time to implement and was hedged in with clauses designed to preserve leeway for the authorities. An official accused of breaking the law could only be prosecuted with the consent of his superior. The government retained the right to take administrative measures outside the regular courts where it deemed necessary. Ministers were quick to express outrage when the courts exercised their independence and defied government wishes, and over the following decades the principles of the statutes of 1864 were freely transgressed. Nevertheless, the reform marked a giant stride in the direction of security under the law.

Two further major reforms affected censorship and education. A statute of 1865 laid down that, for the first time, it was for the courts to decide when the press had broken the law, and pre-publication censorship was significantly reduced. Administrative powers independent of the courts were retained to deal with journals which the regime regarded as particularly dangerous, and these powers too would be freely used in the following decades. All the same, the legal constraints on free speech were loosened and brought much more closely into line with those in the West. The freer atmosphere of the early years of Alexander II's reign also affected higher education. Disciplines forbidden under Nicholas, including philosophy, were reintroduced at university level. Despite the misgivings of conservative ministers appalled at the sustained student unrest of the emancipation period, the universities were granted a significantly greater degree of autonomy in running their own affairs. Here, too, the government retained reserve powers to intervene when it felt necessary. But the clock could never be turned back to pre-reform days, and the academic community would remain a vibrant sounding-board for the country's social and political problems.

The abolition of serfdom and the other 'Great Reforms' of Alexander's early years profoundly affected Russian society. Emancipation itself provided the context for a gradual but sustained acceleration in the rate of economic growth. Economic change brought with it major shifts in the social structure and in the fortunes of different social orders. These shifts conditioned the way in which Russian society reacted to the more open framework of public life.

In the short run, the stimulus given to the economy by emancipation seemed limited. Agriculture was briefly disrupted and the combination of a drop on military orders after the Crimean War, a severe financial crisis in 1858, and a fall in cotton imports during the American Civil War triggered a manufacturing recession which lasted until the mid-1860s. Nevertheless, as emancipation took effect, it slowly removed many of the constrictions which had handicapped the economy, hastening the replacement of forced labour by wage labour and the spread of market relations. Conditions became more conducive to entrepreneurial initiative, capital accumulation, the division of labour, technological innovation, and industrialization. The yield on peasant land slowly rose and a minority of landlords commanded sufficient capital to adapt successfully to farming methods based on hired labour and greater mechanization, thus contributing to a very sharp increase in Russia's grain exports. The peasantry was drawn steadily into the money economy, thereby raising consumer demand and stimulating both handicraft production in the villages and light industries, notably textiles and sugar.

Moreover, the government became more and more firmly convinced of the need to encourage manufacture. The lesson of the Crimean disaster, underlined by Prussia's military triumphs, impelled officials in the Ministry of War to urge that Russia develop strategic railways and reduce her dependence on imported arms. The Ministry of Finance, headed from 1862 to 1878 by the liberal economist Reutern, became equally convinced that only by significant industrial expansion could the regime's chronic budgetary problems be solved. Reutern rationalized the administration of the Treasury, improved banking and credit facilities,

and began to make large loans available, particularly to industrialists willing to undertake railway construction. During Alexander
II's reign Russian industrialists were still largely dependent on
foreign raw materials and machinery. But from the late 1860s the
metal and machine industries benefited from a strong rise in
orders, and the stimulus spread to the textile and other light
industries. The quickening pace of commercial life during
Alexander's reign was reflected in a fivefold increase in joint-stock
companies and a twentyfold expansion of the railway network.

The striking rate of growth should not obscure the fact that the
absolute level of industrial activity was still very low. At the end
of the reign output of coal, steel and pig-iron trailed far behind that
of France, let alone Germany and Britain. Russia's economy
remained overwhelmingly agrarian and, because of the slow rise
in agricultural productivity, its per capita income fell further
behind that of most western countries. The country's industrial
output would continue to fall further and further behind that of
Germany. Nevertheless, Russia was at least entering the lists of
major industrial producers and closing the gap between herself
and second-ranking producers such as France. And by the 1880s
the economy was poised for a dramatic breakthrough. Headed by
Vyshnegradsky in 1887–92 and by Witte in 1892–1903, the Ministry
of Finance began to co-ordinate its tariff, fiscal and investment
policies to attract foreign loans for a massive development of the
railway network. A major stimulus in the industrialization of most
European countries, railways held out particular promise to an
economy uniquely handicapped by vast distances and poor
communications. They linked the empire's far-flung mineral
resources with each other and the centres of population; they
enormously increased the volume of both domestic and foreign
trade; and their construction generated a massive new demand for
coal, steel, iron and manufactures.

The social repercussions of emancipation and accelerated
economic change gave rise to a heterogeneous range of pressures
upon the regime for further reform. For the landed nobility, the
impact of emancipation was deeply disturbing. The loss of
seigneurial rights, of the traditional source of their wealth and
authority, induced among many noblemen a reappraisal of their
role which amounted to a crisis of identity. Moreover, although the
tsar had made abundantly clear his wish that the terms of

emancipation should damage their position as little as possible, the compensation granted them was not sufficient to prevent a steady decline in noble landownership during the decades following 1861. A growing proportion of the nobility lost their ties with the land altogether. This was reflected in the loosening of what had traditionally been a strong correlation between land-ownership and civil and military office, especially at the highest levels. The privileged position of the nobility seemed threatened both by the growing professionalization of the bureaucracy and the far-reaching military reform of the 1870s. Among those who remained attached to the land, the result was a new wariness in their attitude towards the government. They developed a sense of embattlement and, gradually, a new consciousness of a specific 'gentry' interest. And as the level of education and sophistication among provincial noblemen gradually rose, so too did their ability to articulate their interests.

Building on the experience of the dialogue initiated by Alexander II over the method by which to abolish serfdom, they became more assertive and articulate in pressing their claims. Their spokesmen took advantage of the legal and institutional changes of the Great Reforms to express their anxieties. From the 1860s onwards, a major theme of conservative sections of the press was the duty of the state to uphold the position of the landed nobility, to provide financial support for estates in difficulty, and to continue to look to them to staff the upper reaches of the imperial service. At the same time, noble dissatisfaction with the extent of government help coloured the relationship between the newly-formed *zemstvos* and the government. It might have been expected that harmony would have prevailed between the two, since the great majority of landowners were staunchly loyal to the tsar and had no thought of utilizing the *zemstvos* to curb his power. However, the rumbling dissatisfaction among the more conservatively-minded majority, together with their dilatory attitude towards involvement in the work of the *zemstvos*, enabled a minority of more active, liberal-minded and politically assertive noble deputies to take the leadership of several *zemstvos*. In the hands of this liberal leadership, the economic dissatisfaction of land-owners became interwoven with the very different causes of complaint of an emergent civil society.

Along with the development of the urban economy, the

education system and public services the period following the
Great Reforms saw a rapid broadening of the ranks of educated,
urban-oriented society outside officialdom. The quickening pace
of trade and industry provided new opportunities for industrialists
and entrepreneurs, and generated a need for managers, engineers
and clerks of every description. The legal reform led to a sustained
growth in the number and sophistication of those engaged in the
legal professions. The expansion of the reading public, and the
easier conditions for publication, saw a dramatic development of
the world of publishing and in the number of journalists and
writers. The expansion of higher education meant an increase in
the size of the academic community and a substantial rise in the
number of students. It was in a handful of major cities, headed by
St Petersburg and Moscow, that this expansion of the middle
classes was concentrated. But in the provinces, too, new strata of
professionals were adding weight and numbers to 'society'. As
the public services mounted by the *zemstvos* in the provinces
developed, so did the staff of specialists they employed – teachers,
doctors, midwives, economic statisticians, agricultural experts.
This so-called 'third element', distinct from landowners and
peasants, constituted the core of a provincial complement to the
middle class emerging in the major cities.

   The predominant attitude of the educated public towards the
regime was hostile. Rather than satisfying demands for greater
freedom, the era of the Great Reforms had fed the appetite of
'progressive' sections of the public. It had sparked an upsurge in
civic involvement, epitomized by the so-called Sunday school
movement, a voluntary campaign launched in 1859 on a wave of
public enthusiasm for providing workers and their children with
basic literacy and numeracy. As the aspirations of the various
professions, of students, of philanthropists, of the 'third element'
rose, so did their exasperation at continuing official inefficiency,
corruption, and oppression. Repeated infringements of the
principles underlying the reforms generated intense frustration.
Interference with the courts was resented by a legal profession
self-consciously modelling itself upon western practice. The
authorities' attempts to crush recurrent student protest and
disturbances by imposing rigorous discipline upon them alienated
students and staff alike. Censorship remained the cause of
endemic friction with the press and publishing industry. And

as *zemstvo* activity gathered pace, the 'third element' and those noble deputies sympathetic to their work came up against sustained moves by the government to constrain their autonomy and room for manouevre.

As different strata of the educated public became conscious of belonging to a substantial and articulate body of opinion critical of the regime, 'society's' self-confidence grew. Even the more moderate newspapers took officialdom to task for one offence or another. And, although the most radical journalists could be silenced, ministers found themselves gradually having to take at least some account of public opinion. Nowhere was this more dramatically shown than in the field of foreign affairs. During the 1870s the government found it ever more difficult to resist pressure by Panslavist publicists to assert Russia's influence in the Balkans. Worse still was the public reaction to the outcome of Russia's war with Turkey in 1877–8. The terms which Russia attempted to impose on the defeated Ottoman Empire alarmed the other Great Powers and at the Congress of Berlin they forced her to yield many of the fruits of victory. The widespread and open protest at this climb-down, at the failure to achieve the liberation of fellow Slavs from under the Ottoman yoke, dealt a severe blow to the prestige and self-confidence of the regime. The passions inflamed by foreign affairs lent a certain leverage to domestic critics of the social, economic and political ills of the empire. The autocracy was faced with the emergence of a markedly more vigorous and independent public opinion.

For the peasantry, the financial terms of emancipation were a bitter disappointment. They were much harsher than in most parts of central Europe, with the partial exception of Prussia, and ensured that many traces of serfdom lingered long after 1861. Worst off were the private serfs. Although in principle they were to retain allotments equivalent to those they had used before emancipation, in practice the amount of land they retained was significantly smaller, especially in the fertile black-earth regions of the south; there they surrendered almost a quarter of their holdings. In order to compensate the nobility for the labour and services they were losing, the land values on which redemption payments were based were inflated – grossly so in the less fertile provinces where the peasants broadly retained their pre-emancipation allotments. Moreover, it was left to the landowner's discretion to decide when his ex-serfs should pass from the initial status of 'temporary obligation' to outright purchasers of the land. Where redemption did go into effect immediately, the peasantry soon found their allotments inadequate, and their dependence on the nobility was perpetuated by the need to secure access to the pasture, forest and water supplies which often remained in the hands of the landlords.

To make matters worse, pressure on the land was constantly increased by a massive population explosion. During the second half of the nineteenth century the empire's population grew on average 1.5 per cent a year, the total rising from 74 million at emancipation to 126 million in 1897. The result was to force up the price of both renting and buying land. Peasants found themselves compelled to subsidize their incomes by working on noble estates for pitiful wages. It is difficult to generalize about the overall direction of peasant living standards in the post-emancipation period. Yields did gradually increase, the amount of land cultivated grew rapidly, and peasant handicraft in the village expanded. Yet peasant life-expectancy rose very slowly, they proved chronically unable (or unwilling) to meet tax and redemption dues in full, and the high incidence of regional harvest failure (the most notorious being in 1891) created acute rural poverty.

Within individual villages there was a greater differentiation between rich and poor peasant families than in the past. Advantaged households might briefly establish a privileged position within their own commune and rent land from the nobility on their own behalf. But post-emancipation conditions in the countryside precluded the emergence of satisfied and socially conservative strata of peasants comparable to those of France or parts of Germany. It was extremely difficult for the wealthier households that emerged to consolidate their scattered strips or to introduce new methods and seeds. The combination of collective responsibility, periodic land redistribution, a heavy fiscal burden, and a primitive form of farming acutely vulnerable to harvest failure had a constant levelling effect. The overwhelming majority of peasants remained 'middle peasants' directly dependent on their own labour for their livelihood.

Whatever the overall trend in peasant living standards, then, the peasants' sense of injustice and resentment against the emancipation settlement, the burden of redemption dues, and taxation was intense. The gradual spread of market relations did little to undermine their age-old conviction that the land ought to belong to those who worked it. In some respects the slow rise in literacy served to reinforce that conviction, as did such contact as they had with urban and educated society, and the ideas propagated by young radicals and democratically-minded members of the 'third element'.

Yet the Great Reforms opened no avenue through which the peasants could voice their aspirations equivalent to that opened for sections of the educated public. The administrative arrangements adopted at emancipation kept the peasants largely isolated from the world outside. The commune, saddled with responsibility for all peasant obligations, was empowered with a wide range of sanctions over its individual members. Under the crude tutelage of the rural police, the village was left to regulate its own affairs and to administer justice according to customary rather than state law. Even over the local activities of the *zemstvo*, consultation with the peasantry was little more than a formality. *Zemstvo* assemblies met only for a few days once a year; peasant deputies were always outnumbered by their noble colleagues; and they proved extremely reluctant to take any active part in debate. So far as national issues and direct communication with government was concerned, there was no mechanism at all for peasant participation.

Peasant discontent, therefore, continued to be expressed through traditional forms of protest. In 1861 the news that they would have to pay for their allotments was met with angry disbelief, passive and in some areas violent resistance, and recurrent expectations of a 'real' emancipation still to come. From the mid-1860s the number of peasant disturbances declined and remained relatively low until the 1890s. But the uneasy calm was broken by occasional major outbreaks of disorder, notably in Kiev province between 1875 and 1878. Deprived though they were of legal channels to express their discontent, peasant restiveness was widely recognized and formed the backcloth to the politics of the post-emancipation decades.

So far as the urban poor and the small but growing ranks of industrial workers were concerned, they too gained no legal means to press their claims. In the early 1860s, at the height of the reform era, proposals were advanced to regulate the conditions of urban labour. But these were aborted, and the regime continued to treat workers as peasants temporarily absent from their communes. A high proportion of the industrial workforce did indeed retain close links with the countryside. Many left their families in the village, returned for the harvest, and retired there in old age. Yet the fond belief that Russia could avoid what was seen as the western curse of a rootless urban proletariat, or that the rural tie constituted an innoculation against radicalism, proved an illusion. Urban and industrial conditions were as grim as anything seen in the early stages of industrial development in the West. Housing provision was crude, the rate of accidents high, wages pitifully low, discipline harsh and humiliating, and job security non-existent. Moreover, by the 1870s, and even more clearly in the 1880s, some of the distinctive features of the Russian proletariat were emerging. Large-scale manufacture tended to be concentrated in a few industrial areas, and the plants themselves tended to be very much larger on average than at an equivalent phase in western development. This facilitated both the development of a consciousness of common grievances, and an ability to give vent to these grievances. The first major strike, by cotton-spinners in St Petersburg, took place in 1870, there was a significant increase in the number of strikes at the end of the 1870s, and the scale of industrial protest grew ominously from the mid-1880s. Denied the right to engage in collective bargaining, and lacking the moderating influence exerted in the West by traditional craft organizations or a reformist 'labour aristocracy', their militancy soon outran that of their western counterparts. Although even by the end of the 1890s the number of workers in mines and factories had not reached 2 million and constituted less than 5 per cent of the working population, official anxiety over the threat they posed to public order was growing.

It is in the context of mounting criticism of the regime from 'society', and of rumbling discontent lower down the social scale, that the dramatic impact of the so-called 'revolutionary intelligentsia' is to be understood. Drawn from the ranks of the relatively privileged sections of society, the radical intelligentsia took their opposition beyond that of liberal critics to the point of outright rejection of the regime and the whole social structure of imperial Russia. In part their radicalism derived from their own frustration.

The early years of Alexander's reign had aroused expectations which were rudely disappointed. Petty and not so petty intervention by the authorities against student activism, the impediments of censorship, the limited employment opportunities outside dreary and corrupt state service, the myriad legal restrictions subjecting women to the authority of their husbands and fathers drove a significant minority of the young educated élite towards radical politics. During the late 1850s and the 1860s, the works of Herzen, Chernyshevsky, Lavrov and other leading revolutionary thinkers, and a gathering stream of 'Aesopian' articles published legally, and illegal pamphlets and newspapers helped to create a powerful radical subculture. Deprived of any other lever with which to achieve change, the radicals began to identify their own frustration with the predicament of the peasantry. They developed a full-blown vision of a revolutionary transformation in which Russia would be reborn on the basis of free, decentralized, democratic and egalitarian peasant socialism. Alive to the western socialist critique of capitalism, the 'populists' looked for a distinctive Russian path which would avoid the horrors of proletarianization and pass straight to socialism.

During the early 1870s several thousand young idealists sought to make contact with the peasantry. Most famously, in the summer of 1874 they 'went to the people', determined to repay the debt they felt educated society owed the toilers and to enlighten the peasants about the possibility of transforming the status quo. They were quickly lost in the vast peasant sea; the police rapidly descended upon them; and when they did manage to make contact with peasants they were often met with suspicion and even hostility. Mass arrests and successive trials brought the radicals wide publicity, and in 1876 they created the first relatively stable underground organization, 'Land and Liberty', to co-ordinate further efforts. Some of the more militant revolutionary populists stumbled upon the desperate tactic of terror. Initially their goal was often revenge for the indignities inflicted upon imprisoned colleagues. But the sensation which their attacks caused led some to conclude that far-reaching political change and at best even revolution could be precipitated by a sustained campaign of terror directed at key members of the regime. In 1879 a relatively tightly-knit organization taking as its name 'The

People's Will' emerged from within 'Land and Liberty', and devoted its energies to assassinating the tsar himself.

At the end of the 1870s, therefore, just when its authority had been shaken by the furore over the humiliation at the Congress of Berlin, the regime faced a combination of noble discontent, an increasingly assertive and critical public opinion, intermittent unrest in the countryside, unnerving outbreaks of industrial strife, and a sustained terror campaign. Although there was no consensus among ministers and senior officials on how to react, the tsar lent towards those who urged that repression must be accompanied by measured concessions. An important factor in swaying his judgement was the way in which differences between conservative and progressively-minded advisers were interwoven with differences over his irregular private life. Ever since 1864 he had spent as much time as possible with his mistress, Catherine Dolgorukaya. This increasingly public scandal had deeply affronted the tsarevich, who took his mother's side, and the family rift had divided high society. In 1880 when the Empress died, Alexander II hastily contracted a morganatic marriage with Catherine and installed her in the Winter Palace. Traditionalist hostility to Catherine forged a bond between her and more progressively-minded ministers who favoured a flexible response to the complex of pressures bearing in upon the government. In failing health and with a growing sense of embattlement, Alexander II hesitantly sided with this alliance. For a brief interlude, political reform appeared on the government's agenda.

In 1880 the tsar appointed General Loris-Melikov to manage what he saw as a severe crisis for his regime. Loris-Melikov's view was that while the government must act vigorously to suppress all revolutionary activity, its stability could only be secured by widening the basis of positive support for the regime. To that end he introduced a number of reforms and proposed the creation of machinery for a measure of consultation on national issues, with representatives of 'society' drawn from the *zemstvos* and municipal dumas. In themselves, the proposals amounted to very much less than a commitment to constitutional government. But the implication that unvarnished autocracy was no longer sustainable was clear to all, and both opponents and supporters of Loris-Melikov saw the issue as a momentous and possibly irrevocable step along the path trodden by western constitutional monarchies

On 1 March 1881 the tsar consented to the first, tentative moves in that direction. That same day he was assassinated by The People's Will.

The assassination triggered a sharp about-turn in government policy. Alexander II's hesitant concessions were vigorously repudiated and the principle of autocracy firmly reasserted. The government was purged of reformers and office entrusted to staunch conservatives. During the 1880s the regime made plain its determination not only to halt any further movement in the direction of public participation but to crush expressions of dissent and remove earlier constraints on the autocracy. Emergency regulations empowered the government to declare virtual martial law at will. New restrictions upon the *zemstvos* were introduced. New steps were taken to discipline the universities, reduce the number of non-noble students, and intensify censorship. In 1889 a new tier of provincial officials, the 'land captains', were entrusted with both administrative and judicial powers to tighten the administration's direct supervision of the peasantry. Police sections specializing in the prevention and exposure of underground political activity were developed. The new tsar maintained autocracy, and was to bequeath it intact to his son Nicholas II on his death in 1894.

An important ingredient in the regime's determination to resist pressure for political change of any kind was the personality of Alexander III. The contrast between him and his father was sharp, and had been heightened by conflict over Alexander II's relationship with Catherine Dolgorukaya. Alexander III's attitude towards Loris-Melikov and his fellow-reformers was coloured by the support they received from Catherine. As the tsarevich he had gathered around him a circle of reactionary figures whose leading light was Pobedonostsev, his boyhood tutor and, since 1866, procurator of the Holy Synod, the lay official in charge of church affairs. On coming to power, the new tsar was guided in part by simple determination to reverse all his father had done and to model himself upon his idolized grandfather, Nicholas I.

Moreover, resolute reassertion of autocracy was strongly encouraged by conservative opinion within the army, the church and above all the landed nobility. In the aftermath of the assassination it quickly became clear that the most assertive calls for reform from the *zemstvos* had reflected the views of only a minority of the nobility. *Zemstvo* elections following the crisis saw liberal candidates badly mauled. From the start, they had been disproportionately prominent in *zemstvo* gatherings. The broad correlation between liberal leanings, higher education and civic activism had ensured that it was they rather than their more numerous conservative gentry colleagues who took most part in *zemstvo* assemblies and on the executive boards. For most of the landed nobility, the prospect of a severe threat to the authority of the government held no appeal. Disgruntled though they might be by their economic decline, they were too conscious of potential peasant unrest, and of the interdependence between tsarism and their own privileges, to view political instability with equanimity. The 'third element', with their democratic and even socialist tendencies, were regarded with suspicion and hostility. The last thing the landed nobility wanted was for meddling 'do-gooders' to upset the Russian status quo. The new tsar was inundated with noble protestations of loyalty and support.

There is, then, little mystery to the conservative goals of Alexander III's regime. More complex is the explanation for its success in resisting pressure for reform which in the eyes of Loris-Melikov and many had seemed irresistible. One necessary condition for the new lease of life lent to the autocracy was the avoidance of potentially damaging encounters with the other Great Powers. Urged by his finance ministers that the Treasury could not stand the strain of war, Alexander III came to terms with the humiliation of the Congress of Berlin, signed a new alliance with Germany and Austria, and took care to avoid confrontation with the latter in the Balkans. When tension with the Central Powers began to increase in the late 1880s, he moved to shore up Russia's position through peaceful diplomacy, forging an alliance with France which was underpinned by large-scale French loans. It was not until his son rashly took on Japan in 1904 that the regime would once again suffer the dire domestic consequences of unsuccessful foreign engagements.

More fundamentally, Alexander's resolute reaction exposed the limited muscle behind the demands for reform which had so impressed Loris-Melikov. Members of the professions, the more liberal newspapers, the academic community, the 'third element' continued, of course, to yearn for public participation in government and for the extension of civil liberties. Criticism of the regime did not suddenly cease. The rapid expansion of the press and its increasing commercial viability enabled journalists hostile to the government to evade many of the censors' efforts. Concern to present the country in the most favourable light to foreign investors gave the government cause to mollify if it could not silence such critics. Major famine in 1891 acutely embarrassed the regime and gave new momentum to 'enlightened public opinion'. But on their own the liberally-inclined middle-class strata lacked political weight. The division between them and commercial-industrial sectors of the bourgeoisie was profound. For the most part the moneyed classes were politically passive. For one thing, they were themselves sharply divided along regional, ethnic and religious lines. The magnates of the capital and the Old Believers of Moscow viewed each other with suspicion, and the leading figures of the new industries in the south, where much of the most vigorous industrial growth was taking place, were far removed from the political centre. Moreover, beneath a thin layer of sophisticated industrialists, the rank and file of the merchantry remained culturally backward and, as their performance in most of the urban dumas showed, politically deferential. In any case, resistance to working-class agitation for improved conditions formed a bond between the regime and employers which would grow stronger as time passed. Russia's emergent liberal spokesmen lacked an economically powerful constituency.

Nor was adequate compensation provided by pressure for change from lower down the social scale. Under Alexander III the incidence of peasant and working-class protest was not sufficient to force reform back on to the agenda. Tension in the countryside remained real enough, but the regime faced no major crisis there until the turn of the century. As for working-class militancy, although it intensified markedly during the 1880s, it was neither co-ordinated nor sustained. As long as the regime maintained order at home and peace abroad, liberal opposition was relatively easy to rebuff.

The revolutionary intelligentsia, too, found its leverage limited by its failure to attract any wide measure of support. In the 1870s there was some sympathy for the young radicals within educated society and their successors would continue to receive financial and other help from privileged sympathizers. But the resort to terror had itself been in part an admission of their failure to achieve rapport with or effect any organization among the peasantry. During the 1870s the populists had found urban workers more responsive to radical blandishments, and the following decade saw the beginning of a far-reaching reappraisal of the potential for revolution. While recruitment to the radical subculture continued unabated during the 1880s, the increasingly efficient police successfully headed off renewed plots on the life of the tsar. A growing number of radicals began to question not only the tactics of The People's Will but the whole strategy of the populists. The more ready response among urban workers to socialist propaganda, the visible growth of industry and spread of capitalism, and the sheer failure to ignite the peasantry drew increasing attention to the revolutionary prognosis hitherto thought applicable only to the West: that of Karl Marx. From the early 1880s Plekhanov, a populist leader who had rejected the People's Will, spearheaded a sustained assault on the basic populist assumption that Russia could avoid capitalism. He denied the socialist potential of the peasant commune and pointed to the industrial proletariat as the class destined to take the lead in overthrowing tsarism and, in due course, to construct socialism.

By the end of Alexander III's reign, therefore, Russia's political structure had fallen even further out of line with those of the other Great Powers. Instead of accepting the limitations of ruling within the law, and of at least formal consultation with if not responsibility to an elected assembly, government in Russia remained autocratic. Not that the reality of the tsar's control over affairs measured up to tsarist rhetoric. Many of Alexander's cherished goals – to withdraw the judiciary's quasi-autonomy, to cut back the activities of the *zemstvos*, to halt the decline in gentry landownership and the dilution of noble predominance in the upper reaches of the bureaucracy – proved unattainable. Not least among the obstacles to his 'counter-reforms' was opposition from within the increasingly specialized and professional upper reaches of the bureaucracy itself. The more complex and sophisticated became the apparatus of the state, the more narrow became the options open to the tsar. For much of the time his role was that of adjudicating increasingly severe conflicts between one hierarchy and another, between the ministry of internal affairs and those of finance and justice, between the civil service and the military. Under Nicholas II, the unity and coherence of the regime, supposedly guaranteed by the concentration of authority in the person of the tsar, would be progressively eroded.

Moreover, however jealously the autocracy guarded its pre-rogatives, it could not prevent the rapid evolution of Russian society. As economic development accelerated, so social polariza-tion – between landlords and peasants, employers and workers –. intensified. Until the end of the century the regime managed to deny Russia's social classes even minimal freedom to organize and articulate their aspirations. But in doing so, it only exacerbated social tension. Any chance that the conflicting interests of different social and national groups could be mediated through legal channels was ruled out. Gentry frustration and alarm at social instability laid the foundations for the rigidly reactionary noble front of the early twentieth century. Frustration among the professional middle classes yielded Europe's most radical liberal movement. Peasant discontent gathered momentum to the point where, given the chance, it swept away private ownership in land altogether. Russia's working class, lacking any legal framework within which to protect its interests and improve its conditions, provided the kernel of the most militant revolutionary movement the continent had seen. The radical intelligentsia sustained a tradition of revolutionary analysis, underground organization and political propaganda without parallel in the West. Despite the growing cultural, economic and administrative similarities she shared with her rivals, tsarist Russia was impelled down a road of her own.

Further reading

The best general treatment of all but the last decade of the period is D. Saunders, *Russia in the Age of Reaction and Reform, 1801–1881* (London, 1992).

The two most useful economic studies are W. L. Blackwell, *The Beginnings of Russian Industrialization, 1800–1860* (Princeton, NJ, 1968) and P. Gatrell, *The Tsarist Economy 1850–1917* (London, 1986).

Three stimulating interpretative studies at variance with the one offered here are R. Pipes, *Russia Under the Old Regime* (New York, 1974); T. Shanin, *Russia as a 'Developing Society'* (London, 1985) and T. Szamuely, *The Russian Tradition* (London, 1972).

For those without Russian, access to the best Soviet work in the field is now available in the series of translated monographs by P. A.

188 Themes in Modern European History

Zaionchkovsky, including *The Russian Autocracy in Crisis, 1878–1882* and *The Russian Autocracy under Alexander III* (Gulf Breeze, FA, 1979, 1978).
On developments within the state administration both before and after emancipation, see W. B. Lincoln, *In the Vanguard of Reform: Russia's Enlightened Bureaucrats, 1825–1861* (DeKalb, IL, 1982); W. M. Pinter and D. K. Rowney (eds), *Russian Officialdom: the Bureaucratization of Russian Society from the Seventeenth to the Twentieth Century* (London, 1980); and H. W. Whelan, *Alexander III and the State Council: Bureaucracy and Counter-Reform in Late Imperial Russia* (New Brunswick, NJ, 1982).
W. Mosse, *Alexander II and the Modernization of Russia* (London, 1958) remains a useful introduction to the reign, while M. McCauley and P. Waldron, *The Emergence of the Modern Russian State, 1856–81* (London, 1988) presents a wide range of documents.
For the motives behind and dynamics of emancipation, see J. Blum, *The End of the Old Order in Rural Europe* (Princeton, NJ, 1978), who provides comparative perspectives on emancipation; T. Emmons, *The Russian Landed Gentry and the Peasant Emancipation of 1861* (Cambridge, 1968); and D. Field, *The End of Serfdom: Nobility and Bureaucracy, 1855–1861* (Cambridge, MA, 1976).
On other areas of reform, see C. A. Ruud, *Fighting Words: Imperial Censorship and the Press, 1804–1906* (Toronto, 1982); F. Starr, *Decentralization and Self-government in Russia, 1830–1870* (Princeton, NJ, 1972); R. Wortman, *The Development of Russian Legal Consciousness* (Chicago, 1976).
J. Blum, *Lord and Peasant in Russia from the Ninth to the Nineteenth Century* (Princeton, NJ, 1961) is invaluable on rural Russia and should be supplemented with T. Emmons and W. S. Vucinich (eds), *The Zemstvo in Russia: an Experiment in Local Self-government* (Cambridge, 1982), a rich collection of articles which illuminates much more than the development of the zemstvos; and W. S. Vucinich (ed.), *The Peasant in Nineteenth-Century Russia* (Stanford, CA, 1968).
The major work on Russia's emergent middle class is A. J. Rieber, *Merchants and Entrepreneurs in Imperial Russia* (Chapel Hill, NC, 1982), while urban conditions and the fledgling working class are discussed in J. H. Bater, *St Petersburg: Industrialization and Change* (London, 1976) and R. E. Zelnik, *Labor and Society in Tsarist Russia: the Factory Workers of St Petersburg, 1855–1870* (Stanford, CA, 1971).
H. Rogger, *Russia in the Age of Modernisation and Revolution, 1881–1917* (London, 1983) includes a useful overview of the minority nationalities from the perspective of the late nineteenth century, while J. Frankel, *Prophecy and Politics: Socialism, Nationalism and the Russian Jews, 1862–1917* (Cambridge, 1981) skilfully traces reactions among the worst-treated minority.
Volumes 2 and 3 of R. Auty and D. Obolensky (eds), *Companion to Russian Studies* (Cambridge, 1977, 1978) provide an introduction to high culture in the period, while J. Brooks, *When Russia Learned to Read:*

Literacy and Popular Literature, 1861–1917 (Princeton, NJ, 1985) gives a fascinating account of the other end of the cultural spectrum.

On the revolutionary intelligentsia, the most stimulating place to start is the series of essays in I. Berlin, *Russian Thinkers* (London, 1978), while the Polish historian A. Walicki provides a lucid account of ideological developments in his *History of Russian Thought from the Enlightenment to Marxism* (Oxford, 1980).

The basic work on the populists is F. Venturi, *Roots of Rebellion: a History of the Populist and Socialist Movements in Nineteenth-Century Russia* (London, 1960).

On the genesis of radical protest see M. Raeff, *Origins of the Russian Intelligentsia: the Eighteenth-Century Nobility* (New York, 1966), and for recruitment to the underground from the 1860s see D. Brower, *Training the Nihilists: Education and Radicalism in Tsarist Russia* (Ithaca, NY, and London, 1975). Much light on the radical underground in the decade after 1881 is thrown by N. M. Naimark, *Terrorists and Social Democrats: the Russian Revolutionary Movement Under Alexander III* (Cambridge, MA, 1983) and D. Offord, *The Russian Revolutionary Movement in the 1880s* (Cambridge, 1986).

7

Progress, prosperity, and positivism: cultural trends in mid-century

MICHAEL BIDDISS

Ideas of progress are deeply rooted in the history of western civilization. Yet they have never been more frequently and confidently proclaimed than during the middle decades of the nineteenth century. Here is the message at its clearest: 'Progress is not an accident but a necessity . . . Surely must the things we call evil and immorality disappear; surely must man become perfect.'[1] The words are those of the British philosopher and liberal pundit Herbert Spencer; the date is 1850, the year before the Great Exhibition of the Works of Industry of all Nations was held at Hyde Park. This essay will examine how the enhanced plausibility of such progressive ideas in much of Europe around that time can be related to contemporary perceptions, not just of economic and political improvement but also of scientific and technological achievement in particular. It will also survey the implications of such a linkage for some wider aspects of European intellectual and cultural life. This involves some reference to religious issues, as well as to the work of certain social thinkers, novelists, and painters who were active during the heyday of the movements known as 'positivism', 'realism', and 'naturalism'.

Between the revolutions of 1848, which came at the end of a decade known as 'the hungry forties', and the so-called 'great depression' of the mid-1870s Europe enjoyed a period of remarkable economic expansion. This greater prosperity was not evenly spread, either geographically or across the social structure: it excluded many artisans (such as hand-loom weavers), and proved generally weakest in the southern and eastern regions of the continent. Yet, viewed overall, this was for most Europeans an epoch of material advance, during which there was an ebbing in those tides of revolutionary anger that had reached danger levels in 1848. Although those who led the risings of that year were often inspired by ideas of 'progress', this was not a notion instantly derivable from the realities of their preceding experience – that is, from life in a Europe dominated by Metternich and afflicted by widespread disease and scarcity. Those who lived through the following decades, however, found it easier to forge a link between everyday actuality and their belief in improvement. Many convinced themselves that such ills as grinding poverty and premature mortality, even where these still happened strongly to survive, need not indefinitely prevail as normal features of the human condition. Change became more frequently identified as advance, the course of history more easily interpreted as moving not only onwards but upwards.

The indications of material progress around the mid-century were evident on many sides. It was true that, as Friedrich Engels and many other critics stressed, the processes of industrialization accelerating since the later eighteenth century had a shadow-side of misery and exploitation. But they were associated also with a most dramatic enlargement of productive potential and the prospect of a richer and more varied pattern of consumption; in short, they launched perhaps the most far-reaching set of changes to have affected the everyday life of Europeans since the tool-making innovations of the Neolithic Age. Even before 1850 the impact of industrialization had already been quite widely felt in Britain and Belgium. Now other countries, particularly France, Prussia, and some of the smaller German states, would also become more rapidly involved. This growth of industrial capitalism was certainly accompanied by a tendency towards inflation. The level of the latter remained, however, generally compatible both with the encouragement of expansion by entrepreneurs and with the maintenance or increase of the average real wages paid to their employees. European population too continued its rise (from around 260 million in 1850 to about 325 million in 1880, and now due more to changes in rates of birth than death), yet it did so in a way that was seemingly immune from the worst of the miseries earlier predicted by Malthus as the eventual penalty for such a demographic boom. As the balance between rural and urban habitation also shifted, such innovations as gas-lighting and mains drainage began to improve the quality of life for those dwelling in and moving to the rapidly expanding towns. Standards of health started to benefit not just from better sanitation measures but also from the introduction of surgical anaesthesia and antiseptic procedures. Nutrition was vital too, and here the age-old problem of obtaining sufficient food was eased by good prospects of profitability to farmers, by further developments in 'scientific' agriculture (especially as applied to feeds and fertilizers), and by progress in the mechanization of equipment. Not least, the task of actually transporting supplies to points of need was advantageously transformed by the new train systems.

The railway was, amongst all the symptoms of advance, perhaps the most widely visible and audible to townspeople and countryfolk alike. Europe's rail track was expanded from 14,000 km in 1850 to 65,000 km by 1870. The construction of this network involved truly monumental feats of tunnelling, viaduct-making, and city station-building. Thus in its preliminary infra-structure as well as in its subsequent operation the railway was a stimulus to many other sectors of the economy, such as the enterprises devoted to the extraction of coal and iron ore and those engaged in the production of steel by the Bessemer process first developed in the 1850s. It also generated a need for capital, on a scale far surpassing that which had arisen during the earlier stages of industrialization. That demand was met, swiftly and relatively cheaply, by an increasingly sophisticated system of company organization and of banking and credit services. The dominance enjoyed by the leading European countries in an increasingly global system of commerce was assisted by their pre-eminence in other aspects of improved communication besides the railway. They developed not only electrical telegraphs and cable systems, but also steamships. European ownership of the latter leapt from 186,000 tons in 1850 to 1.5 million tons twenty years later, and soon afterwards the figure surpassed that for ships powered by sail. During the same period world trade multiplied by 2.6; global output of coal by 2.5, that of iron by 4; and global steam-power increased nearly fivefold. The opening in 1869 of the Suez Canal (itself a triumph for new mechanical methods of construction engineering, and for the technocratic reputation of the French entrepreneurs and politicians who had inspired it) both symbolized and practically assisted the projection, whether by trade or war or migration, of Europe's ascendancy over other continents. By then the world had become divided, as Eric Hobsbawm says, 'into a smaller part in which "progress" was indigenous and another much larger part in which it came as a foreign conqueror'.[2]

Already in the late 1830s Alfred Tennyson's poem *Locksley Hall* had epitomized this kind of confidence through the famous line, 'Better fifty years of Europe than a cycle of Cathay'. Such perceptions were certainly underpinned by a sense of material prowess, best illustrated in those techniques of manufacture, navigation, and sheer fire-power which were aiding the consolidation of formal or informal empire. But that kind of belief has to be related, in turn, to a structure of progressive ideas with an even broader base. Not least, prosperity was viewed as going hand in hand with political, and even moral, improvement. Many believed that the experience of Britain, above all, pointed the way forward. Her leadership in trade and industry, including the extension of economic influence overseas, was interpreted as the product of a 'liberal' spirit whose material and political strands were closely entwined. The 'Manchester School' of Richard Cobden and John Bright, which in 1846 had won such a famous campaign to repeal the Corn Laws, increasingly attracted continental converts to the view that the freedom and prosperity of the greatest number might best be promoted by serving first the political and economic interests of the industrial and commercial middle class. This was perhaps easier to believe during the 1850s and 1860s than ever before, or since.

The resultant liberalism meant different things to different people. Critics saw it as a dangerously negative or merely compromising force – it seemed impatient with traditional conservatism on the one hand, and yet fearful about more thoroughgoing change on the other; it seemed to favour equality before the law, while becoming far more cautious when radical socio-economic egalitarianism raised its head; and it seemed to support the allocation of greater power to parliamentary institutions, while usually refraining from endorsement of universal suffrage, which might well be the precondition for any sovereignty of the people at large. Liberals themselves did, however, lay claim to a core of real conviction, centred on the belief that individual and collective happiness could be maximized progressively through the development of freer economic competition and of political institutions directly representative of the many who had some sure, and usually propertied, stake in society. Enlarged freedom in belief and expression, fuller education and greater literacy, moderately broadened franchise, and more responsible government were all welcomed as auspicious omens. During the 1860s, for example, it was possible (though not invariably wise) to put a favourable gloss on the erosion in France of the more authoritarian features of the Second Empire, or the creation of a new Italian kingdom by Piedmont at the expense of Naples, or Bismarck's use of free-trade policies in outmanoeuvring Austria, or the concessions eventually made by the Habsburg emperor to his Magyar subjects, or – even in benighted Russia – the pursuit by Alexander II of a reform campaign which included the emancipation of millions of serfs. There was also a temptation to interpret as wars of liberation at least some of those military campaigns which otherwise threatened so bloodily to disturb the progressive harmonies of this period. With hindsight, it may be clear to us just how naïve was much of this optimism. But, for those who actually lived through these years, it was far from implausible to believe that broadly liberal values, though still weak in eastern and even in much of central Europe, were enjoying an advance in the West which must herald their eventual conquest over minds and institutions elsewhere.

Our understanding of mid-nineteenth-century ideas of progress can be further sharpened by exploring not just their material and political foundations but also their association with notions about the march of science. This kind of link was well captured in 1867 by Walter Bagehot who observed that 'a certain matter-of-factness' was growing upon the world and that it characterized very similarly 'the two greatest intellectual agencies of our time', which he then identified as business on one hand and physical science on the other.[3] During the nineteenth century many aspects of material advance became increasingly dependent upon a more sophisticated understanding of natural phenomena: take, for example, the work done by physicists on the principles of electromagnetism as then translated into the development of the dynamo, and the researches into the principles of chemistry as then exploited to promote the manufacture of new alloys or the refinement of the steel-making methods that we connect with such names as Bessemer, Siemens, and Thomas-Gilchrist. Science was emancipating itself from 'natural philosophy'; becoming more organized as a distinct specialism (indeed, soon, as a series of specialisms); asserting itself as a greater force in higher education, especially in Germany and France; and creating a more sophisticated network of professional contracts for national and international scholarly communication. Not least, the intellectual achievements of the scientists were being constantly converted, by means of applied technology, into inventions and processes that seemed already to be improving the quality of life for many, and to be capable in the longer run of bringing benefit to all.

This was the kind of context within which, as early as 1837, the most famous of Whig historians composed his eloquent and revealing essay on Sir Francis Bacon – a figure who, over 300 years before, had made his own influential contributions towards man's age-old quest to achieve domination over the realm of nature. In that piece we find Thomas Macaulay writing thus of science:

> It has lengthened life; it has mitigated pain; it has extinguished diseases; it has increased the fertility of the soil; it has given new securities to the mariner; it has furnished new arms to the warrior; it has spanned great rivers and estuaries with bridges of form unknown to our fathers; it has guided the thunderbolt innocuously from the heaven to earth; it has lighted up the night with the splendour of the day; it has extended the range of human vision; it has multiplied the power of human muscles; it has accelerated motion; it has annihilated distance; it has facilitated intercourse, correspondence, all friendly offices, all dispatch of business; it has enabled man to descend the depths of the sea, to soar into the air, to penetrate securely into the noxious recesses of the earth, to traverse the land in cars which whirl along without horses, to cross the ocean in ships which run ten knots an hour against the wind. These are but a part of its fruits, and of its first-fruits; for it is a philosophy which never rests, which has never attained, which is never perfect. Its law is progress.[4]

Here is another passage, written eleven years later:

The subjugation of the forces of nature, the invention of machinery, the application of chemistry to industry and agriculture, steamships, railways, electric telegraphs, the clearing of whole continents for cultivation, the making of navigable waterways, huge populations sprung up as if by magic out of the earth – what earlier generations had the remotest inkling that such productive powers slumbered within the womb of associated labour?[5]

The authors, this time, are Karl Marx and Friedrich Engels. Their interpretation of progress was more complex than Macaulay's and certainly less complacent about the miseries that still abounded. But even they assumed that there must ultimately be some convergence between material and moral improvement. Moreover, despite all its hostility towards the contemporary capitalist order, not even their *Communist Manifesto* could refrain from expressing admiration for the recent scientific and technical achievements that had been registered under the leadership of the European bourgeoisie during the epoch of its class hegemony.

Such advances were nowhere better displayed than in the series of international exhibitions held during these years, starting with that London spectacle of 1851 mentioned at the outset of this essay. Some 14,000 firms were represented at Hyde Park, and that figure had doubled by 1862 when Britain hosted a second celebration of this kind. Paris (1855 and 1867) and Vienna (1873) also joined the list of venues, while the rapidly rising stature of the USA as a competitor in industrial and technical improvement was reflected through the huge Philadelphia Centennial Exhibition of 1876. It may be helpful to think of the Crystal Palace, which Joseph Paxton designed for the first of these events, as a giant glass-case in which the public could examine the multiple specimens of the species, Progress. Yet his structure might also be regarded as a sort of secular cathedral – thus symbolizing something of the tension, or even hostility, which many contemporaries believed had inevitably to operate between the march of science and the maintenance of religion.

How far might the former be sustained only at the expense of the latter? The middle decades of the nineteenth century were certainly ones in which Christianity went through a particularly severe crisis of authority. On the organizational and social front, the churches were having to face the challenge of adapting their pastoral ministry to an environment changing with unprecedented rapidity towards greater urbanization and industrialization, and towards the enlargement of state influence in matters such as education. But their problems in that regard were made worse by a more or less simultaneous confrontation with the forces of intellectual modernity, embodied above all in the advance of science. Here actual discoveries were matched in importance by the model of scientific method and technique underlying them, and by its potential for application far beyond the realms of physics and biology. Science seemed increasingly capable of emancipating itself from theology; but it was more doubtful whether theology dared stand so independently of science. Christianity claimed to be purveying statements about reality, but many of these fell far beyond the ambit of scientific validation. It was now increasingly tempting to dismiss discourse on such topics as divine creation, the human soul, the afterlife, and the miraculous suspension of natural laws as mere rhetorical flourishing. A recurring characteristic of 'revealed truth' had long been a brand of revelation which, according to the criteria of science, denoted precisely what was *not* revealed in any experimental or other controllable sense. More than ever before, this was being taken adversely to matter.

The increasingly questionable status of the Bible itself is a central illustration of the problem. Already by 1830 such geologists and palaeontologists as Georges Cuvier and Charles Lyell were indicating the need vastly to enlarge the time-scale postulated for the universe, and were thus undermining belief in the literal truth of one fundamental part of the biblical story. The cogency of Charles Darwin's *Origin of Species* (1859), with its exposition of 'natural selection' as the principal mechanism of biological evolution, can only be understood within the context of such a longer span. Its author struck devastating blows against literal interpretations of the Genesis account of creation, and threw into doubt – for some, even into absurdity – the doctrine that mankind originated as the object of a special act of divine creativity. The cousinship between human beings and apes implied by Darwin's book made it notorious even before his *Descent of Man* (1871) discussed this delicate topic explicitly. Moreover, regarding the natural order at large, the stress in both volumes upon blind and impersonal struggle seemed to make redundant any approach to biological development which might still rely upon the concept of a continuing divine purpose. The development of 'higher criticism', which applied far more rigorous standards of textual and historical scholarship, also called sceptically into question the status of biblical truth. Meanwhile, studies in anthropology and comparative religion – their popularity enhanced by Darwinistic debates – tended to diminish the uniqueness and even the dignity of Christianity through exploring its close kinship with pagan and 'savage' practice and with the symbolism and mythology of other cultures.

The panic which this whole range of challenges, both social and intellectual, could elicit is best exemplified by that blanket denunciation of modernity which was embodied in the papal encyclical of 1864, *Quanta Cura*, and in the accompanying *Syllabus of Errors*. Here Pius IX denounced the belief that 'the method and principles by which the old scholastic doctors cultivated theology are no longer suitable to the demands of our times and to the progress of the sciences', and shuddered against the thought that 'the Roman Pontiff can, and ought to, reconcile himself, and come to terms with progress, liberalism, and modern civilization'.[6] It was open to debate whether such assertiveness was more the product of desperate weakness than any sign of real strength; and similar doubts surrounded the decision, taken six years later by the Vatican Council, to proclaim the pope as actually infallible in matters of faith and morals.

To the extent that such figures as Pius IX found themselves on the defensive in intellectual matters, it was not simply because of any particular findings of the natural sciences; the situation also arose from the fact that those disciplines now seemed to offer, overall, a mode of understanding and explanation no less systematically applicable than that which Catholic or Protestant theologians had traditionally sought to supply. At the heart of this emerging synthesis was an image of the universe, largely derived from Newtonian principles, where material bodies existed in separate spatial and temporal dimensions of the sort familiar to everyday experience. The basic units of matter were viewed usually as billiard-ball atoms of fixed weights, capable of being lumped together in many different ways. Explanation of their movements was structured in terms of a mechanistic dynamics. This described the forces operating between pieces of matter, and in all its mathematical neatness it conveyed the harmonies, regularities, and constancies innate within that logically-ordered external reality which science was now deemed to be portraying. The most significant mid-nineteenth-century work in physics, from that undertaken in the late 1840s by William Thomson (later Lord Kelvin) on the first and second laws of thermodynamics to that published in the early 1870s by James Clerk Maxwell on electricity and magnetism, served to confirm the potential of science to reveal the seamlessness of some overarching structure of connections. The periodic table of the elements, logically expounded in the late 1860s by the Russian chemist Dmitri Mendeleyev, seemed to dictate the same conclusion; so too did the contemporaneous advances in physiology and organic chemistry spearheaded by the Frenchmen Claude Bernard and Louis Pasteur. Similarly, the work of Darwin did not simply lock more tightly together the study of animals and of men but also demanded that the discoveries of the earth sciences be related to both; further, it presented an evolutionary biology which might soon prove capable of being subsumed within a physics that could tie the activities of living organisms to the overall framework of atomic motion as cases of mechanical and chemical energy.

Some of the major implications of all this have been most lucidly summarized by Leszek Kolakowski, when expressing his belief that around the 1860s 'European intellectual life entered a new phase':

The natural sciences appeared to have reached a point at which the unitary conception of the universe was an incontestable fact. The principle of the conservation of energy and the laws governing its transformation were, it appeared, close to providing a complete explanation of the multiplicity of natural phenomena. Studies of the cellular structure of organisms gave promise to the discovery of a single system of laws applying to all basic organic phenomena. The theory of evolution afforded a general historical scheme of the development of living creatures, including man with his specifically human attributes . . . The day seemed close at hand when the unity of nature, hidden beneath the chaotic wealth of its diversity, would be laid bare to human view. The worship of science was universal; metaphysical speculation seemed condemned to wither away.[7]

That last point crystallizes precisely what Pius IX had come to fear. Put another way, he was leading the Catholic church at an epoch when perceptions of progress were becoming ever more closely entwined with the rising reputation of 'positivism'. We can define this as the belief that the method of natural science provides the principal, or even the sole, model for the attainment of true knowledge; and, conversely, that any insights claimed by other disciplines and domains can be valid only to the extent that they incorporate, or at least imitate, the procedures of natural science. In its more modest forms, when striving to establish certain consistencies in the sources and methods of knowledge, positivism could usefully scour away much nonsense; but in its less critical guise, when constructing over-ambitious unitary systems of actual quasi-scientific conclusions, it would eventually prove capable of sowing errors of its own. Meanwhile, Christians had not simply to appreciate that positivism threatened to render their own religion redundant; they also had to face the danger that science, by virtue of its triumphs both as the basis for intellectual synthesis and as the leading agent of practical material improvement, might be getting erected into nothing less than a directly competing cult – a 'secular religion' whose rivalry was powered by notions of inexorable progress.

The work of Auguste Comte, who himself invented the term 'positivism', certainly illustrates that challenge. But it also commands interest because it embodied such a direct effort to bring the whole *social* domain beneath the aegis of natural science, and did this in such a way as to exemplify very well both some of the merits and some of the defects of the positivist enterprise. He developed Henri de Saint-Simon's intimations about every branch of human knowledge tending to progress according to a 'law of three stages': from the theological phase (explanation via supernatural agency) to the metaphysical one (explanation via abstract forces), and then to the epoch of 'positive' understanding where the vanity of all absolute notions and underlying causes is recognized and the mind applies itself through rational observation to studying the invariable relations of succession and resemblance among phenomena. Comte's reputation as a valued founding father of modern sociology (another word which he coined) is based primarily on his relatively cautious treatment of this process in the six-volume *Course of Positive Philosophy*, which he brought out between 1830 and 1842. But by the time that the four volumes of *The System of Positive Polity* were appearing (1851–4) the tone had altered. Now Comte was attempting to refine his scientific laws of society in a form that was also congruent with his so-called 'religion of humanity'. The mystical excesses of this cult, which included a secularized version of the Blessed Virgin, alienated John Stuart Mill together with many other earlier sympathizers. T. H. Huxley dismissed the outcome as being, in a famous phrase, 'Catholicism without Christianity'. However, Comte's own lapse was insufficient to discredit generally a pervasive positivistic mood which had so many other factors working in its favour. Indeed, as Owen Chadwick has written in his significantly titled study *The Secularization of the European Mind in the Nineteenth Century*, 'The name of Comte became a symbol, like the names of Darwin or Voltaire; a symbol which by 1870 carried a power far beyond the intellectual influence of the lectures which he gave or the books which he published.'[8]

Comte's aspiration to produce some grand system of social explanation with solid roots in science was characteristic of much mid-nineteenth-century social, political and historical thinking. The ambitiousness of the works produced may have had a great deal to do with the quasi-religious functions which they increasingly seemed to fulfil under conditions of 'secularization'. Isaiah Berlin has indeed interpreted this drive to systematize as being a response to the deep human desire 'to find a unitary pattern in which the whole of experience, past, present, and future, actual, possible, and unfulfilled is symmetrically ordered'.[9] The resulting explanations were not only allegedly scientific in some sense but also, typically, both monistic and total; that is to say, each referred back to one primary category of causation, and treated it as containing the master-key to a formulation of general laws and to an understanding of all social processes. On this basis the study of history would be fully scientific (and how – we might ask – distinguishable from sociology?) only when it revealed these regularities, not just as operative in the past but also, by extrapolation, as predictively applicable.

That is the spirit in which the most ambitious mid-century exercises in positivistic historical or sociological synthesis were conducted, by writers as diverse in their particular choice of explanatory mechanisms as Spencer, H. T. Buckle, Hippolyte

Taine, and Arthur de Gobineau. Here is the last of these exemplifying this kind of approach near the opening of his *Essay on the Inequality of the Human Races* (1853–5):

> I have become convinced that the race question dominates all the other problems of history, that it holds the key to them, and that the inequality of races from whose fusion a people is formed is enough to explain the whole course of its destiny . . . It is now my belief that everything great, noble, and fruitful in the works of man on this earth, in science, art, and civilization, derives from only one starting-point, develops from the same seed, is the result of a single thought, and belongs to one family alone, the different branches of which have dominated all the civilized countries of the globe.[10]

If the stark pessimism of Gobineau's eventual conclusions about the imminent twilight of the Aryans is untypical of the epoch, his system-building is not. Once we substitute the struggle of classes for that of races, we then find ourselves dealing with that alternative thread which the most influential of all historical positivists, Marx and Engels, offered to their contemporaries as the only safe guide through the labyrinth of the past.

It is not surprising that, after 1859, the name of Darwin too should have been used to promote this whole quest for a framework within which to unify the advance of social and natural science. Indeed, as the century went on, no feats of synthesis were more readily invoked than those associated with him on one hand and with Marx on the other. It was widely ignored that Darwin had sought to write neutrally of adaptation, not progress, and to deal wherever possible in terms of contexts not absolutes. No less alarmingly, he was taken to be pronouncing upon virtually everything, and thus to be providing (in W. E. Mosse's words) 'a major ingredient in a new secular universalist philosophy'.[11] Most doctrines, old or new, about human conduct could gain in plausibility through being presented in the jargon of 'social Darwinism'. By this means, almost any opinion about rivalry and struggle could bask in the glow of science. Such plasticity of application was perhaps social Darwinism's most fundamental characteristic. Its implications varied according to the chosen unit of competition; and then, again, according to whether the stress was on struggle within or between such units. While Spencer and

Bagehot used it to support ideas about *laissez-faire* and individual initiative, others highlighted its supposed vindication of beliefs about more collectivist modes of action that were inimical to liberalism.

Most particularly, there could be asserted a degree of positive congruence between social Darwinism and Marxism itself. Each was, for instance, at odds with prevailing religious orthodoxy. Each embraced a form of materialism. Each claimed to expound a fundamental and unifying scientific law of social development. Within that process each raised doubts about the status of individual freedom and choice, about the balance between blind conflict and rational effort. Moreover, each had as its developmental dynamic a form of unremitting group struggle. If classes were indeed taken as the most operative units of competition, then it was easy enough to formulate a 'dialectic of nature' that would bring Darwinism into very direct alliance with Marxism. The desire to forge such a union was indeed exemplified within the oration which Engels gave at his collaborator's graveside in 1883: 'Just as Darwin discovered the law of development of organic nature, so Marx discovered the law of development of human history.'[12] Thus did the speaker seek to draw more tightly around himself the mantle of a distinctively scientific socialism.

What *else* might contemporaries seek to clothe in science? Positivism, by the very nature of its claims, was not easily to be limited in potential scope. Thus the cult of science came to impinge significantly even on the apparently remote sphere of imaginative literary and artistic creation. This final section of the essay will seek to indicate that connection by noting – with reference especially to the novel and (more briefly) to one aspect of painting – some further significant expressions of the idea that progress in any field must somehow be assimilated to the master-model of advance in the natural scientific one. At issue, here, is not so much positivism itself as the nature of its extension and transformation into the more 'cultural' phenomena loosely identified under the labels 'realism' and 'naturalism'. (The debate about the relationship between these two terms is not pursued here, but readers might find it helpful to note that most cultural historians tend to use the former chiefly in regard to the period 1848–70 and the latter for the years 1870–90.) This is the context within which the art critic Jules Castagnary observed that certain paintings shown at the Paris

Salon of 1863 represented 'truth bringing itself into equilibrium with science'; and it is the atmosphere within which the comparable exhibition of 1866 stimulated the young French novelist Émile Zola to declare: 'The wind blows in the direction of science. Despite ourselves, we are pushed towards the exact study of facts and things.'[13]

This whole shift has been splendidly surveyed by Linda Nochlin, who writes of its historic significance in these terms: 'It was not until the nineteenth century that contemporary ideology came to equate belief in the facts with the total content of belief itself: it is in this that the crucial difference lies between nineteenth-century Realism and all its predecessors.'[14] The contrast with the Romanticism of the earlier nineteenth century is particularly evident. Its religious and metaphysical concerns, together with such other features as its fondness for the past, seemed to the realists like symptoms of mere escapism from actualities that needed to be faced. As Zola put it in 1872,

> If you are no longer sure of heaven, you are bound to believe only in a human art . . . That is the guiding spirit of the modern naturalist school, which alone advocates the abandonment of the ancient fables. The mendacious art that thrives on dogmas and unassailable mysteries is gradually dying away as the tide of science rises.[15]

Men of his ilk often conceded, rightly, that the battle was not yet won. But, having once uttered the war-cry '*Il faut être de son temps*' ('we have to be people of our own time'), they never doubted their eventual victory.

The claim to be 'contemporary' involved issues both of technique and of subject matter. In each of these linked respects the situation was more complicated than the realists supposed. Their methods of observation certainly aspired to reflect those qualities of exhaustive precision and objective impartiality which seemed to characterize scientific advance. However, particularly if we recollect the muddle to which Comte had succumbed, sceptical questions are unavoidable. Did realists too not sometimes delude themselves about the degree to which their activities could truly remain 'value-free'? How far was their professed objectivity eroded by what Eric Hobsbawm has identified as the 'social demand that they should act as all-purpose suppliers of spiritual contents to the most materialist of civilizations'?[16] To some (such as the English critics Matthew Arnold and John Ruskin, or Jacob Burckhardt, the great Swiss historian of the Renaissance) it was indeed all too painfully evident that the realists were in fact zealots of a new pseudo-religious heresy – of a 'philistinism' that betrayed everything in art and literature which ought to transcend the merely material.

The contemporaneity of realism also seemed clear from the very topics towards which its techniques were directed: bars and boulevards, mines and factories, railway stations and department stores, all the hubbub of the here-and-now. In that sense, the movement could again look like a straightforward celebration of the triumphs being registered by bourgeois civilization – indeed, by realism in the hard-headed entrepreneurial sense as well. Thus there seemed to be here some reinforcement of current com-placency about the indissoluble link between prosperity and progress, and some confirmation of what George Steiner has termed 'a trust in the unfolding excellence of fact'.[17] However, just as Marx had managed not merely to admire the dynamism of the middle classes but also to protest against their exploitative urge, so too did much of artistic and literary realism critically question, rather than simply reflect, the values of the age. Thus it must be strongly stressed that any deep concern with 'the real' meant exposing, albeit usually with confidence about improving, the seamier side of life. In Linda Nochlin's words, 'Stone-breakers, rag-pickers, beggars, street-walkers, laundresses, railway-workers and miners now began to appear in paintings and novels, not as picturesque background figures but in the centre of the stage.'[18] A typical village scene is now one of peasant sweat, not rural idyll; and, even as other aspects of Romanticism weaken, its sense of the artist as an *alienated* figure retains some force.

Whereas the principal literary achievements of the Romantics had been registered in the form of lyric poetry, those of the realists centred on the novel. If creative fictions still had any role to play in that matter-of-fact world which Bagehot saw emerging, then it was perhaps best to convey them through this fittingly prosaic mode of expression. That was the spirit in which already, during the years of Louis-Philippe's 'bourgeois monarchy', Honoré de Balzac had quite consciously pursued a finely-detailed anatomiza-tion and classification of pre-1848 French society, through the

huge sequence of novels and shorter stories known collectively as
La Comédie Humaine. Its author was an enthusiast for all that was
most fashionable in the latest scientific advances (even for
investigation of such blind alleys as phrenology), and he believed
his 'studies' to be completely consistent with the objectives of the
new positivistic philosophy and sociology. Engels, for one,
claimed that from Balzac's probings into the morally corruptive
effects of the contemporary lust for material gain he had learned
more than any historian, economist, or statistician could ever
teach him. Over the thirty years or so following Balzac's death in
1850 that potential of the novel to dissect, indeed evaluate, the
'reality' of a whole society or epoch was exploited by significant
authors in all the major European literatures. Notable examples,
especially from the later part of the period, are Gottfried Keller (a
Swiss) and Theodor Fontane in German, as well as Benito Pérez
Galdós in Spanish and Giovanni Verga in Italian. However, most
literary historians agree that the greatest monuments to realism
and naturalism in literature were those raised by a number of
English and Russian authors, and also by certain Frenchmen who
built still more directly upon the Balzacian legacy.

Among the English novelists who come most readily to mind
within this context are four figures, all of whom were born in the
second decade of the century: William Thackeray, Charles
Dickens, George Eliot (Mary Anne Stevens), and Anthony
Trollope. *Vanity Fair* (1847–8) by the first of these and *Hard Times*
(1854) by the second represent two major examples of realism from
the earlier part of our period. The masterpiece of Eliot, who had
earlier been much influenced by Comte, is *Middlemarch* (1871–2)
which has as one of its principal tragic characters Dr Lydgate, the
doomed man of science. Trollope's contribution to the naturalistic
genre is best seen in *The Way We Live Now* (1875), where the
sordid commercial career of Augustus Melmotte becomes the
vehicle for an attack upon the nineteenth-century equivalent of
the 'loadsamoney' ethic. Already in 1860 the work of this novelist
had been properly characterized by the American author Nathaniel
Hawthorne as 'solid and substantial, written on the strength of
beef and through the inspiration of ale, and just as real as if some
giant had hewn a great lump out of the earth and put it under a
glass case with all its inhabitants going about their daily business,
and not suspecting their being made a show of'.[19] As for the

Russian novel, its triumphs in the realistic vein are associated chiefly with the names of Ivan Turgenev (for example, *Fathers and Sons*, 1862), Leo Tolstoy (for example, *War and Peace*, 1863–9; *Anna Karenina*, 1873–7), and Fyodor Dostoyevsky. The third of these brilliantly illuminated the confusion in contemporary values through a series of works culminating in *The Brothers Karamazov* (1879–80). In *Crime and Punishment* (1866), which he called 'a novel of contemporary life' where 'the action takes place this year', Dostoyevsky produced arguably the greatest of all detective stories. Since the murderous guilt of the student Raskolnikov is made clear at a very early stage, the question is not the usual 'Who done it?', but rather 'Why, and with what craving for the joy of confession and punishment?'. This is a novel which takes us into a realism of interior rather than merely exterior description. As Dostoyevsky himself declared: 'I am called a psychologist – that is wrong. I am only a realist on a higher level. In other words, I describe all the depths of the human soul.'[20]

On the French scene the figure of Gustave Flaubert looms large. Though reluctant to be pigeon-holed as a realist, he did produce two major novels which rendered it difficult for contemporaries to avoid identifying him with the tendency to bring the domains of literature and science ever closer together. The first, *Madame Bovary* (1857), led Flaubert to be tried on a charge of offending public morals and to obtain an acquittal which itself boosted the stock of literary realism. The book presented the tale of Emma Rouault who, having married an infatuated but utterly dreary provincial doctor, engages in a self-destructive revolt against the stifling conventions that society seeks to impose on her. That rebellion is all the more passionate because of the gulf that she experiences between the tedium of actual everyday living and the expectations of Byronic adventure falsely aroused by her earlier romantic reading. Flaubert's second masterpiece *Sentimental Education* (1869), pivoting around the revolutionary events of 1848, also pursues the theme of youthful hope betrayed. Here it is expressed through the disappointments of Frédéric Moreau, a hero who is just as naïve about the fruits of love as he is about those of revolutionary liberation. F. W. J. Hemmings concludes,

> *L'Education sentimentale* qualifies as the supreme masterpiece of French realism not merely on technical grounds – Flaubert's

doctrine of impersonality was never better observed than in this novel – and not merely because it fulfils so admirably the aim of every great realist, to paint an exact and comprehensive portrait of the age of which he has the widest personal experience. Its best title to supremacy is, after all, that it stands as an embodiment of the realist critique of whatever runs counter to realism: that is, of romanticism, political idealism, and in general all philosophies of life that wilfully disregard the real conditions of life.[21]

Prominent amongst other Frenchmen who directly preached the need to face up to those very circumstances were the brothers Edmond and Jules de Goncourt. Famed above all as social diarists, they also wrote in their novel *Germinie Lacerteux* (1864) what its preface called 'a clinical study of love', based on the debauched life of their own maid: 'We asked ourselves whether there should still exist, be it for writer or reader in these times of equality, classes too unworldly, sufferings too low, tragedies too foul-mouthed, catastrophes whose terror is not sufficiently noble.'[22] Faced by that question they felt obliged, despite their own conservative inclinations, to offer a negative, therefore liberating, answer.

Such too was the response of Zola, whose enthusiasm for the cause of positivistic realism-naturalism was noted earlier. The characters in his startlingly violent *Thérèse Raquin* (1867), dominated by their animal instincts and seemingly devoid of moral sense, appeared to be mere pretexts for quasi-physiological observation. It was, however, his twenty-volume cycle of novels, *Les Rougon-Macquart* (1871–93), which came to constitute the principal monument to this brand of literature. Inspired partly by Claude Bernard's writing on experimental medicine, it was subtitled significantly 'A Natural and Social History of a Family' – the ideal social grouping within which to explore the transmission of hereditary weaknesses from generation to generation. The afflictions that beset the Rougon-Macquart clan reflect, in microcosm, the features of a society much more generally diseased. Paris of the Second Empire – its slums and brothels, its stores and finance-houses – is here the chief, and painstakingly observed, environment with which heredity must interact. Yet there is also excursion into provincial life. Indeed, the most famous volume within the whole series – *Germinal* (1885) – explores, with

uncompromising coarseness, the miseries of the mining communities near the Belgian border. Whatever the setting, Zola
presents figures ensnared in the trammels of heredity and
environment, where each person seems to be the passive product
of conditioning rather than any kind of active moral agent.
As for the novelist himself, his 'inquiries' become (in theory
at least) ever more indistinguishable from those of the experimental scientist.

The Paris of Zola was also by the 1860s the major spiritual capital
of European painting and art criticism, a city where the polite
frequenters of the *salons* had already been shocked by the visual
versions of realism associated with such figures as Jean François
Millet, Gustave Courbet, and Edouard Manet. From there in 1874
a new epoch in the history of art was inaugurated by an exhibition
featuring prominently the names of Claude Monet and Auguste
Renoir. The fact that 'impressionism' began as a term of abuse
symbolizes the hostile reception which first greeted the work of
their group. Some critics regarded the Impressionists' degree of
enthusiasm for everyday urban topics as indicating insufficient
appreciation of what was artistically dignified. As for matters of
technique, the first spectators tended to view the new art as one
of blob and smudge. They remained to be educated in nothing less
than a new manner of seeing. For us it is the way in which this
vision related to contemporary views about the status and nature
of science that constitutes much of Impressionism's intellectual
fascination. Emerging at an epoch still deeply influenced by
positivistic assumptions, this movement became associated with
attempts to improve upon the realism both of Courbet and of the
camera. In short, these artists aspired to establish a truly scientific
form of visual representation.

Zola, a friend to many of the painters involved, readily
applauded Impressionism as an ally of literary naturalism in
the search for quasi-scientific procedures and findings. The
artists, for their part, certainly felt the challenge of conveying
accurately the complexity of optical experience. They responded
by analysing each seeming visual whole into its component
elements. Shadows assumed hues that offended the orthodox,
and colour in general was treated independently of its associations with particular material objects. As Zola declared in
1880,

These men propose to leave the studio where painters have cooped themselves up for so many centuries, and go forth to paint in the open air, a simple act of which the consequences are considerable. In the open air, light is no longer of a single sort, consequently there are multiple effects which diversify and radically transform the appearance of things and beings. This study of light in its thousand decompositions and recompositions is what has been called more or less properly impressionism, because a picture becomes the impression of a moment experienced before nature . . . Here then is what the impressionist painters exhibit: exact research into the causes and effects of light, flowing in upon the design as well as the colour.[23]

In this spirit, Monet believed it important to explore such subjects as the west front of Rouen cathedral and the lily-pond at Giverny in as many conditions of light as possible. For him and his associates studio studies seemed generally less challenging than work conducted (or, at least, begun) outdoors, where from minute to minute tones and values vibrated and were transformed. As Linda Nochlin observes, 'The "instantaneity" of the Impressionists is "contemporaneity" taken to its ultimate limits. "Now", "today", "the present", had become "this very moment", "this instant" '.[24] Attending to the ephemeral chromatics of sun and snow, of showers and steam, these artists hoped to capture moments of time and vision about to be lost. Moreover, in the paintings of horses and dancers undertaken by Edgar Degas we witness an art that is, if anything, even more explicitly addressed to the problem of simultaneously freezing and expressing movement and change.

With hindsight we can see that the grandiose scientific pretensions originally embraced by, or thrust upon, the Impressionists were doomed to failure. Paradoxically, the movement's success resided not in any prosaic ability to complete an experiment but in a more poetical capacity to suggest mood and atmosphere. As the century drew to a close and a 'revolt against positivism' itself gathered force, it became increasingly clear that, in terms similar to the new 'symbolist' and 'expressionist' challenges to naturalism within literature, the talent of the Impressionists was a matter less of objective description than of subjective evocation. The manner in which those painters intimated that perceptions of the flux of reality were personal – in terms both of time and space – inspired all who followed in every field of intellectual and cultural innovation. Nor was the Impressionists' achievement without some relevance to the revolution now imminent in the sphere of scientific ideas themselves. For, in the very process of escaping the influence of the old science, Impressionism was stressing the uniqueness of each single observation. It was thus anticipating, however unconsciously, the principles of relativity and discontinuity that were central to an understanding of the kind of physics being developed around 1900, particularly by Max Planck and Albert Einstein. Theirs was a revolutionary achievement comparable in scale to the Newtonian one which they were now, in many senses, challenging. In the early twentieth century European intellectuals and artists might still be tempted to seek a certain inspiration or orientation from science. However, they could no longer expect to obtain from it the sort of grandiose answers which it had appeared to offer so readily just a generation or so earlier, during the epoch of progressive positivism upon which this essay has concentrated.

Notes

1. Herbert Spencer, *Social Statics: or, the Conditions Essential to Human Happiness* [1850] (London, 1868), p. 80.
2. Eric Hobsbawm, *The Age of Empire, 1875–1914* (London, 1987), p. 31.
3. Walter Bagehot, *The English Constitution* [1867], as quoted in R. N. Stromberg (ed.), *Realism, Naturalism, and Symbolism: Modes of Thought and Expression in Europe, 1848–1914* (New York, 1968), p. 31.
4. Thomas Macaulay, 'Lord Bacon', in *Critical and Historical Essays* (London, 1883), pp. 403–4.
5. Karl Marx and Friedrich Engels, 'The Communist Manifesto', in D. McLellan (ed.), *Karl Marx: Selected Writings* (Oxford, 1977), p. 225.
6. See generally A. Fremantle (ed.), *The Papal Encyclicals in their Historical Context* (New York, 1963), pp. 135–52.
7. Leszek Kolakowski, *Main Currents of Marxism: its Origins, Growth and Dissolution*, Vol. 1 (Oxford, 1978), p. 376.
8. Owen Chadwick, *The Secularization of the European Mind in the Nineteenth Century* (Cambridge, 1975), p. 233.
9. Isaiah Berlin, 'Historical Inevitability', in *Four Essays on Liberty* (London, 1969), p. 106.
10. Michael Biddiss (ed.), *Gobineau: Selected Political Writings* (London, 1970), pp. 41–2.

11. W. E. Mosse, *Liberal Europe: The Age of Bourgeois Realism, 1848–1875* (London, 1974), p. 52.
12. K. Marx and F. Engels, *Selected Writings*, Vol. 2 (Moscow, 1962), p. 167.
13. Linda Nochlin, *Realism* (Harmondsworth, 1971), pp. 41, 42.
14. Ibid., p. 45.
15. F. W. J. Hemmings, *The Age of Realism* (Harmondsworth, 1974), p. 180.
16. Eric Hobsbawm, *The Age of Capital, 1848–1875* (London, 1977), p. 333.
17. George Steiner, *In Bluebeard's Castle: Some Notes Towards the Redefinition of Culture* (London, 1971), p. 16.
18. L. Nochlin, op. cit., p. 34.
19. W. E. Mosse, op. cit., p. 75.
20. A. Hauser, *The Social History of Art*, Vol. 4 (London, 1962), p. 146.
21. F. W. J. Hemmings, op. cit., p. 179.
22. L. Nochlin, op. cit., p. 34.
23. 'Naturalism in the salon', as quoted in Stromberg, op. cit., pp. 156–7.
24. L. Nochlin, op. cit., p. 28.

Further reading

The best form of further reading involves studying the various 'primary sources' from the nineteenth century itself which have been mentioned in the course of the essay. As for secondary works, most of those that follow have good detailed bibliographies of their own.

Among general histories, some already referred to, that deal well with intellectual and cultural issues are: A. Briggs (ed.), *The Nineteenth Century: the Contradictions of Progress* (London, 1970); E. H. Hobsbawm, *The Age of Capital, 1848–75* (London, 1977) and *The Age of Empire, 1875–1914* (London, 1987); and W. E. Mosse, *Liberal Europe: the Age of Bourgeois Realism, 1848–1875* (London, 1974).

Useful books focusing principally on intellectual developments include: M. D. Biddiss, *The Age of the Masses: Ideas and Society in Europe since 1870* (Harmondsworth, 1977); O. Chadwick, *The Secularization of the European Mind in the Nineteenth Century* (Cambridge, 1975); L. Kolakowski, *Main Currents of Marxism: its Origins, Growth and Dissolution*, Vol. 1 (Oxford, 1978); G. L. Mosse, *The Culture of Western Europe: the Nineteenth and Twentieth Centuries* (London, 1963); and W. M. Simon, *European Positivism in the Nineteenth Century: an Essay in Intellectual History* (Ithaca, NY, 1963).

For 'cultural' matters, see A. Hauser, *A Social History of Art*, Vol. 4 (London, 1962); F. W. J. Hemmings, *The Age of Realism* (Harmondsworth, 1974); H. Honour, *Romanticism* (Harmondsworth, 1981); C. Morazé (ed.), *History of Mankind: Cultural and Scientific Development*, Vol. 5, *The Nineteenth Century*, Parts I–III (London, 1976); L. Nochlin, *Realism* (Harmondsworth, 1971); F. Novotny, *Painting and Sculpture in Europe, 1780–1880* (revised ed., Harmondsworth, 1978); and J. Wintle (ed.), *Makers of Nineteenth-Century Culture, 1800–1914* (London, 1982).

8

Shifting patterns of political thought and action: liberalism, nationalism, socialism

B. A. HADDOCK

Europe in 1830 was still struggling to come to grips with the traumatic events that had embroiled her in the previous fifty years. Not only had the various states to accommodate vast structural changes – urbanization and industrialization on a new scale, unprecedented increase in population – but at the ideological level very many of Europe's trials and torments had seemed to be self-inflicted. The *Declaration of the Rights of Man and the Citizen* of 1789 had confidently proclaimed that 'men were born and remain free and equal', enjoying 'natural and imprescriptible rights', with a collective identity in the nation which constituted the only legitimate source of political authority. But it was far from clear at the time, and became less clear as the revolution progressively unfolded, precisely how these principles might be translated into viable political institutions. What the *Declaration* provided was a series of rallying cries rather than closely argued political and constitutional proposals. And, indeed, nothing so terrified the established princes of Europe as the spectre of the French revolutionary armies demanding 'liberty, equality and fraternity' for all men, everywhere. Such ideological motivation was a new phenomenon in 1789, comparable only with the hideous enthusiasm generated by earlier wars of religion. It cut across traditional territorial and dynastic claims, leading the political map of Europe to be redrawn according to new and uncertain standards.

When the principles of the *Declaration* were examined in detail, however, they were found to be intrinsically unstable. It very soon became plain that commitments to liberty and equality could in practice be mutually incompatible. And attempts by small factions to justify their conduct by claiming to embody the spirit of the nation (the 'general will') were readily seen for what they were – transparent presentations of authoritarian policies in 'democratic' disguise. To conservative critics such as Edmund Burke and Joseph de Maître the absurdity of revolutionary principles was but an illustration of the larger folly of supposing that states could be fashioned to satisfy the capricious demands of individuals. Not the least of the effects of the revolutionary years was a general discrediting of democratic and radical ideas. Indeed, the dire warnings of conservatives and reactionaries seemed to be vindicated by the course of the revolution itself, staggering from the lofty principles of 1789, through the terror of 1793, to the Napoleonic dictatorship.

The revolution, then, had excited a general reaction. Many established interests, tired of convulsion and uncertainty, welcomed the collapse of Napoleonic France as an occasion to turn the clock back. Traditionalism had become a dominant motif in political thought, championed by Burke and Coleridge in England, de Maître and Bonald in France, Cuoco and Savigny in Italy and Germany. The situation seemed ripe in 1815 for a return to the safer (and more familiar) style of dynastic politics. In truth, however, the attempted restoration of the status quo ante was no more than a precarious holding operation. Not only had the politics of the *ancien régime* been challenged at the theoretical level; its effectiveness as a mode of political and administrative organization had also been called into question.

Two factors, in particular, imposed limits upon the style and character of any viable state. In the first place, there was a need to seek justification for the state beyond the accident of family inheritance. Monarchies which had once been successfully challenged could not simply fall back upon a tacit assumption that hereditary rule was a part of a natural or divinely ordained scheme of things. Order itself, as well as reform or revolution, had to be defended at a theoretical level. The second factor concerned the scale and organization of the state. Changes in economy and society required dynamic political management. What this involved at the practical level was a mobilization of populations on a larger scale than had been the case before 1789. Such mobilization need not, of course, take overt political form. It was not simply a question of extending the franchise or involving wider groups in decision-making. Most people's contact with the state would be through local or national bureaucracies. The point to stress, however, is that the state, in responding to changing circumstances, was impinging upon a wider range of interests. And explaining and justifying its procedures would necessarily involve recourse to broad principles. To speak of 'popular' politics in the early nineteenth century would be anachronistic. Yet we can see the beginnings of a process which has continued into recent times, with ideological arguments becoming a crucial dimension in the cut and thrust of practical debate.

Attempts to establish a viable political consensus after 1815 thus involved a variety of factors, both practical and ideological, which continued to threaten further revolutionary or reactionary turmoil. Nowhere was this tension more apparent than in France, where the grant of a charter by Louis XVIII in 1814 (which might have been construed as a significant concession to liberal con-stitutionalism) was qualified by the contention that 'all authority in France resides in the person of the king'. The constitution itself, far from being regarded as the political expression of a people's natural right, was described in the declaration as a gift bestowed by the king upon his people of his own free will. And, of course, what had once been given could always be revoked if circumstances changed and different interests needed to be accommodated.

The 1814 charter was very much a compromise. Just how precarious an achievement it had been became clear in 1824 with the accession of Charles X to the throne. Supporters of the traditional rights of Crown, aristocracy and church had never ceased to regard even the semblance of constitutionalism as wholly tainted by the atrocities of the revolution. The advent of a monarch sympathetic to such views sharply polarized positions, with a seemingly unbridgeable gulf developing between liberals, republicans and anti-clericals on the one side and the various species of traditionalist on the other. The tensions and hostilities which had marked the revolutionary years were still as entrenched as ever. What was at issue was not so much the propriety of adopting this or that policy as the character of political life itself.

The emergent ideologies were precisely a response to a political situation that had yet to assume a settled form.

Nor were these difficulties unique to France. The experience of revolutionary wars had taught both radicals and reactionaries that international frontiers were no defence against ideologies which challenged the rationale of a state. Rising groups excluded from a political establishment would exploit new arguments in order to justify a measure of political power or influence commensurate with their social and economic significance. France had essentially established terms of political reference which would dominate the thought and practice of the first half of the nineteenth century. A political disturbance on the streets of Paris in 1830 or 1848 would thus be an event of European significance.

The ideological alliances which emerged in Paris in 1830 served as a pattern for wider European conflicts. A reactionary and obstinate monarch had forced opposition groups into the position of supporting revolutionary claims, despite the modest nature of their practical proposals. Liberals, in fact, were anxious to disavow any connection between their own ideas and the principles of 1793. The limit of their ambitions was a return to something like the constitutional principles embodied in the charter of 1814. Through Madame de Staël and Benjamin Constant, they had come to associate popular government with tyranny. In a seminal lecture delivered in 1819 Constant had specifically contrasted ancient liberty, which stressed popular involvement, with modern liberty dominated by the idea of the rule of law. The civic republican ideal was peculiarly suited to the small-scale states of antiquity, where a sizeable proportion of the citizen body might plausibly meet to resolve issues. What Rousseau (and more especially his Jacobin followers) had done, in Constant's view, was to lift the ancient view of citizenship out of context. In attempting to apply ancient ideals to the modern world, they had failed to recognize the practical difficulties which made the modern state a different political species from the ancient *polis*. The scale of the modern state, and the diversity of interests it represented, dictated a modification in political and constitutional principles. A cult of virtue, for example, of the kind associated with Robespierre or Saint-Just, might very well be a fitting reflection of the cultural homogeneity of an ancient republic. In a state the size of France in the nineteenth century, however, an insistence on moral or political uniformity would necessarily involve the suppression of a plethora of interests and points of view.

The crucial point at issue in Constant's contrast of ancient and modern liberty is the characterization of the proper relations between individual and state. Rousseau and the Jacobins had insisted that each individual had a right either to participate in government or at least to authorize the actions of a government. What this meant in practice was that a government claiming to derive its authority from the people would be blessed with unlimited theoretical powers. An isolated individual opposed to specific policies would place himself in the position of opposing the collective will of the community. This would mean that opposition could be construed as an assertion of narrow self-interest; moreover, since the collective will of the community would simply be a partial interest which had succeeded in presenting itself in the guise of the collective interest, there would be ample scope for a determined minority to dominate the many interests of the different groups within the community.

Constant's solution to the dilemma was to treat the state not as an instrument for the realization of liberty in any abstract sense but rather as a guarantor or protector of the very many liberties which might be enshrined in a way of life. In any civilized society men enjoyed a variety of rights (to be subject to the law rather than the whim of individuals, to be free to express opinions, to pursue a profession, to associate with others, to be foolish or frivolous in the quiet of their homes). The principal role of the state in this scheme of things was to preserve a system of constitutional guarantees which might enable individuals to go about their business in their own way. Vested interests, which had been viewed by the Jacobins as a series of obstacles to the inculcation of public virtue, would have to be respected as a tangible means of containing the state within proper bounds. In general, private life would be regarded as the principal focus of an individual's endeavour and ambition. Political devices served merely to facilitate the private realm, ensuring sufficient stability and security for the pursuit of a multitude of individual ends.

Privacy and pluralism became central themes in the liberal defence of the individual against the creeping encroachment of the potentially tyrannical state. Liberals were less certain on the value of popular participation in political life. Though Constant denied that political participation was an end in itself, he saw a measure of participation as a necessary means of securing the state in its rightful role. But this was far from the standard liberal position. If in 1830 French liberals were obsessed by the threat posed to the principle of constitutionalism by an authoritarian monarch, they had not forgotten that an unholy alliance of radical intellectuals and the Paris mob could lead a movement of political reform to degenerate into revolution. What they feared above all was that political liberty would not survive attempts to put the state at the head of a radical programme of social and economic transformation. The limits of their political ambitions were very much set by a concern to preserve the prevailing balance in society.

The overmighty state was only one of the dangers menacing liberty in the 1830s. Subtler forces were at work in economy and society which, by degrees, threatened to undermine an individualist culture at its source. The adaptation of industry and commerce to the demands of an emerging mass society led to a levelling of standards. And with uniformity of taste came a tendency towards moral conformity, stifling energy and initiative and encouraging a dull, bureaucratic mentality. Constitutional guarantees had clearly only limited value in dealing with dilemmas of this order. Part of the problem was that men had begun to look to the state for a solution to all their difficulties. Yet it was precisely reliance on the state and its cumbersome apparatus that seemed to compromise political liberty in the longer term.

The prognosis for liberalism was far from encouraging. Alexis de Tocqueville, for example, surveying the course of recent history, saw an inexorable advance of the principle of equality at the expense of liberty. Political liberty in the past had been secured by a balance of powers within society, with vested interests (aristocracy, church, municipalities, etc.) constituting bulwarks against the central authority. In modern times, however, a whole series of factors had served to erode hierarchy, rank and privilege. In France, successive monarchs had pursued levelling policies in their efforts to assert themselves against the aristocracy. In the wider European context, the Protestant Reformation had given a religious sanction to egalitarianism. And the transformation of industry and trade since the late eighteenth century had made the egalitarian ethos of the bourgeoisie the dominant influence in French society.

Yet it would be futile for liberals simply to deplore the modern world and all its works. In his seminal *Democracy in America* (1835–40) Tocqueville set himself the task of distilling the lessons of American political experience. Whereas in Europe a commitment to equality had almost universally involved the sacrifice of liberty, the Americans had contrived an egalitarian society without the slightest trace of political tyranny. Much of this success could be explained by reference to the origins of the United States. But there were political lessons from which the old world could profit. Popular participation at national, state and local level had given political life a massive solidity which kept extremist adventurers at bay. Administration itself was so thoroughly decentralized that there was little risk of a single focus of power and influence emerging. And respect for legal procedures was a deeply ingrained habit of mind. It would not be possible, of course, to resuscitate European liberalism simply by selectively applying the best features of American political culture in the vastly different situation which prevailed in Europe. But Tocqueville hoped that an understanding of democracy in practice would, at least, help France and Europe to avoid the immediate peril of political tyranny.

There was little in Tocqueville's analysis to encourage optimism. To the traditional liberal suspicion of the state had been added the more insidious threat of a tyranny of the majority. While practical exigencies gave every opportunity for further centralization, liberals found themselves unable to reverse the trend. From Wilhelm von Humboldt to John Stuart Mill and beyond, freedom was treated as a precious commodity, more likely to be lost through inadvertence than to be brought down by direct political action. Tocqueville himself, in the face of the revolutions of 1848, was filled with foreboding. A shift was evident in people's attitudes and expectations. Where once the defence of political liberty had been the first concern of the articulate classes, attention was now given to substantive social and economic questions. It became clear to him that the principles of classical liberalism had begun to appear quaintly old-fashioned. If the choice were between basic freedoms and a redistribution of property, too many people would have little hesitation in opting for the latter.

Nationalists in France had always been able to embrace change with more confidence. At the outset of the revolution, Sieyès in

his influential tract *What Is the Third Estate?* (1789), had identified
the French nation with its active and productive members. And
throughout the revolutionary years the habit persisted of treating
rank and privilege as enemies of the true French nation. Unlike
liberals, the French nationalists had no quarrel with the idea of
equality. What obsessed them was the lurking presence of the
enemy within. The great historian Jules Michelet, for example,
saw the events of 1789 as the purest expression of the spirit of the
French people. He was aware, of course, that that spirit had
suffered distortion at the hands of men such as Robespierre. But
the reign of terror remained for him an aberration. Responsibility for the crimes of history could normally be traced back to
monarchs, aristocrats and priests. Writing in 1846 he could still see
the restoration of the lustre of 1789 as his principal task. He sought
to make the revolutionary tradition a source of inspiration for the
political strivings of subsequent generations of Frenchmen. His
motivation, however, was far from parochial. His association of
the French republican ideal with a universal justice made France
pre-eminent among the nations, a leader of the civilized world.
The contrast with the political language of the liberals should be
clear. Attention had shifted away from the best means of
advancing the interests of Frenchmen towards the cultivation of
a certain image of France. Indeed, France's mission was described
in religious terms, with little or no consideration of the practical
difficulties which might transform righteous enthusiasm into
zealous persecution.

French nationalism was distinctive only in its introspection. The
nation state could be taken for granted in the quest for an ever
purer expression of the popular will. Elsewhere the hegemonic
position of the Austrian Empire dictated a rather different
configuration of ideological alliances. Both liberal and nationalist
aspirations were thwarted by Metternich's intransigence. And
while there was little common ground between them on such
crucial issues as the constitutional form of a legitimate state or the
extent of popular participation in political life, they could discern
in the absolutist system a threat to both political liberty and
national autonomy. The extent of their common interest was
predicated upon recognition of a common enemy.

There could be no doubting, however, that the current was
running away from classical liberalism. The liberalism of the

post-restoration period had always been narrowly class-based. Popular enthusiasm, which had on occasion been harnessed to dramatic effect, was notoriously difficult to control. And the last thing the liberals wanted was to see their limited political demands swamped by more far-reaching social changes. Nationalism, by contrast, was cast in broader terms. Though, like liberalism, it was very closely associated with the newly emerging professional and business classes, nationalism as an ideology was never simply a political guise for their social and economic interests.

The roots of nationalism, indeed, should be sought beyond the sphere of politics. It had initially emerged in the eighteenth century as a reaction against the predominance of French culture in the literary world. In the minds of most intellectuals France and the Enlightenment had been identified as the acme of civilization and refinement. To critics such as Herder, however, especially in his early writings (1769–74), French cultural supremacy was viewed as intellectually and morally ruinous. Enlightenment thinkers had tended to adopt an abstract, generalizing vocabulary, blind to the subtle distinctions and nuances embedded in local cultural traditions. What made matters worse was that German or Italian or Czech writers were being encouraged to couch their work in an idiom and style which derived essentially from France. Peoples were being alienated from their roots. The only way to halt the decline was to foster local cultures. Herder himself spent a great deal of time seeking to restore national traditions through collections of folktales and songs. He loathed the 'good taste' and 'decorum' of high (French) culture and admired instead the 'natural' products of unsophisticated cultures. Homer and Ossian were his favoured poets, not Pope and Racine. Above all, it was language that distinguished natural cultural units. Individuals identified with their language at the most basic level. A cultural programme which countenanced neglect of so much that was important to them ran the risk of moral and intellectual atrophy.

A concern with roots and identity became a leading theme in later nationalist writings. So, too, did Herder's rejection of the idea of progress. Where Enlightenment thinkers had tended to see the past as a succession of types of society culminating in the present, Herder, instead, saw a society as a unique focus of a particular way of life. His nationalism, indeed, was of a deeply apolitical kind. He thought in terms of cultural diversity, language, shared myths and traditions rather than in specifically political categories. He had a profound suspicion of the modern state as a vast bureaucratic machine which would tend either to ignore or to trample upon the distinctive customs of local communities.

What transformed nationalism into a political movement was the reaction against the attempt to return to a system of dynastic politics in 1815. Peoples had grown accustomed to new styles of political thought and practice and new loyalties had emerged. Problems were most acute within the sprawling Austrian Empire. Educated Slavs, Hungarians or Italians simply could not identify with rule from Vienna. Within these suppressed nations (for that is how they began to regard themselves) movements arose with a very clear political objective – to rid the nation of foreign rule. The ideal of national self-government was thrust to the forefront of political debate, with the question of the kind of constitutional arrangement which might be appropriate for a community being treated as a secondary issue.

The most striking representative of this new style of nationalism was Giuseppe Mazzini. His bent was much more for propaganda than systematic social or political theory. In 1831 he had created the organization *La giovine Italia* (Young Italy), geared to the creation of a united Italian republic through popular insurrections. And, indeed, throughout his career, much of it spent in exile in England after 1837, he was indefatigable in keeping the idea of a united Italy before the educated public in a stream of impassioned publications. Despite a deep personal commitment to republican principles, he always stressed that he would support any movement devoted to the liberation of Italy from foreign rule. He insisted, however, that liberation should be the work of Italians themselves and not the product of a fortunate concatenation of diplomatic circumstances. The manner in which Italian unity was finally achieved in 1861 thus deeply disappointed him. And he remained an embittered and isolated man until his death in 1872.

Mazzini's nationalism had a specifically political focus. Yet he shared many of the assumptions which had informed Herder's view. He rejected, for example, abstract 'scientific' analysis of history and society, focusing instead on identification with the non-reflective attitudes and dispositions which are the foundation of a way of life. He also opposed the narrow individualism which the Enlightenment had bequeathed to liberal thought. What mattered to him was not so much that individuals should be enabled to pursue their particular interests but that they should be aware of the ties which bound them to their communities. Harmony and co-operation were his watchwords. The stress on competition and conflict in contemporary liberal and socialist doctrines was for him a principal obstacle to the well-being of communities. Instead he contended that individuals would only grow in moral stature by co-operating in a common enterprise. It was hence crucial that a people's sense of identity (formed through the medium of language, cultural traditions, etc.) should be reflected in their political institutions.

Nor was Mazzini's nationalism narrowly Italian in scope. In 1834 he had formed an organization, 'Young Europe', as a sister movement to his 'Young Italy'. He envisaged in a distant future a kind of federal republic of European nations. Each nation would have rid itself of foreign rule and would henceforth be able to co-operate with its neighbours in peace. Once a nation had acquired its own political institutions, it would have no further need to assert itself. Internal security and war, the preoccupations of the politics of the *ancien régime*, would have faded from the scene along with kings. Mazzini pictured a delightful harmony in which each nation made its distinctive contribution. This view probably reached its zenith in 1848 as the Austrian Empire began to crumble. But the later history of nationalism was a much more sombre and sinister affair.

Nationalism had assumed the guise of a liberation movement in response to the challenge of imperial rule. As a political movement, however, it embraced a variety of positions, ranging from radical claims for direct democracy to defence of the most extreme forms of authoritarianism. This flexibility, of course, was essential to the appeal of the movement. Nationalists could set their ideological or constitutional differences aside in a common commitment to the contention that communities with a sense of their own linguistic or cultural identity should have a political voice. Here were tantalizing possibilities for established authorities. Through identification with the state as a symbol of the nation, a sense of political participation could be attained without any real extension of popular involvement in government. Nationalism could thus generate from within its own resources a remarkable transfiguration from an ideology of liberation to the official doctrine of a repressive state.

There had, indeed, always been a darker side to the history of nationalism. Fichte, for example, writing at the very beginning of the nineteenth century, saw the nation in such exclusive terms that a national state would be justified in pressing its claims not only against other states but against its own people. The bond between people who spoke a common language was seen to be so crucial to their fulfilment that nothing could be allowed to distract them from their sense of common purpose. In *The Closed Commercial State* (1800) Fichte argued that an individual's noblest qualities would only flourish in a state which controlled all aspects of a way of life, while in his *Addresses to the German Nation* (1807–8) he fiercely rejected any accommodation of one language-based community to another. These were ideas which, with the leaven of social Darwinism later in the century, could warrant the most aggressive policies. Nations could be pictured maximizing their moral and political energies in competition with one another, with individuals subordinating their interests, and sometimes their lives, to the pursuit of a common good. Once the interests of the state had been identified with the needs of the nation, it was but a small step from a view of a world of diverse nations, each finding a political outlet for their energies, to that of a world in which a nation is justified in asserting itself against other nations. What Mazzini had conceived as a recipe for international harmony and co-operation could be transformed into a pretext for imperial adventures and war.

Nationalism had diverged markedly from liberal beliefs and values in its rejection of individualism. Where liberals would judge institutions and practices in terms of their capacity to enhance the well-being of individuals, nationalists would look instead to the community as the focus of value in social and political life. Nor is it difficult to appreciate why an ideology which was especially adapted to the interests of an independent and resourceful entrepreneurial class should seem irrelevant to a broader spectrum of classes, ranging from established landed interests to the working masses gathered in the burgeoning industrial cities. In an age that had to confront increasingly complex problems of integration and control in the economy and society, it was natural that politically articulate groups should turn to ideologies which stressed the collective rather than individual dimension in political life.

Nor was it only in relation to nationalism that liberalism's lack of popular appeal was evident. In the early decades of the nineteenth century arguments had been mooted urging a high degree of central planning in the organization of an economy. Robert Owen and Saint-Simon, for example, contended that scientific and technical progress had created alternatives to capitalist production which were both more efficient and more humane. Problems which had in the past been treated as the 'natural' concomitants of human life – poverty, exploitation, crime – were, on this view, attributable to an outmoded social and economic system. Replace anarchic competition with rational planning, coercion in the factory with co-operation, and not only would productive capacity be increased but there would be no further need for the state to assume a repressive role.

Ideas of this kind were growing in popularity, especially among educated workers in London and Paris in the 1840s. They constituted a frame of reference in which substantive political, social and economic demands could be advanced – for universal male suffrage and annual parliaments among the Chartists, for a radical redistribution of property among the Paris workers. But, far-reaching though the practical implications of these demands might be, they were thoroughly reformist in tone. These were arguments for justice and fairness which right-minded liberals might be persuaded to accept. The contention was that by amending specific institutions and practices, wholesale benefits would accrue to working people. What transformed socialism into a deadly threat to the liberal order was the supposition that meaningful change could not be achieved within the confines of a capitalist system. Tinkering with this or that abuse might, indeed, strengthen the status quo by distracting the working class from their revolutionary task. Where reformists had sought to convince a ruling élite of the justice of their cause, revolutionary socialists vested their hopes for the future in the working class. Capitalism had created, along with unparalleled wealth, an impoverished and brutalized industrial proletariat. With dawning awareness of the logic of their class position, however, the proletariat would suffer a metamorphosis. The passive victims of capitalist exploitation would assume the direction of a new era.

Karl Marx was the principal architect of a class-based socialism. In his early writings he targeted his criticism on the view, central to liberal theory, that moral and political principles have a universal validity. The conception of rights embodied in the *Declaration of the Rights of Man*, for example, which purported to be a statement of the necessary conditions for the rounded political and social development of human beings everywhere, was seen by Marx as a defence of the sorts of conventions which might best advance the interests of the emergent bourgeoisie. Champions of the *Declaration* would not, of course, recognize the narrowness of their perspective. In arguing for certain rights, they meant what they said. What they had not grasped, however, was that the view individuals form of their predicament (expressed in moral, political, philosophical, religious, aesthetic or whatever terms) was a product of their place in a complex of social and economic roles.

Marx, at this stage of his career, was engaged in the kind of unmasking exercise which had occupied his slightly older contemporaries, Strauss and Feuerbach, in their analyses of religion. Religion had always been taken as a statement of perennial truth. Yet, according to Strauss and Feuerbach, it should be treated as an idealization of a conception of human nature prevalent in a particular historical culture. Marx extended this analysis to the political realm. The dominant political philosophy of his youth, that of Hegel, had portrayed the state as the concrete expression of the universal good of the community. Marx, instead, saw it as the protector of the economic and social interests of a dominant class. Faced with any statement of formal principles, Marx would always look to the class interest which had generated it. The whole of the ideological realm was (for him) but a reflection of more fundamental conflicts and developments in economy and society.

Marx's shift of perspective involved a quite different conception of political argument. The ingenuity which past philosophers had devoted to the justification of abstract principles was clearly misplaced. What was required was not a titanic confrontation of concepts – divine right against natural right, liberty against equality – but an explanation of the economic changes which had brought forth particular ways of speaking about political life. Marx, writing in collaboration with Friedrich Engels, drew his early ideas together in a pamphlet, *The Communist Manifesto*, which became a model for the new style of argument. Conceived as a contribution to the turmoil of 1848, the *Manifesto* sought to raise the revolutionary consciousness of the industrial proletariat by explaining the economic basis of their new-found political strength. Marx's initial premise was that all conflicts in society could be traced back to class divisions. These divisions could be complex in pre-capitalist societies, with subtle distinctions of status and rank changing slowly in relation to the distribution of economic power. With the advent of mature capitalism, however, a new phenomenon had occurred. The interrelationships of earlier societies were tending to be replaced by a basic division into two broad classes, the bourgeoisie and the proletariat, with implacably opposed interests. The bourgeoisie, as owners of the means of production, would be intent upon maximizing their profits in order to survive the rigours of competition. The proletariat, on the other hand, who were propertyless, would be forced to sell their labour for subsistence wages. Since, according to Marx, the exploitation of the workers was the only source of profit in a capitalist system, it followed that the inexorable logic of competition would compel the bourgeoisie to squeeze ever more production out of the workers in return for the lowest possible wages.

But here we see problems looming. Economies of scale dictated that production be concentrated in ever larger factories. Yet the discipline of factory life would accustom the proletariat to working together as a body. And it was but a small step from recognition of the interdependence of the system of production to recognition of the proletariat's collective interest as a class. As competition among producers became more intense, so extra pressure would be put upon the workers. The workers would be forced by their poverty to resist that pressure, first in the factory and subsequently (as political awareness grew) at national and international levels. Capitalists, in their restless pursuit of profit, would have created the conditions for their own undoing.

The *Manifesto* was no more than a schematic account of the economic context in which modern political battles were being fought out. Marx's crucial point was that the political position of the proletariat would be improved not by appeals to principles but through a realistic appraisal of the shifting balance of economic power. Capitalism had created a technology with vast economic potential; but that potential could not be fulfilled within the established legal and political order. The task of the revolutionary intellectual was to bolster the proletariat by showing precisely why capitalism would collapse under its own weight. In his later writings, culminating in the first volume of *Capital* (1867), Marx broke new ground in economic history by charting in detail the development and prospective demise of capitalism. But his researches were always guided by a political goal: the demonstration of the inevitability of the triumph of the proletariat.

Marx's specific predictions were not, of course, to be realized. The revolution which he had confidently expected in 1848 receded in his later writings to a more distant prospect. Nor can it be said that the states which have proclaimed themselves to be 'Marxist' in the twentieth century emerged in quite the way Marx had anticipated. But the fact remains that Marxism has signally enriched political debate. As an analytical tool, it has enabled historians and political theorists to set the conventional terms of political discourse in a novel and perhaps more critical context. More important, at the practical level, it has furnished a theoretical framework which lends political significance to ordinary events in working people's lives. Grinding experience of home and work had never been more than a background condition in liberal thought, an incentive to individuals to try to better themselves, but without positive political value. In a broader context, however, the lessons of life's daily round could assume a national or international relevance, extending the horizons of the working class without detaching them from their immediate circumstances. By the 1860s the impact of an organized labour movement was beginning to be felt. Groups which liberalism had largely disregarded were now demanding both a concrete improvement in their working conditions and a more active role in political life. And while there was nothing in liberal doctrine which denied the validity of the widest possible participation in politics, the substantive claims being advanced by workers' organizations were scarcely translatable into the formal language of classical liberal theory.

The success of Marxism is best measured in terms of the breadth of its impact. Groups which would not describe themselves as Marxist could profit from the new emphasis on the politics of labour. Nor was Marx's direct legacy uniformly revolutionary. Soon after his death in 1883, leading intellectuals (Labriola and Croce in Italy, Sorel in France, Bernstein in Germany) were debating the practical implications of Marx's theories. It became evident that, when due attention was given to particular political contexts, Marxism could be used to justify an evolutionary as well as a revolutionary road to socialism. What had originally been presented as the doctrine of a small revolutionary sect could by the 1890s function as the theoretical foundation for a broad-based ideology, embracing a multitude of diverse groups and associations.

Between nationalism's emotive appeal and socialism's direct relevance to working people, liberalism was being squeezed on two fronts. It could (and did) adapt itself somewhat, stressing the significance of participation and self-government in addition to legal entitlement. English liberalism after John Stuart Mill took important steps away from the earlier preoccupation with *laissez-faire*. T. H. Green and his school in the 1870s and 1880s championed a much more interventionist role for the state than had been the fashion among mid-century liberals. It was no longer regarded as heresy to argue that the state should actively support disadvantaged groups within society, especially in the field of labour relations, where the 'free' contract agreed between an individual worker and an individual employer had always been heavily loaded in favour of the latter. On health and welfare issues, too, it was accepted that the state should restrict the freedom of some groups in order to enhance the welfare of the most vulnerable.

A similar pattern emerged in other European states. In Italy after 1876 the ruling liberals rejected the idea of a night-watchman state in favour of direct governmental sponsorship of industry and commerce. The *Kulturkampf* in Germany, too, saw liberal opinion supporting a role for the state in the spheres of morality and culture that would have been anathema in the days of Wilhelm von Humboldt's influence. And throughout Europe in the 1880s we see states pursuing aggressive foreign policies, especially in Africa, designed both to promote economic interests and to sustain a certain conception of what went with 'great power' status.

Liberalism was clearly no longer making the political running. Its principal role in the future was rather to 'domesticate' nationalism and socialism than to set the tone of political debate. Yet liberalism displayed a remarkable flexibility in responding to changed circumstances. Traditional liberal policy priorities were reversed throughout the developed European states: free trade giving place to state intervention in the economy, foreign policy assuming a higher profile in domestic politics, state-sponsored welfare schemes beginning to replace self-help. But the structural features of liberal polities remained largely intact. Liberal states were still distinguished by commitments to constitutional procedures and the rule of law. Insistence on maintaining established channels for the pursuit of ends rendered all manner of political beasts docile. Liberals, indeed, found little difficulty in making common cause with nationalists across a broad spectrum of issues. What united them was a fear of socialism's subversive potential, both politically and economically. In the last resort, however, the threat of socialism was seen off by the resilience of capitalism itself. Capitalism was able to adapt to the new collectivist ethos without significant traumas. Its capacity for wealth generation was one of the principal factors which gave liberal states a wide range of options in seeking to accommodate demands from organized labour. In the longer term, of course, the relationship between capitalism and the state was to present a whole series of new problems to the liberal order. For the time being, at least, liberal states had been secured, even if liberal policies had had to be sacrificed. Just how far liberalism would be able to adjust to the dawning age of mass politics remained to be seen.

Further reading

There is no satisfactory overall study of political ideologies in the nineteenth century. But the student is fortunately better served by an extensive literature on particular movements and theorists.

Among general treatments of liberalism, Guido de Ruggiero, *The History of European Liberalism*, trans. R. G. Collingwood (London, 1927), remains outstanding. Two more recent introductions, directed rather more to the student of political theory than the student of history, can be recommended: John Gray, *Liberalism* (Milton Keynes, 1986) and D. J. Manning, *Liberalism* (London, 1976). Liberal ideas are set in a novel frame of reference in Nancy L. Rosenblum, *Another Liberalism: Romanticism and the Reconstruction of Liberal Thought* (Cambridge, MA, 1987).

Students of the subject would benefit from examining the work of specific thinkers for themselves. See Benjamin Constant, *Political Writings*, ed. Biancamaria Fontana (Cambridge, 1988) and Alexis de Tocqueville, *Democracy in America*, ed. J. P. Mayer and Max Lerner, 2 vols (New York, 1966).

For commentary see Jack Lively, *The Social and Political Thought of Alexis de Tocqueville* (Oxford, 1962) and Stephen Holmes, *Benjamin Constant and the Making of Modern Liberalism* (New Haven, 1984). The standard introductions to nationalism are Peter Alter, *Nationalism* (London, 1989); Elie Kedourie, *Nationalism* (London, 1960); and K. R. Minogue, *Nationalism* (London, 1967). The arguments advanced in Benedict Anderson, *Imagined Communities: Reflections on the Origin and Spread of Nationalism* (London, 1983) and Ernest Gellner, *Nations and Nationalism* (Oxford, 1983) are rather more polemical but no less arresting. Detailed historical background is provided in Hugh Seton-Watson, *Nations and States: an Enquiry into the Origins of Nations and the Politics of Nationalism* (London, 1977).

Among specific writings by nationalists, see: F. M. Barnard (ed.), *Herder on Social and Political Culture* (Cambridge, 1969); Jules Michelet, *The People*, ed. J. P. Mckay (Urbana, 1973); and H. S. Reiss (ed.), *The Political Thought of the German Romantics* (Oxford, 1955); Gaetano Salvemini, *Mazzini* (London, 1956), is a spirited reconstruction of Mazzini's thought.

The literature on socialism is vast. Among general introductions see R. N. Berki, *Socialism* (London, 1975); George Lichtheim, *The Origins of Socialism* (London, 1968) and *A Short History of Socialism* (London, 1970). More advanced students should not miss Leszek Kolakowski, *Main Currents of Marxism*, 3 vols, trans. P. S. Falla (Oxford, 1978).

Marx is clearly the dominant figure in the socialist tradition. One should read (at least) Karl Marx and Frederick Engels, *The Communist Manifesto*, available in many modern editions but perhaps most conveniently in *Selected Works* (London, 1968). From the wealth of modern commentary see Shlomo Avineri, *The Social and Political Thought of Karl Marx* (Cambridge, 1969); Isaiah Berlin, *Karl Marx: his Life and Environment*, 3rd edn (London, 1963); Terrell Carver, *Marx's Social Theory* (Oxford, 1982); Michael Evans, *Karl Marx* (London, 1975); and David McLellan, *Karl Marx: his Life and Thought* (London, 1973).

9

Steam: revolution in warfare and the economy

BRUCE WALLER

In two fields, those of economic and military affairs, the nineteenth
century saw change of such gigantic proportions as to make
previous advance dwindle into insignificance. We deal here not
only with this, but also with the introduction of a new dynamism
which in our century is threatening to consume us – the still-
evolving economy and military have clearly become cancerous.
We shall see that at the beginning the outlook was very different.
We take the revolution in the economy first.

What was the Industrial Revolution? If we mean a sudden burst
of industrialization which wrought decisive, swift, revolutionary
change, we will find none. In no country was the pace of
industrialization quick enough to alter society significantly within
a generation. Individual facets, sometimes several, were altered
in this time-span, but society as a whole was slow to respond. If
one recalls that the economy and society were gradually evolving
in the pre-industrial period, the strides of progress over one
generation look unimpressive. If, however, we take a period of
three generations after the onset of industrialization the transformation is remarkable. We do, in fact, have 'revolutionary'
change not only to the economy, but to social relationships,
people's minds and the physical environment. How can one
account for the revolutionary impact of, say, seventy-five years of
only 2 per cent annual growth? This was the rate at which the
global economy of the major powers expanded once industrialization started. The difference from the past was that growth was
continual, being subject to only short interruptions. Previously,
lean periods had invariably followed fat ones, bringing things back

to square one. Under the force of industrialization the cycle of such alternation stopped. This was new and unexpected, and brought to ordinary people the profoundly un-Christian optimism of eighteenth-century intellectuals. Not only was the economy of pre-industrial Europe undermined; so also were its beliefs.

When we talk of the Industrial Revolution we use the expression as shorthand for sweeping changes on a broad front. The alteration in industry is conspicuous to the untrained eye: that the village blacksmith could not have built the Eiffel tower is obvious. Other things were not so obvious. There were great, though gradual, improvements in agriculture, without which there would have been no Industrial Revolution. There was in addition a surge in the population. In most of Europe outside of France it grew with uncomfortable rapidity. Many regarded the resultant outward flow of emigrants as healthy, since pressure for work or possessions at home slackened. There was also a commercial, communication, transport and banking revolution. Finally, connected with this and partly derived from it, there was the great military revolution of the nineteenth century. All these things were related; they stemmed from the same sources, and with the passage of time they reinforced one another. Wherever they ran parallel with political forces and the might of ideas, their influence on society and therefore history was irresistible. In other words the Industrial Revolution was merely the most conspicuous element of a much larger movement: the application of systematic logic to an ever-widening circle of problems, some practical, others theoretical. It was the legacy of the Enlightenment.

The Industrial Revolution had a unique configuration in each country and occurred at different times. If we keep this in mind, we can save ourselves from the pitfall of ranking countries solely according to their progress *à l'anglaise*. It is, for instance, customary to decry the poor French performance in the previous century. In heavy industry, where Britain excelled, France was second best. Yet overall French economic growth and per capita performance were quite respectable. All things considered, the balanced French economy was much stronger in the twentieth century than could have been the case if the critics of France are right.

That cotton textiles should have been the 'leading sector' at the beginning is understandable. They are simple products with an enormous potential market. It merely took a calculating and practical mind to devise the necessary gadgetry. Britain was well placed to capitalize on this because the possibility of a world-wide market existed, and the other related aspects of the Industrial Revolution were already well underway. But by the beginning of our period the driving force of industrial transformation was steam. More than any other single invention, the harnessing of steam changed our lives. To produce the increasingly sophisticated engines a great coal and iron industry grew up and banking became transformed. Steam not only drove all kinds of machines, it also transported people, material, ideas and even disease with a hitherto and subsequently unattained acceleration. Taking into consideration the two factors of speed and dependability, the locomotive and steamship brought absolute savings which can never again be equalled. Of course the best stage-coach and clipper ship could be nearly as fast. But with them conditions were rarely ideal. Steam, however, propelled train and ship in bad as well as good weather. The revolution in transport also had further indirect effects, to be discussed later. The point to be retained here is that steam – damp, hot air – changed men's lives and man himself.

If we take a long view of the Industrial Revolution, two characteristics stand out. First of all, the economy did not leap ahead. As previously mentioned, progress was slow and fairly steady over several generations. Secondly, within this period there were three longish waves. There was relative recession from Waterloo to 1848; then a period of more vigorous growth till 1873; and finally until 1896 a further twenty-three relatively poor years. Scholars and public figures have long realized that the economy is subject to annual fluctuations and that over very long periods, say a century, one can discern upward or downward trends. But it was not until our own century that Kondratieff uncovered the generation-long swings in the economy. The more industrialized and integrated Europe became, the more perceptible these swings were. The picture from 1830 to 1848 is patchy: the recession was clear in central Europe, not so clear in the West. Taken as a whole, however, the period was not vigorous. The upswing to 1873 had more of a fully European character. Subsequent ups and downs affected most countries, in one way or another – not, of course, automatically because each state had special circumstances. The various annual indices of trade and industry show that the fluctuations are not large. But the impact of small alterations in international trade, industrial output, or the price of grain, on society and on individuals was far from negligible. People's approach to politics and economics at the beginning and end of our period was defensive. Everywhere they attempted to 'catch up' with Britain or other rivals, and therefore the tendency to protection was strong. The national movements were inward looking. There were of course imperial conflicts, but serious war was avoided. Pessimism characterized both periods of recession, the second especially.

The mid-century boom, however, was very different. It was a period of ebullient optimism; economic advance seemed almost automatic. Statesmen were assured and, if need be, warlike. Their outlook was also liberal in politics and the economy. Liberalism is the philosophy of people convinced that restraint is artificial and that through struggle a higher harmony will eventually emerge. It is quite wrong to think of liberalism as the philosophy of Quakers. It was the philosophy of the man on the make and was neither peaceful nor democratic. The spirit of the nineteenth century therefore underwent rapid and profound transformation from 1830 to 1890. What we should note here is that the various European countries were influenced in different degrees by these economic and psychological swings, depending on the extent to which they had industrialized. France and Britain had been heavily influenced by the eighteenth-century Enlightenment and its optimistic creed. Their economies had developed to a considerable degree by 1850. So the impression made by mid-century optimism and liberalism was very strong. The others were less profoundly influenced by these movements. Russia was 'at the end of the queue' and therefore very little affected by liberalism. Germany stood not far behind France and so was influenced, but in a different way, by the mid-century 'high': its pioneering and entrepreneurial spirit received a great boost; the legal and social structure was gradually transformed; new techniques, new organization and gadgetry were especially well applied in the military sphere. So when the trial of strength came with France of the Second Empire – a country surrounded by the aura of revolution – victory was seen as a triumph over unrest. In consequence, a German state was established which bore a recognizable resemblance to the old Prussia.

The connection of the economic ebb and flow with political events is too striking to be overlooked. The more evolved the individual state economy, the greater was the lasting impression of mid-century liberalism on it. By the time of the 'great depression' from 1873 onwards, Europe had become sufficiently integrated for movements to appear on a continental scale. In most European states apart from Britain the government began to interfere increasingly in the economy so as to resuscitate it. The move to protection and then to imperialism as defensive measures was a European-wide phenomenon motivated more by worry than by exuberance. This fitted well into the general trend for groups in all areas of society to form and to consolidate: the workers increasingly joined hands with one another; capitalists built ever larger companies and then, finally, cartels; protective tariffs established a kind of national cartel; imperialism worked in the same direction, founding on the international plane an exclusive brotherhood. The character of international affairs changed considerably from the turbulent 1850s and 1860s to the more peaceful 1870s and 1880s. The construction of a vast alliance network in the 1880s, tending to immobilize Europe at home (but not abroad), again contributes to this picture of an uneasy and disillusioned continent.

On the domestic scene there was the appearance or strengthening of groups aimed at the persecution of outsiders. The word 'anti-Semitism' was coined in 1878, and anti-Jewish behaviour assumed a more virulent character. But not only the Jews were persecuted or harrassed; other minority groups were as well. Much of this was clearly anti-liberal agitation. But there was, paradoxically, also a link with the liberals, many of whom were proudly and ungenerously anti-clerical. So in some ways they offered an example and justification for the persecution of Jews, Poles, Slovaks, socialists, or others. This set of reactions to the great depression is clear enough and must not be overlooked, but the downswing had this profound effect on people because other influences were working in a similar direction. For instance, optimism was increasingly seen as a slender reed. In the realm of politics several nation-states had been created which began vying with one another abroad for pre-eminence of empire, while in

Europe itself a series of barely viable submerged nationalities threatened ever more to upset the domestic and the international balance. The social structure too was rapidly changing: a myriad of mutually dependent groups was being transformed into much fewer mutually antagonistic classes.

It is sometimes argued that with the spread of industrialization and the creation of a truly European economy, international specialization will naturally emerge to enhance stability and efficiency. This half-truth is all too frequently accepted without reflection. Nineteenth-century Britain is a good example of one-sided development, and demonstrates some of the problems. There was first of all the need to switch quickly from one speciality to another, for instance, from cotton to iron. It was also necessary to move from one market to another in search of outlets or raw materials. Throughout the last century Britain rose to the challenge. The economy was strong and flexible. But as the indispensable investment in capital and manpower steadily increased, room for manoeuvre also inevitably diminished. Specialization necessitates adaptability, but in the long run this is increasingly arduous. As Europe developed materially, one-commodity suppliers were encouraged. The globe is now strewn with the wreckage of such economies, which were well adapted for one thing at one time, but could not easily adjust to other circumstances. The inherent strength of the less specialized French institutions should be remembered. The Austrian and Russian economies were in some ways similarly balanced, although less industrialized, and were therefore perhaps not quite so weak as might be assumed. Germany and Italy lay between the specialized British and the balanced French approach and so had some of the drawbacks and advantages of each. Italy made steady progress in agriculture, had expertise in silk, and towards the end of our period developed the manufacturing sector. The Germans perhaps most successfully of all peoples moved from the age of steam, with its iron and steel industries, to the age of chemicals and electricity. Both Italy and Germany combined flexibility with specialization and with the cultivation of other strengths.

Not until after the defeat of Napoleon I did Europeans realize that Britain's industrial innovations were a threat. One reason for European industrialization was the attempt to ward off British competition and to emulate the leader. So there was an element of artificiality everywhere. The later the onset of industrialization, the more apparent that was. France and the Low Countries were advanced in the eighteenth century and so could emulate the British with a fair amount of self-assurance. The pre-industrial German economy was also well-developed, but the country was disunited and disputatious. Conditions were a good deal better under the Confederation established in 1815, but it took almost another twenty years for a spirit of co-operation to emerge. The foundation of the *Zollverein* (Customs Union) in 1834 is tangible evidence of this. The first German railway was built simultaneously, so it is a moot point whether the expansion of the Customs Union or the railway network was more important. Surely the force of the one not only added to, but multiplied, the other. The point here, however, is that, although the German base was sound, rapid industrialization started later than in France, at about 1850. Not surprisingly, it was then to proceed very rapidly. Germans knew that they had the required skills, but they keenly felt their late start. This led to that extra exertion which was absent in France and the Low Countries. The educational system did an excellent job. In addition to the traditional schools, very good technological institutions were established. And the German banks proved especially helpful; they participated much more actively than their British opposite numbers in running both the economy and individual companies as well. They lent money not only on a short-term basis, but also for the longer term, and they frequently had seats on supervisory boards. This backing channelled capital and financial acumen in the right direction. The fear of being left behind encouraged the co-operation of big business with large landowners from the mid-1870s on. Together they pushed for a protective tariff. Later in the 1880s the industrialists made increasingly formal cartel agreements and grain producers got higher tariffs. Initially the motive was fear, but soon the instinct for survival turned into a desire to exploit. So, apart from a keen and efficient approach generally, German industrial development displayed distinctive features; there was the important role of the banks and the tendency to cartelization. Despite their impressive success, the Germans remained acutely conscious of the precariousness of their position.

The Italians had a similar problem; although development in Italy was retarded in comparison with Germany, the extra effort made by men in government and business to catch up was roughly comparable. Cavour was a great believer in deficit spending, but his approach was more or less standard *laissez-faire* in other respects. It did not seem to work very well; indeed the Italian example shows us that liberalism can impede the industrialization of late-comers and even condemn them to the role of permanent suppliers of primary products. Italy finally went over to protection in 1878, and a higher tariff was adopted nine years later. After the great banking collapse in 1893 the government in Rome looked to Berlin for financial assistance. In consequence banks of the German type were started, and soon afterwards a sustained development followed. Apart from a sporadic but vigorous attempt at railway construction and some support for heavy industry in the 1880s, this was as far as the government went in the direction of interference.

The backward south, the dearth of raw materials and the heavy preponderance of agriculture (even though it advanced fairly steadily despite much peasant unrest) sufficed to keep Italy well behind Germany and the West, given the lack of a concerted government push to counteract these factors. The modest Italian performance was perhaps a lesson that late-comers would have to try that much harder if they wanted to draw alongside the leaders.

Turning to Austria, there are three things to note at the outset. First, on the eve of industrialization the economy was moderately strong. There were some backward areas, as in every country, but other regions, for instance Bohemia, were promising. In fact the first important railway in central Europe was built in Austria, and not in Germany proper. Second, Austrian economic development was modest but steady throughout the century. Finally, the more rapid development in Prussia was not disastrous for Austria since the former drew swiftly ahead only after the great divide of 1866. Until then Austria suffered mainly from poor political leadership and indifferent military achievement. (Afterwards the ailment was nationalism.) The economy was held back by these forces; it did not directly contribute to ineffectiveness in battle or strife at home.

Like Germany, and a good deal more than Italy, Austria was affected by the long economic waves. By the onset of the great depression Austria was well integrated into the international economy despite the reasonably self-sufficient nature of the state economy as a whole. The political and military defeats of the previous decade and a half brought the seriousness of the depression home to Austrians, who in the first part of the century had apparently not realized that their country was losing ground in relation to others. The reaction to the depression was rather stronger than in many other areas. There was a general upsurge in nationalism and related to this a morbid growth of anti-Semitism. In addition, the trend towards cartelization was, if anything, more pronounced than in Germany. These things were partly the legacy of political mistakes and military defeat; they were also affected by the more recent growth of nationalism throughout Europe and the realization of relative economic insufficiency compared with other states.

The size of the Russian economy was altogether different and enabled the concentration of effort in selected spheres coupled with that same neglect in other areas which we have seen in our own century. In some respects, for instance, in iron production, Russia was well to the front in the late eighteenth century. So there can be no question of its starting from scratch in the long and arduous process of industrialization. Russia had its own necessary raw materials – including coal and iron – waiting for exploitation. The rivers, unfortunately, mostly flow in the wrong direction; the construction of railways, however, was not difficult despite the length of track needed for a network. In addition, the iron hand of censorship had a perhaps unexpected consequence: many aspiring intellectuals sought refuge in science. So once industrialization started, it could advance rapidly, although it did not make much headway until liberalism was waning and the clouds of depression were already on the horizon. It is natural that a proud country immersed in tradition and accustomed to autocratic rule should from the 1870s resort increasingly to protection and state guidance on a large scale, in the tremendous and promising effort to catch up. At the very end of our period some sectors of the Russian economy, such as basic industries, and certain features, for example, factory size, were beginning to look impressively modern. The paradox of Russian industrialization was that ample government guidance was needed to get it going and to keep it moving, but the government could not, and did not, view favourably the social results of industrialization.

Looking at the period from 1830 to 1890 as a whole, it is clear that Britain was regarded as the economic and industrial leader; but failure to conform to the 'British standard' must not now be necessarily regarded as a deficiency in the long run. It is important not only to note each country's relative stage of development, but the effect on it of the long economic swings, and even more, the effect on people's minds. Industrialization was a slow and laborious process, proceeding differently in each country; liberalism might not be an appropriate long-term gauge of success or failure.

Revolution in warfare: cause, character, effect

If Alexander the Great could have been brought from the tomb to witness Napoleon at Austerlitz, he would have been impressed by the size of the operations and terrified by the noise and destructiveness of the cannon. But otherwise the battle would have been broadly comprehensible. Had he been led by Haig through the trenches of Flanders in 1916, he would have wished himself back in the grave – not because of the horror, but simply because warfare had changed so much as to be unintelligible. He would have understood 1805, but not 1916. For him the First and Second World War would be much the same – very different from anything he had known. The character of warfare changed more from 1850 to 1918 than it had throughout all previously recorded history.

From ancient times till the fifteenth century the art of war had not advanced very much. The weapons remained familiar; the classical texts were still assiduously studied, so the theory was much the same. Discipline, the greatest military virtue and one of the Roman strengths, had been badly neglected for a thousand years. So from the point of view of the military arts, ancient history in a sense lasted until the fifteenth century.

Then two important changes simultaneously occurred. First, the Swiss pikemen brought the art of war back to the peak of Roman practice: discipline was valued again. Second, the introduction of guns, muskets and cannon, introduced a new element, Previously a well-prepared defensive position had been very hard to defeat. Guns now made attack easier and so the medieval forts quickly lost their purpose. Cannon had battering power and so did a two-ounce musket ball, but both were cumbersome and quite inaccurate except at point-blank range. The famous Spanish musket needed two men to fire it. Frederick the Great's best trained musketeer could not fire more accurately at 300 yards than an expert English archer. Nor could he fire as fast.

In the late seventeenth century the ring bayonet was introduced. It could be fixed to a musket and so eliminated the pikeman. Previously the musketeers fired at the advancing enemy, and pikemen finished them off in hand-to-hand combat. In Napoleon's time, ten shots at most were fired by each solider in a battle and then the bayonet decided it. Napoleon made what was for his day massive use of artillery. But every big First World War artillery barrage fired more shot than all Napoleon's armies put together. This is not to say that small guns and cannon had not improved over four centuries. They certainly had, but not to a startling degree. A skilled archer might still have had a chance in 1850!

We have already noted that the fifteenth-century Swiss pikemen showed what discipline could do. In this direction there was vast room for improvement, and by the eighteenth century the ability to organize large troops and keep them supplied had been improved beyond recognition. These intangible things were the modern aspect of the pre-1850 armies. So if in military science ancient history continued until the fifteenth century, medieval history lasted till 1850.

After about mid-century change was rapid. The concept of obsolescence had not so far really existed. Subsequently it was on everyone's lips. One apparently pedestrian change can illustrate this. In the Crimean War (1853–6) the Russians still used muskets. The allies had muzzle-loading rifles – arguably not much better. In 1870 both the French and Prussians had breech-loading rifles. Now it has been calculated that a rifle is five times as accurate, and has a far better range than a musket. But if it has to be muzzle-loaded, it is slower firing, so the advantage is doubtful. The breech-loading rifle, however, fires at least five times as fast. It can also be fired lying down. So it would not be wrong to say that a breech-loader is twenty-five times as effective as a musket. In practice the advantage is less because other factors (for example, the soldier's state of mind, or his training, or the weather) are important. In close combat it is also immaterial whether a bayonet is affixed to a rifle or a musket. Two Roman legionaries would have had a sporting chance against one of Napoleon's musketeers. Five of them, however, would not have had a ghost of a chance against one of Louis Napoleon's riflemen. For the first time in history it was possible for one man easily to kill another without seeing the white of his eyes. The infantry rifle's range, accuracy and rate of fire were further refined by 1914 so that a company of riflemen would be more than a match for a regiment of musketeers. The improvement in the arming of the lowly foot soldier was without precedent. But this was only one of a series of important changes.

First let us ask what was behind the biggest change in warfare ever. One is tempted to attribute it to the social and political inheritance of the French Revolution. This ultimately altered many things, even music and art, so why not warfare? It brought the 'nation to arms' and the knowledge how to organize, supply and lead it. After this Napoleon made little technical advance, and only part of his strategic and tactical skill could be taught or imitated. So the French Revolution did bring changes, but only within the existing system.

Let us look instead at the Industrial Revolution and the rational cast of mind behind it. Indeed, the Industrial Revolution produced the new technology, and practical minds saw how to apply it. Armies can take advantage of innovations originally devised for some other purpose, and it was so with the steam engine and the telegraph. The old-fashioned army had rarely travelled more than fifteen miles a day, the soldiers each carrying between 30 and 40 kgs of equipment on their backs. This had not really changed over the millennia. But by rail large numbers of troops could travel over 100 miles in a day with minimal losses. Small detachments could go much further. If they did not stray too far from the railhead, supply was no problem.

One of the reasons for the French defeat in 1870–1 was that Prussia understood far better than France the significance of the railway. The Prussians quickly assembled and supplied their troops. The telegraph facilitated co-ordination between units and command, which was no longer on a nearby hilltop but in some cases many miles away. All subsequent improvements in transportation and communication taken together have been less important, relatively than the advantage given by the initial use of the railway and telegraph. The superiority of air transport over rail, or radio communication over the telegraph can be exaggerated.

So much for the changes affecting strategy. Let us turn now to tactics. The metamorphosis of the smooth-bore musket into the repeating rifle has already been mentioned. This was the result of ten or twelve important innovations occurring in the middle and second half of the nineteenth century. Cannon experienced a similar development, from a battering-ram into a very long-range accurate and rapid-firing instrument.

Towards the end of the century machine guns appeared. Although they were heavy and susceptible to jamming, they appreciably strengthened the defensive. When the infantry and artillery developed this kind of fire-power, cavalry as an instrument of shock had no place any more, despite the unwillingness of soldiers to recognize this fact. The real tragedy of the Light Brigade's charge was not the frivolous sacrifice of excellent men to a misguided concept of duty. Its terrible significance was that it showed how in 1854 cavalry could well prevail even if all the rules of military tactics or even common sense were disregarded. The charge was, after all, a success! The men rode out to silence some Russian guns. Not only was this accomplished but the adversary was demoralized as well. That success strengthened the faith in mounted soldiers and led probably to subsequent, even more appalling and easily avoidable blunders, in other words, the use of old-fashioned shock tactics against seasoned troops armed with modern weapons. At Vionville in 1870 Bredow succeeded but lost half his men. His famous 'death ride' was the last victorious charge in Europe. A few days later the French imperial cavalry displayed surpassing courage at Sedan. It lost the battle and practically all its men but won the accolade from William I: *'Ah, les braves gens!'* What was foolish but still feasible in 1854 was murder in 1870. The Polish cavalry charge in 1939 with sabre gripped and lance lowered was simply quixotic. Certain things the generals learned quickly. But the experience of two millennia of shock tactics was not very rapidly thrown out.

So far we have spoken only about the army because it, especially the infantry, usually settled accounts. But the navy was more quickly, and more profoundly, affected by some of the changes mentioned. Until the fifteenth century fast and manoeuvrable galleys were the most effective warships. They fought by ramming and boarding. But they were doomed when sailing ships began to mount numerous cannon on their sides because the galleys could be sunk before contact was made. Henceforth naval battles were fought at a distance, and boarding was rare. The principle of fighting at a distance is modern and the navy in sail was more advanced than the army of its day. But it too was transformed by steam, iron construction, naval rifles and the improved exploding shell. Henceforth naval battle took place beyond the range of small arms. By the end of the nineteenth century only technologically sophisticated countries could construct an effective fleet. The need to build battleships proved a very strong incentive for all-round technological and economic advance. The improvements in weaponry were immediately adopted by most navies, whereas in the army there were many generals who still believed in the bayonet charge. Such men were fools, and there were more of this kind of fool in the army than in the navy. They were present even in the Prussian army. The gentle slopes before St Privat bear witness to this, for there the flower of the Prussian aristocracy was cut down in twenty minutes on a summer day in 1870. The army was still led by conventional gentlemen who were not very interested in new gadgetry. The navy was run by the more open-minded middle classes who were very much quicker in this respect. The Somme and Jutland are permanent memorials to this point; along the river one futile clash followed another, whereas off the Danish shore two fleets superbly equipped had but one encounter, and afterwards each possessed the good sense to avoid another.

So in our period the navy was more swiftly affected by innovation. In turn, it increasingly stimulated advances in the economy. It encouraged a more outward-looking attitude in general which led partly to a genuine interest in the rest of the world. But it also helped to export European quarrels. At the end of the nineteenth century the army was still less modern than the navy although land warfare had altered radically. The nineteenth century started with a bayonet charge; it ended in a machine gun salvo. There was no longer personal contact, although the average soldier frequently saw the enemy. At the beginning of the century the average sailor saw his opponent; at its end he rarely did.

A third aspect is worth mentioning: the development in medicine, hygiene and nutrition. The horrors of the Crimean War were merely repetitions of those of previous wars. In all but the shortest campaigns more men died of illness than on the battlefield; even minor wounds were usually fatal. A soldier's life during hostilities was worse than that of a farm animal. By the end of the nineteenth century this had radically changed. It became possible to care for the man in uniform and a concerted effort to do so was made; each state did what it could and the Red Cross, founded in 1864, provided some international co-operation. Few soldiers died of illness and many recovered even from serious wounds. The terrible folklore about the Flanders trenches of the First World War is well known, but even there the soldier's daily existence was better than in earlier periods.

The improvement in medicine has made war more humane in many respects. It helps to compensate for the vast improvement in fire-power. The compensation is so striking that, if we put aside ideological genocide and Russian casualties in both twentieth-century World Wars, we may argue that they were not more costly in human lives than some previous conflicts, such as the Thirty Years War; the number lost, seen as a percentage of the population, is not disproportionately greater. But the point is that the nineteenth-century revolution in warfare did not necessarily make it so much more horrible than it had been in the past. In some ways the noisy, but indiscriminate firing of large and small weapons is roughly comparable to the Indian war cry. Its purpose is as much to terrify as to kill. As the population grew, so did armies. Battles have been big in this century, but the opponents were well separated from one another. Enormous quantities of gadgets and supplies were used but to little effect. Because of the vast amount of equipment which was so unintelligently used, state bureaucracies increased, taxes mounted and armaments industries flourished. Increased mobility required extensive planning in peacetime, absorbing a great deal of effort.

The French defeat in 1871 encouraged all states to copy Prussian methods. Apart from universal military service, this meant the systematic application of the human mind to the solving of military problems. Training, planning and organization became very much better, for indeed this attitude spread throughout society. In this respect the businessman and the soldier worked for the same purpose. As in the period after the advent of the Swiss pikemen, this intangible aspect was very important. The emphasis was ever less on enthusiasm and personal courage. Even as late as Napoleonic times morale was a large element of success on the

battlefield. By 1914–18, however, there was only grim determination. During most of the nineteenth century the complacent
and dull officer dominated all ranks in every army but the
Prussian. And even there he was at home in the lower ranks. After
1870 these men began to disappear. By 1900 all the great armies
were very much more professional than they had been in 1850.
Commissions could be bought in mid-century Britain. Elsewhere
the system was slightly less commercial but not very different in
essence: command was a game. By 1900 one had to work for a
commission, and thereafter at the job itself.

We may summarize the revolutionary changes in warfare under
six headings:

1 Troops were very much better organized, supplied and led.
   The scientific and even middle-class businesslike spirit over-
   took the easygoing aristocratic approach.
2 Weaponry was much more deadly and accurate, but combat
   occurred at increasing distances.
3 The odds against dying on the battlefield shortened. But the
   chance of dying off the battlefield was steadily reduced.
4 Large segments of the male population received military
   training and were liable to war service.
5 Powerful state bureaucracies grew up to recruit, organize,
   supply, plan and pay for the military establishment. State
   intervention was mounting.
6 The improvement in navies led to more world-wide involvement.

The territorial adjustments occurring in our period were
determined by whichever power was, in each particular conflict,
superior in technology and efficiency. This emerges clearly out of
the Crimean, Austro-French, Austro-Prussian, Franco-Prussian
and Russo-Turkish wars. The creation of Italy and Germany were
in a sense 'modern' achievements. Had rapid changes in warfare
not occurred, these states might well not have appeared. One can
also partly explain those territorial alterations which failed to occur
by reference to new military technology and efficiency. The Poles
rose twice unsuccessfully against the Russians, and the Italians
(until they gained powerful allies) were no match for the
Austrians. The United States survived the Civil War, although the

qualities of dedication and leadership were more evident on the side of the rebels. The Northerners were badly prepared and they ran home at Bull Run not once but twice. Still, the North had more men, a stronger economy and better organizational skills. The old-fashioned assets of enthusiasm and leadership were not equal to this.

In the seventeenth and eighteenth centuries all the general European wars were fought on American soil as well. This is an often neglected, but important fact. And the wars in the middle of the eighteenth century extended over three continents. Despite this, it is still true that the technological and intellectual changes in the late nineteenth century facilitated the spread of European wars over the globe. They also made Europe vulnerable to outside attack, for the first time since the defeat of the Turks by the Polish King John Sobieski in 1683 at the gates of Vienna.

Strangely, the creation of mass armies based on conscription facilitated not only the growth of nationalism and fascism, which is self-evident, but also democracy and socialism. It gave the common man training, seriousness of purpose and a certain amount of dignity which he did not hitherto possess. His full co-operation was needed for the army. He expected to make a contribution in peacetime as well. Disciplined and self-confident participation was possible. Socialism benefited not only from the brotherhood of the trench, but from the paternalistic attitude of the army and the state in war. The extensive state regulation during the First World War enabled the army to fight and society to be controlled for a common purpose. So here as in many other fields one can see that reality is complex. The modern army encouraged business interests as well as socialism – totalitarianism as well as democratic rule; it glorified male virtues, yet led to a vast increase in women's rights and place in society; it helped to consolidate some states, and to destroy or revolutionize others.

Further reading

ECONOMIC HISTORY: GENERAL TREATMENTS
The Cambridge Economic History of Europe, Vol. VI, H. Habakkuk and M. Postan (eds), (Cambridge, 1965–6); Vol. VII, P. Mathias and M. Postan (eds), (Cambridge, 1978) – the most authoritative account; C. Cipolla (ed.),

The Fontana Economic History of Europe, Vols III and IV (London, 1973) – the most useful general survey.

W. Ashworth, *A Short History of the International Economy, 1850–1950*, 3rd ed. (London, 1975) – still useful; T. Kemp, *Industrialization in Nineteenth Century Europe*, 2nd ed. (London, 1985) – intelligent interpretation with excellent critical bibliography; A. Milward and S. Saul, *The Development of the Economy of Continental Europe, 1850–1914* (London, 1977) – a descriptive work with much quantitative information; S. Pollard, *Peaceful Conquest: the Industrialization of Europe, 1760–1970* (Oxford, 1981) – an imaginative regional analysis.

I. Berend and G. Ranki, *The European Periphery and Industrialization, 1780–1914* (Cambridge, 1982) – deals with the parts other surveys do not reach.

SPECIAL ECONOMIC AND SOCIAL STUDIES

J. Blum, *The End of the Old Order in Rural Europe* (Princeton, NJ, 1978) – stresses the archaic motives of the eighteenth and nineteenth century reforms; H. Habakkuk, *Population Growth and Economic Development since 1750* (Leicester, 1971) – a brief survey dealing with the broad issues; D. Landes, *Unbound Prometheus: Technological Change and Industrial Development in Western Europe from 1750 to the Present* (Cambridge, 1969) – brilliantly written, authoritative; T. McKeown, *The Modern Rise of Population* (London, 1976) – emphasizes importance of hygiene and nutrition; W. Rostow, *The Stages of Economic Growth: a Non-Communist Manifesto* (Cambridge, MA, 1960) – a seminal but controversial statement; P. Stearns, *European Society in Upheaval. Social History since 1750*, 2nd ed. (London, 1975) – good mix of social and economic history with useful bibliography.

ECONOMIC HISTORY: INDIVIDUAL COUNTRIES

F. Carron, *An Economic History of Modern France* (London, 1979) – assumes prior knowledge, confirms picture of slow and steady growth; T. Kemp, *Economic Forces in French History* (London, 1971) – skilful Marxist analysis covering the nineteenth century; P. O'Brien and C. Keyder, *Economic Growth in Britain and France, 1780–1914: Two Paths to the Twentieth Century* (London, 1978) – states the French case.

H. Rosenberg, 'Political and social consequences of the great depression of 1873–1896 in central Europe', in *Economic History Review*, xii (1943) – argues that the long economic down-swing crucially affected most things; S. Saul, *The Myth of the Great Depression, 1873–1896* (London, 1969) – minimizes the effect of the depression.

W. Henderson, *The Zollverein* (London, 1959) and *The Rise of German Industrial Power, 1830–1914* (London, 1975) – two accurate but merely descriptive works; M. Kitchen, *The Political Economy of Germany, 1814–1914* (London, 1978) – up-to-date interpretative survey from the 'Fischer' point of view.

C. Clough, *The Economic History of Modern Italy* (New York, 1964) – largely factual; D. Good, *The Economic Rise of the Habsburg Empire, 1750–1914* (London, 1984) – full and sympathetic account with international comparisons.

W. Blackwell, *The Beginning of Russian Industrialisation, 1800–1860* (Princeton, NJ, 1968) – well researched account of the early period; M. Falkus, *The Industrialisation of Russia before 1914* (London, 1971) – most useful brief introduction.

MILITARY HISTORY: GENERAL WORKS

G. Best, *War and Society in Revolutionary Europe, 1770–1870* (London, 1982); B. Bond, *War and Society in Europe, 1870–1970* (London, 1984) – two serviceable surveys; J. Gooch, *Armies in Europe* (London, 1980) – treats briefly the period between the eighteenth century and World War II, putting the subject in the wider social and political context; M. Howard, *War in European History* (Oxford, 1976) – exceptionally well-written, the briefest and best introduction; W. McNeill, *The Pursuit of Power: Technology, Armed Force and Society since A.D. 1000* (Chicago, 1982) – brings out the broader issues; T. Ropp, *War in the Modern World* (New York, 1962) – especially good on technical matters; H. Strachan, *European Armies and the Conduct of War* (London, 1983) – covers the same period as Gooch and has useful bibliographies.

MILITARY HISTORY: SPECIAL TOPICS

M. van Creveld, *Supplying War: Logistics from Wallenstein to Patton* (Cambridge, 1977) – fine account of an important but neglected subject; M. Pearton, *The Knowledgeable State: Diplomacy, War and Technology since 1830* (London, 1982) – underlines the significance and ambiguities of technological advance; D. Showalter, *Railroads and Rifles: Soldiers, Technology and the Unification of Germany* (Hamden, CT, 1975) – excellent technical discussion.

MILITARY HISTORY: INDIVIDUAL COUNTRIES

D. Porch, *Army and Revolution, France, 1815–1848* (London, 1974) – shows how the army came to terms with the restored monarchy, and *The March to the Rhine: the French Army, 1870–1914* (Cambridge, 1981) – mostly on the period after 1890.

G. Craig, *The Politics of the Prussian Army, 1640–1945* (Oxford, 1955) – a well-written survey; M. Kitchen, *A Military History of Germany from the Eighteenth Century to the Present* (London, 1975) – more up-to-date than Craig; G. Ritter, *Sword and Scepter*, Vols I and II (Coral Gables, FA, 1969–70) – a classic work; vol. I is on Prussia, vol. II has short sections on other countries.

G. Rothenberg, *The Army of Franz Joseph* (West Lafayette, IN, 1976) – fair rendering of the highs and lows of the Austrian army; J. Whittam, *The Politics of the Italian Army, 1861–1918* (London, 1976) – lacks analysis but stresses the importance of the army in domestic politics; J. Gooch,

Army, State and Society in Italy, 1870–1915 (London, 1989) – the most recent treatment.

J. Curtiss, *The Russian Army under Nicholas I, 1825–1855* (Durham, NC, 1965) – sound study of the unreformed army; F. Miller, *D'nitri Miliutin and the Reform Era in Russia* (Vanderbilt University Press, 1968) – looks at the work of Russia's greatest nineteenth-century army reformer.

10

Relations between states and nations

BRUCE WALLER

The term 'international relations' is relatively modern. A nation is a group of people with similar characteristics and aspirations. It is not the same thing as a state, and every Celt will tell us that. Many nations now have their own state. This was less true in the nineteenth century and hardly true at all in earlier periods. In the eighteenth century 'international' relations amounted to relations between princes; in the nineteenth century relations between patricians; in our century relations between plebeians. We have therefore a social evolution in addition to the change from the non-national to the national state. There is an intellectual dimension as well. During the Enlightenment politics between princely states had a certain cool rationality that had been absent during the religious struggles in the early modern period and which became submerged after the onset of the French Revolution. The Romantic Movement affected not only literature, the visual arts and music, but politics as well. So too did the succeeding movements of realism and, at the end of our period, naturalism. Trends of thought and movements in art are not altogether out of step with politics. Finally, in the nineteenth century there was the emergence of an international industrial economy. This necessarily had a profound impact on relations between states and nations.

We must not therefore assume that diplomacy by public insult which we know so well now was typical of the nineteenth century, to say nothing of the eighteenth century. The concept of the nation-state was virtually unknown in the eighteenth century. Today we have democracies of one kind or another – liberal, social or dictatorial. There was none before 1792. Woolly sentiment or 'conviction' dominates politics now; two hundred years ago 'reason' was in higher esteem. Our world is firmly tied together by rails of steel, ribbons of concrete or threads of vapour in the sky. Two centuries ago a distance of fifty miles – two days' journey on foot – frequently sufficed to seal one area from another. The period between 1830 and 1890 saw the old world vanish and the new one appear.

In 1830 there was much about foreign affairs reminiscent of the previous century, most obviously the personnel of diplomacy, the aristocrats. This was the feature of the old regime which most obstinately refused to go; by the First World War the diplomatic corps was little changed. It would still, perhaps, be aristocratic today but for the arrival of American businessmen and Russian commissars masquerading as diplomats. Throughout the nineteenth century the diplomatic corps was not only high-born, it was also incestuous. The representatives of the different monarchs were frequently related to one another and had comparable backgrounds. It was perhaps unusual that the Gablenz brothers should simultaneously run errands, one for Prussia and the other for Austria, and that Waddington and Derby, the foreign secretaries at the same time for France and Britain respectively, should have been to Rugby together. It was also peculiar that Beust should have been foreign secretary of Saxony and then of Austria. But it was not odd that Metternich was from the Rhine (not Austria) or that Capodistrias, the Russian foreign secretary, was from Corfu. Nor was it strange that in 1914 the German and Russian ambassadors in London were cousins and that both were distantly related to George V, who in turn had family ties with the Austrian ambassador. The ideas of these people on all kinds of subjects were similar.

High society in Britain was an exception to the rule that French was the lingua franca, even more than English is today. Interpreters were not needed, except in Constantinople where, as dragomans, they were 'narrow-gauge' ambassadors in their own right. They were intermediaries not only between the French and Turkish languages, but also between the ideas and civilizations of East and West. The diplomatic service was cosy; it lived an almost cocoon-like existence, seemingly unaffected by the sweeping changes on all sides.

Eighteenth-century ambassadors represented one monarch to

another. The prince was more important than the state or his
people, a fact that few then disputed. Throughout the nineteenth
century, ambassadors continued in theory to represent monarchs.
In practice they began increasingly to mediate between states; they
became bureaucrats. There was not only the obvious difficulty of
accommodating the French republics in the old scheme although
their ambassadors were naturally also noblemen. There was also
the increasing significance of the state and its bureaucracy, and
the diminishing role of the prince. A graphic example of this can
be seen in the relations between Prussia-Germany and the Russian
Empire. Their rulers were especially powerful, and their blood ties
especially close. Throughout our period they were represented to
each other by both an old-style ambassador – the military
plenipotentiary who was treated as a member of the family and
had little political influence – and the new-style ambassador who
did most of the work. In fact, ambassadors became the agents of
states which were falling under the dominion of the wealthy
middle classes.

The origin of 'national' as opposed to 'state' representation can
be seen not so much in the diplomacy of Bismarck and Cavour –
they were more interested in aggrandizing their own states and
were not enthusiastic nationalists. Ireland was a domestic British
matter. Poland had been divided in stages during the eighteenth
century by Russia, Austria and Prussia. The attempt at restoration
of a divided Poland was therefore by definition an international
problem. Instead of encouraging a 'national' approach – diplomacy
aimed at nation-building – the representatives of the eastern
empires discouraged it because those who had profited by
subduing the Poles united to keep them suppressed. The
'national' motive in diplomacy came from the European fringe,
mainly that tangle of nations called the Balkans where the
situation was very different. Turkey had Europe's most enduring
empire, and in early modern times it was vigorous and advanced.
Subsequently decay set in. But the Serbs in the mountain citadel
of Montenegro had never been effectively subdued. For them
battle with the Turks was partly crusade, partly pastime and partly
destiny. Their example and that of the French inspired their
kinsmen to rebel. By 1817 they had succeeded in establishing an
autonomous Serbian state centred in Belgrade under Turkish
suzerainty. There were then two Serbian states, Serbia and

Montenegro, neither of them completely free, but neither completely under the Turkish yoke. The area between these two states and to the south was also inhabited by Serbs; that to the north-west, mainly by Croats, who were cousins. They have since joined in a 'south Slav' state: Yugoslavia. Throughout our period both Serbian states followed a 'national' policy and were bent on expansion and the annexation of 'Serbia Irredenta'. The French revolutionaries had shown what force nationalism could unlock, but the inspiration for the Balkan peoples was indigenous. Nationalism there was not simply a French import. The drive for national liberation and unification spread to the Greeks, who obtained a measure of independence through war in the 1820s but continued to work for more territory throughout the nineteenth century. The Romanians were next to obtain independence piecemeal. The process was also not complete until the First World War. The Bulgars began gradually obtaining independence in the 1870s. The one remaining nationality, the Albanians, made no progress until after 1900. The pattern is clear: diplomacy centred on the 'nation' rather than on the state received its strongest and most consistent impetus from the Balkans and not from the older, larger and more sophisticated nations in west and central Europe.

The policy of Austria was necessarily and firmly state-oriented. The Russian line was almost as consistent in this respect. France, Spain and Britain were nation-states of sorts and so special reference to the popular needs of the nation was not needed. Although neither Bismarck nor Cavour was an outright nationalist their work did powerfully boost nationalism. Two things however ought to be noted. First, in both cases the work of unification was completed in one decade. It was therefore an episode and not a continuing factor throughout the century. Second, Italian and German unification came when the Balkan movement was well under way. The point is merely that our twentieth-century identification of states with nations owes much more to Balkan history than many of us realize. An important modern force was at work in the backward Balkans.

If the object of diplomacy changed from personal disputes between rulers to the state and then the people themselves understood as nations, so too did the subject. Foreign policy before 1789 was governed by princes who carefully calculated what was in their own and their state's interest. *Raison d'état*, in other words rational policy, was oriented on the prince as well as the state. Some princes were conservative, others liberal, but there was no political doctrine and no organized party behind it. As social, political and economic power slipped from the hands of princes and into those of patricians, political doctrine became important. First the liberals formed loose associations, and then in reaction the conservatives did as well. In line with the Romantic Movement ideological politics gained ground which was, as ever, mixed with considerations of self-preservation and self-advancement. Until the failure of the 1848 revolutions international politics bore the stamp of ideological conflict. The Holy Alliance of the Eastern Powers was by no means as silly as is often argued. It was a force for stability. The opponents of the Eastern Powers favoured gradual change in a vaguely liberal (but not democratic) direction. Britain, France, and for a while, the two Iberian countries (the 'Quadruple Alliance') formed a less cohesive group since although they favoured some change, they also were very suspicious of one another. There can be no doubt, however, that the moderately liberal group opposed the conservative one and that ideology, general political philosophy, was far more important than in the eighteenth century. During the 1848 revolutions ideology on all sides seemed ineffective and so both the conservatives and the liberals became more hard-headed, that is, more realistic. In international affairs the sea change came during the Crimean War and will be discussed briefly later on. The course of the revolution a half-dozen years beforehand suggested a tougher approach to politics. The diplomats tried it out in the Crimean War. The new 'realism' is what we call *realpolitik*. It is associated with Bismarck but he was not its author, nor was the approach to politics especially German. Indeed the trend towards realism can be seen in many fields and many countries.

We may regard the ideological politics of the pre-1848 period as that of the articulate noblemen pushed by the advancing well-to-do middle classes. When they realized in mid-century that the path of political advancement was stony, they sought another avenue. It was a shift in attitude amongst conquering patricians. The leading diplomatists, all naturally noblemen, were able to steer events. Many tried to continue their way on familiar conservative tracks, but some set their compass in a more realistic direction. The first fifteen years of *realpolitik* were hectic. Four major, but brief, wars followed the Crimean conflict, and the map of central Europe was completely redrawn. These changes were all reasonable, for nowhere did the victors overreach themselves. They neither sought nor attained anything merely for the sake of conquest. But when the mid-Victorian boom was followed by an economic down-swing after 1873 lasting twenty-three years, attitudes hardened. Statesmen thought that, if a bit of realism had worked well, more of it would work even better. Rivalry between the powers intensified and the vision of statesmen narrowed. They looked for something to snatch on the cheap. A sign of the changing atmosphere was the war in 1877–8 between Russia and Turkey. It profoundly modified the Balkan peninsula: Montenegro, Serbia and Romania gained independence; the first two and Greece acquired extra territory; the nucleus of a Bulgarian state was established. The results were not unreasonable, and so fit into the pattern of the previous five conflicts, but they emerged from an important climb-down by Russia following its attempt at a more revolutionary change. In Africa the going was much easier. The 'scramble' for that continent in the 1880s was that degenerate form of realism which we may call naturalism. Thus we move from rather lofty idealism interwoven, to be sure, with self-interest, through a kind of realism in some ways reminiscent of the eighteenth century to serious and less cautious greed. In the 1880s this scramble caused no immediate harm in Europe, but the underlying narrow selfishness led, almost inevitably, in the direction of serious confrontation. In the 1880s men with vision could foresee trouble. The era of the patricians was waning. Rather than inheriting the liberalism and optimism of some of them the plebians took on the self-centred hardness of the others. By 1890 they had begun to challenge the patricians for political power, but could not replace them until after the First World War.

One does not have to be an economic determinist to believe that these trends were connected with the accelerating pace of the Industrial Revolution, which destroyed autocratic Europe and enabled the patricians to advance and then to be overtaken by others. One can also see the connection with the long waves in the economy. The cautious nature of international and domestic politics during the first part of the century reflects an economy lacking vigour. The mid-Victorian boom was the first sustained continental boom in modern times and documents clearly the increasing integration of Europe. That this period of supreme optimism should have witnessed a series of calculated rather than outrageous wars is not surprising. Nor is it odd that during the first long European depression which followed, peace at home was maintained but was accompanied by a wild and in some ways pointless scramble for African territory.

When Napoleon's Empire collapsed in 1814 and its make-shift revival was defeated at Waterloo a year later peace with France was concluded on each occasion in Paris. These were the first and second treaties of Paris. The map of Europe was concurrently redrawn in Vienna. If we regard all three agreements for the sake of simplicity as the Vienna settlement, there are two important things to be said about it. First, it was by far the most important and enduring peace settlement in recent history. There was nothing comparable in the hundred years preceding or succeeding Vienna. The Congress of Paris (1856) and Berlin (1878) were by contrast of little significance. The Congress at Versailles (1919) attempted similarly great things, but within two decades its work had crumbled, and the statesmen in Versailles were not entirely blameless. After the Second World War there was neither a congress nor a peace agreement with Germany. Indeed almost all of the following dozens of smaller conflicts still await a formal peace settlement.

Second, the Vienna agreement created a balance of power in Europe. A balance, meaning a true equilibrium of several powers, had not been achieved by earlier treaties, nor would it be achieved by later ones. The uniqueness of Vienna is worth noting because none of the statesmen at the Congress really wanted a true balance – not even Castlereagh, who very largely got his way as far as the European balance was concerned. He reckoned, correctly, that his country's non-European holdings were worth more in the long run than territorial gains in Europe.

An equilibrium in Europe of five approximately equal powers was a new situation. The 'natural' state of Europe in modern times seemed to be one in which one ruler dominated the rest. First it was a Habsburg, and for almost two hundred years prior to Vienna a Bourbon king. He had the ascendancy and his state enjoyed a hegemony justified by cultural, economic and military pre-dominance. The idea of a *prépondérance légitime* was not challenged as such. The leading power usually only faced an opposing coalition when it overreached itself. The smaller powers would unite, not to oppose ascendancy, only outright domination. We have a good example of this during the twenty-five years of turmoil before the Congress of Vienna. European statesmen therefore faced an entirely new situation after 1815. They had to devise a means of voluntary co-operation amongst relative equals. France was the traditional leader and still had considerable inherent strength, but the others were determined to thwart any aspirations for revived hegemony. Russia was the only other country with sufficient military might to aspire to ascendancy, but it was backward politically, economically and culturally and so caused a good deal of fear rather than mere animosity. Much effort at Vienna had been expended to keep the tsar from benefiting excessively from the peace settlement, and uneasiness about Russian ambitions remained until the Crimean War.

Before the advent of Louis Napoleon neither France nor Russia dared make a direct challenge in Europe. But each sought to probe the possibilities by an active policy in the Mediterranean. France tried to extend its influence in Spain and Egypt and make firm annexations in Algeria. Russia wanted to fight or to dominate Turkey. France had been a traditional friend of Turkey and was apparently willing to concede the Russians something there, but when it came to a trial of strength between Turkey's vassal, Egypt, and the sultan in 1840, France supported the former and Russia the latter. Europe's two restless powers collided in Turkey. In Europe itself they were more cautious.

Given the unsteady equilibrium in Europe after 1815 it was possible for Metternich to dominate international politics. Austria was weaker than Russia or France but more wedded to the status quo than either of these two powers. Prussia was nearly as strong as Austria at this stage, and quite prepared to follow rather than lead. The Habsburg emperors were the traditional leaders in Germany, having been the Holy Roman Emperors until 1806. And Austria had the key role in the German Confederation which was set up in 1815 to replace the defunct empire. Austria also possessed in Metternich Europe's most skilful diplomat. His policy was to keep the powers united on the basis of a virtually unchanging status quo. The Holy Alliance was one way of doing this since it tied one of the restless powers to it. Given the co-operation of three out of five great powers, periodic meetings, or congresses, would work in the same direction. There were early eighteenth-century precedents for such meetings, but the idea seemed practicable anyhow and emerged out of the intense negotiations between the powers towards the end of the Napoleonic wars and then, of course, the Vienna Congress itself. The first meeting at Aachen in 1818 went well and brought the French back into the system. In 1820 trouble began during the second meeting at Troppau in northern Moravia. There were revolutionary disturbances that year in Spain, Portugal and Italy which could, if they progressed, disturb the international balance. It was decided to suppress them. Lack of trust among the allies led to suspicions that the intervening powers would perhaps fish in troubled waters. Britain was the first country to withdraw from military co-operation, but not because of any fondness for revolution. Although British statesmen were less worried about it than the others, suspicion of them was the real motive. After the successful 1830 Revolution in France Europe became divided into two informal camps, a 'liberal' West and a conservative East. Each group contained a restless power, biding its time but nevertheless inclined more to action than to inaction.

Since the powers had little experience in the politics of give and take, the status quo was precarious. As the memory and fear of a European-wide war gradually receded, the likelihood of a new trial of strength increased. It is not true that economic growth had led to an appreciable shift in power relationships by mid-century. These changes occurred, for the most part, after 1870. The relative strength of the powers was pretty much what it had been in 1815 or 1816.

The importance of the Crimean War lies in the fact that it was a trial of strength between the two contenders for ascendancy in Europe, Russia and France. It eliminated the one and thus boosted the other into a slightly elevated position above the rest, the first step to true ascendancy. The war also marked an appreciable change in the approach to international politics. A series of further trials of strength followed which could have led to the re-establishment of true French hegemony, but they did not. The Crimean War was the great divide in international relations during the nineteenth century. For that reason a few words about its origin, its effects and the character of the diplomatic exchanges during its course would be in order.

With the collapse of the 1848 revolutions those who had hoped for or feared change began to strip off their idealism and don sturdier clothing. The change in approach was immediately visible in international affairs: solidarity amongst conservative powers seemed less important than the struggle for power. Before 1848 the Prussian kings, Frederick William III until 1840 and then Frederick William IV, had slavishly followed the lead of the Austrian emperors, Francis till 1835 and Ferdinand afterwards. In 1849 and 1850 Frederick William IV challenged Francis Joseph, the new emperor, by putting forward a plan for German unity without Austria. This led to a famous showdown between Austria and Prussia in November 1850 at Olmütz in Northern Moravia, where Russia firmly backed Austria and forced Prussia to capitulate. Many Prussians keenly felt the humiliation. The Holy Alliance powers were clearly and deeply divided. Relations between France and Britain, the liberal West, were characterized by similar insouciance. The Don Pacifico affair, also in 1850, was supremely trivial, yet it led to the withdrawal of the French ambassador from London. Pacifico was a shady character of doubtful British nationality who sought redress for a personal wrong which had occurred in Athens. This was not the only time that Palmerston played the role of diplomatic picador, but at mid-century he seemed inordinately fond of empty victories, when emphasis instead on liberal solidarity with France might well have dampened some of Louis Napoleon's ambitions. The unifying force of the ideals of liberalism and conservatism was on the wane.

We can see the new recklessness most clearly in the policy of Nicholas I and Louis Napoleon. The crisis leading to the Crimean War was mainly their doing. In 1829, when the Turks had been beaten by Russia, and some of the Greeks had gained independence, Nicholas decided to dominate the Turks through diplomacy rather than with his armies. He followed this line for twenty years. The experience of 1848 and its aftermath convinced him that Russia was strong, for it had intervened and restored order in central Europe and Turkey. Nicholas thought he had proved his superior strength and earned the gratitude and therefore the compliance of Austria and Prussia. Napoleonic France would be paralysed by Britain – which he believed was friendly as well. The time had come therefore to steal a march on the others and tip the European balance in his favour; the reward, ascendancy in Europe, was a lustrous prize. Nicholas knew that any serious attempt to snatch it would probably lead to war which he was hoping to avoid. Nevertheless from December 1852 on he carefully considered it. The dispatch in February 1853 of his special agent, Menshikov, to Constantinople, who started roaring like a lion and ended bleating like a lamb, was quickly followed by the occupation of the Danubian principalities, soon to become Romania but then a part of Turkey. Instead of concealing his warlike intention Nicholas exaggerated it with a display of faultless clumsiness. A few years earlier Russia had been, it seemed, the hinge on which conservative Europe turned. When it fractured so too did the belief in conservative solidarity.

Nicholas was prepared for adventure. But so was Louis Napoleon, and he was first off the mark. He wanted to keep on good terms with Britain and so avoid at least one of his illustrious uncle's mistakes. He also wanted to move France ahead of the other European powers by undermining the 1815 settlement. A challenge to Russia at Constantinople was brilliantly calculated to serve this purpose. When in the spring of 1850 Napoleon advanced claims on behalf of Turkish Christians he knew that Russia would take offence. The vast majority of them were Orthodox, and Russia had acted as their protector of sorts for many years. Napoleon was perfectly aware of this, but he forced his claims on the Turks with Palmerstonian bluster. In December 1852 the Turks yielded. Russia rose to the challenge. Like Nicholas, Louis Napoleon hoped to gain the trick without war, but like Nicholas he pursued a goal which virtually necessitated it. The Crimean War was therefore no accident. The constraint of ideological solidarity had only just kept European rivalry in check beforehand. Both France and Russia put it aside, and in the spirit of post-1848 rigour, reached for Europe's greatest political prize: hegemony.

The role of Britain and especially Palmerston and Stratford Canning (who went to Constantinople just when the trouble started) has been carefully studied. The reason for this is not that they were the crucial actors – because they were not. It is because a good deal more source material is available. Access to the Russian archives is not easy and in any case Nicholas was by no means as straightforward and consistent as is usually thought. Russian policy, therefore, is not readily traced. Napoleon too was always secretive; the surviving material can be seen but leaves plenty of room for uncertainty. So we know the workings of British policy best. Public opinion was much more aroused than in France. However, it did not cause the war; British policy was influenced only a little by it. The cabinet felt simply that of the two dangers to the peace – the French and the Russian threat – the second one was the more substantial. The peril was not really ideological since from a Christian and liberal point of view the tsar was probably preferable to the sultan. It was a question of power politics.

The war between Napoleon and Nicholas ended the period of 'unnatural' and tense balance. The purpose of the struggle was to see which would subsequently lead Europe. The magnitude of the final victory would determine the relative strength of the dominant power.

Otto von Bismarck was the Prussian delegate to the German Confederation which met in Frankfurt. He exhorted his government to follow a virile policy of state egoism, known as *realpolitik*. But of all the great powers at the time Prussia's policy remained closer to the pre-1848 pattern. The king and his ministers did not want to spoil relations with either Russia or Austria and so followed a statesmanlike policy of wavering neutrality. The other cabinets followed a 'realistic' line. The head of the Austrian government, Buol, who ran the Foreign Ministry as well, was the only leading statesman who sincerely worked for peace. He realized, as had Metternich before him, that Austria needed stability. He tried as much as he could to bring the opponents together at the conference table. But it was apparent that his heart was with the West: although he talked conciliation he also threatened the Russians repeatedly. He forced them to evacuate the Danubian principalities at the start of the conflict and his ultimatum at the end finally brought them into the conference room. He did indeed, as Schwarzenberg had promised, astonish the Russians with his ingratitude. Although his intentions were pure, his approach was tough, and the result in the short run was favourable to Vienna. In the long term it was not. In the 1860s Austria could have used Russian support, but failed to obtain it.

When the crisis broke, the British were on the sidelines, but as war approached, and during it, they became more belligerent than the French. Napoleon had started the tussle with his religious demands and his troops made the major contribution to ultimate victory. But after the fall of Sebastopol in September 1855 he worked for peace. Throughout, the French and British bullied the Austrians and Piedmontese and tried to outwit one another. Palmerston's beau ideal (war aims) and Napoleon's plans to revise the European map were far-reaching and remarkably similar in many respects. Each forged revolutionary nationalism into a weapon against the tsar. The fairly liberal *entente cordiale* of pre-1848 days had crumbled to an unscrupulous power struggle with revolution as an ingredient.

The Piedmontese joined the struggle fearing that if Austria also did, and they did not, they would have to face two large and disagreeable neighbours. France and Britain made this clear. The hope of subsequent reward gained from allying with the western powers was a less important motive than fear of isolation. Here the pattern of short-term calculation repeats itself.

Russian policy leading to war was of the new type – assertive and calculating. Once war came, it reverted to the old pattern of attempting to reanimate the Holy Alliance and save national honour. This was an interlude, lasting until Gorchakov finally replaced Nesselrode a year after the death of Nicholas and when the Paris Congress came to a close. Gorchakov had been ambassador in Vienna and thus witnessed at first hand not only the 'treachery' of Austria, but also the machinations of political realism. As Foreign Minister he tried to marry realism to Russian nationalism. And it was through the tutelage of him, the Russian 'Caravaggio', that Bismarck – the 'Raphael' as Gorchakov generously and colourfully put it – refined his knowledge of politics.

There is much for soldiers to learn from the military events of the war. The lesson for politicians was clear and simple; it was that Russia's pretensions had outstripped its power. The challenge to the status quo had been genuine but it was easily checked.

Nicholas had foolishly forced the pace from the start. When he died early in 1855 his very much more intelligent adviser, Nesselrode, could influence his son, the new tsar Alexander II. They were wise enough to conclude peace before defeat had become decisive. As a result, French domination in Europe for the next fourteen years was also less secure than it might have been. The international balance, created in 1815, had after all not been completely overturned, although for the rest of his reign Napoleon was Europe's leading statesman.

With a slight French advantage over the other powers after Crimea, Europe was nearing its 'customary' state in which one cabinet exercised hegemony. The Austro-French war of 1859 and its aftermath brought it closer. The origins of this war are the purest example we have of nineteenth-century *realpolitik*. It was rationally calculated and precipitated. The diplomatic conspirators, Louis Napoleon and Cavour, remained in complete control until almost the end, when Napoleon pulled out of the war prematurely. In the short run each got less than he had bargained for, but by 1861 each had more. Piedmont acquired an almost united Italy, at the expense of Austria's informal empire. In addition to some territory (Nice and Savoy) France gained in standing where Austria had lost. During the Crimean War and at the Congress Napoleon had toyed with the idea of a major redrawing of the European map which would have involved Austria losing its direct Italian possessions (Lombardy and Venetia) and gaining the Danubian principalities (Moldavia and Wallachia) in exchange. In the event, not only did the Habsburg Empire lose some territory and much influence in Italy; the Danubian principalities united and strengthened at the same time. So it lost out both ways. The eclipse of Russia after Sebastopol and the intense dislike of Vienna in St Petersburg were only minor factors in 1859–61. Italy surely would have been united anyhow and so also, perhaps, would Romania. Russian neutrality during the three subsequent wars was very much more important. The German policy of Nicholas and Nesselrode had been to work for a balance between Francis Joseph and Frederick William in central Europe, which would enable Russia to play a decisive role whenever needed. Between 1848 and 1850 Prussia seemed on the verge of getting the upper hand, so the tsar sided with Austria to even the balance. After Sebastopol this policy remained unchanged. But the new tsar, Alexander II, was more anti-Austrian. Prussia was the only significant power in the mid-1850s not hostile to Russia so when a revolution broke out in Russian Poland in 1863, it alone was outwardly friendly, in fact embarrassingly so. During 1848 and its aftermath Russia had interfered diplomatically to keep Prussia well away from the straits between Denmark and Sweden by opposing it on the Elbe Duchies, Holstein in the south, which was completely German, and Schleswig to the north, which was half German. In contrast, when Austria and Prussia went to war against Denmark in 1864 and took Schleswig-Holstein, Russia was nervous but did not interfere much. Vienna and Berlin co-operated, so the dispute did not seem to affect the balance between the two in central Europe, and, after all, Prussia had fully earned some consideration from Russia.

At the time of the Danish war most statesmen believed that the chief danger to peace and the European status quo emanated from France. It had just annexed Nice and Savoy, and was keen, it seemed, to take advantage of civil war in the United States and to build a Mexican empire.

When war broke out between the two erstwhile allies in 1866, most observers anticipated a long struggle, such as that which had taken place in the eighteenth century. Napoleon, certainly, thought he would have plenty of time to make plans and would anyway be able to move in at the end and possibly annex the left bank of the Rhine. The Russians were not on the Austrian side but they also did not foresee a rapid Prussian victory. That victory, when it came, ended the German Confederation. Prussia annexed some territory and set up The North German Confederation, which it then dominated. This was a state covering the northern half of the former *Bund* and so seemed inconsiderable. It is clear to us now that the decline in Austrian power during the previous seven or eight years was precipitous, though at the time it did not seem so great.

As part of his programme to redraw the European map and, incidentally, add bits to France, Napoleon had backed the Italian, Romanian and Polish national movements. With the Prussian victory of 1866 it looked very much as if the Germans were rapidly moving towards unification. Had Napoleon been ideologically consistent, he should have supported it. But there was a different problem here. There were at least as many Germans as Frenchmen. United they might well be powerful rivals in a way that the Italians, to say nothing of the Poles or Romanians, could not be. Since the break-up of the great German Empire after Frederick II in the high Middle Ages French security had depended to a large degree on a disunited and therefore weak central Europe. The Prussian victory in 1866 did not, as it happened, immediately alter the situation sufficiently to make much difference, but Napoleon knew that a greater degree of unification would. He knew also that Bismarck was not averse to a move in that direction and that a successful war against Prussia might well be the kind of undertaking which could complete French hegemony in Europe. Louis Napoleon lacked not only the military genius of his uncle, but also his demonic determination to see his adventures through. In the Crimea he withdrew when he had achieved his main goal, although his British allies were keen to press on. He pulled out of the Italian war for a similar reason. He retreated from Mexico when America threatened to make things hot for him. These three abrupt policy reversals are a sign of political astuteness: they were the right decisions. But the kind of man who would get these things right would go wrong when it was a question of working unrelentingly for hegemony. Napoleon wanted to play Europe's first fiddle, but he lacked determination, consistency and flair. He knew that the French army needed reforming, that is, more men in uniform and better artillery, and he worked for improvements. But he did not try hard enough. He thought that the French army was better than the Prussian forces. It probably was, but it was also badly outnumbered.

Napoleon did not lack courage, so when the crisis came in July 1870 he was prepared to try his luck, as was Bismarck. Neither had worked unremittingly for war, but each was fully prepared to let things go that far. The struggle on the French side was for hegemony, on the German side it was for unification. The result of the German victory was that the two contenders swapped relative power positions. Bismarck obtained the sort of slight advantage that Napoleon had possessed during the last fourteen years of his reign.

It was likely that the Germans would at some stage try to turn their slight advantage into full hegemony. There were two ways of doing this. War was the traditional method, and this the Germans tried in 1914. The other method was new: economic and demographic development. Germany's slight edge on the others in 1871 was vastly extended by 1914. Superiority in numbers and economic as well as military ascendancy had been attained, but political dominance had not. This was the missing ingredient. The late 1870s and 1880s were a period of almost continuous depression which dampened German economic growth. This was also a period of mass emigration, so population expansion was kept within bounds. By 1890, therefore, the power position in Europe had not yet appreciably changed since 1871: the Germans had a slight advantage, and the inherent instability of the system remained.

There was only one further war, from 1871 to 1890 – the Russo-Turkish contest in 1877–8, one which has already been mentioned. The war marked the re-entry of Russia on the international scene. By this time that scene had radically changed: Russian power was much less, relatively, than in the first half-century, even if Russian pretensions were not. But it was much more important that the dominant power, Germany, was now on the Russian frontier. And Austria had sunk in relative power through its own defeats and through Prussian victories. The disparity in economic development was also beginning to matter. The Habsburg monarchy was simply falling behind in the race for economic improvement. After the Franco-Prussian war Gorchakov tried to resume the policy of balancing Austria against Germany. So the eighteen years of Siberian frigidity between Vienna and St Petersburg from mid-1854 to September 1872 rapidly thawed. This was the necessary prerequisite for a more active Russian policy in the Balkans which was adopted again in 1875. But this revived tension with Austria. Gorchakov's policy of a central European balance had therefore to be supplemented by a Europe-wide balance. He looked to France as much as to Austria for some counter-weight to Germany.

In summary, the twenty-five years after 1830 were a period of a fairly true balance of power in Europe. During the next fourteen to fifteen years the French had a slight ascendancy. For the final nineteen years the Germans had that fragile advantage the significance of which before 1890 must not be exaggerated.

Bismarckian Europe, of the 1870s and 1880s, was inherently more stable than the preceding period. Unlike Louis Napoleon, Bismarck was determined to maintain his tenuous hold on leadership, without a series of wars. That is because he had a more realistic view of what was possible. Whereas Napoleon strove erratically for hegemony, Bismarck had a very keen sense of Germany's precarious position. The country was after all only united in 1871 and had risen rapidly to that point, that is, there was no tradition of domination to look back on. In the nineteen years between unification and his retirement in 1890 Bismarck's main problem was simple, and he must be given credit for facing it. He could seek hegemony – in some ways the most natural line to follow; or he could make the existing unstable situation work for him; there was also a third alternative: he could relax and withdraw inside fortress Germany. These policies involved varying degrees of activity, and each of the three was inherently risky. Clearly, the first, adventurous line was most hazardous. Bismarck had led his country through three short wars. He had benefited from the fact that would-be opponents were more concerned about possible French aggression or other problems than they were about Prussia. After unification his opponents were much more on their toes. During the first four years Bismarck considered, rather hesitantly, the possibility of an ambitious foreign policy. He knew the dangers, but he thought he could probe the limits, and try the patience of others to see what he could get away with. There was no plan of aggression, he was merely examining his options.

After their defeat in 1871 the French were recovering rapidly. Bismarck sought to slow this down by a policy of random sabre-rattling, and early in 1875 by calculated bullying. The climax in May 1875 was a celebrated war-scare in which Germany was isolated. This was a situation which could lead to war, but did not. Bismarck had the sense to back down: faced with a choice of war or humiliation, he chose the latter. Subsequently his line was active but generally cautious. He attempted to perpetuate tension in Europe for his own purpose, that of attaining security through balancing and not trying to abolish tension. The risk here was clear: if tension remained high, small problems could easily lead to more than a flare-up. There was no guarantee in the long run that statesmen would be as able and as conscientious as they were in the 1870s and 1880s. Bismarck's policy realistically aimed at the preservation of peace and thus the furtherance of German security. But he sailed perilously close to the wind, and his tactics could be erratic and harsh. His imitators, like his bard Treitschke, saw his vigour but not his fundamental reasonableness. There was an element of inevitability in the deterioration of his approach to naked power politics, or naturalism. But it was less his fault than that of his successors.

Bismarck's third alternative would have been a policy of watchful self-limitation. The danger here was that rivals would profit from German modesty and make such gains as to outstrip the new empire. Bismarck was by nature and conviction unwilling to consider this approach, and the position of his country was perhaps too uncertain to make it viable in 1871. But after a very few years it should have been clear to all that the likelihood of the empire being outstripped rapidly dwindled. Bismarck's immediate successor in office, Caprivi, realized this, but of all the imperial chancellors he was the only one to do so.

If the first part of our period bore the impress of Nesselrode and Metternich and the second that of Louis Napoleon, the third was shaped to an even greater degree by Bismarck. His three predecessors experienced failure and disgrace. Bismarck did not. His approach was not 'politics with the idealism left out', but to many it did look this way. Nothing succeeds like success. Bismarck's toughness stood out; his moderation did not. So the one was copied, the other was not.

Further reading

SURVEYS
R. Albrecht-Carrié, *A Diplomatic History of Europe since the Congress of Vienna* (London, 1973) – inelegant but very sound; M. Anderson, *The Eastern Question, 1774–1923: a Study in International Relations* (London, 1966) – an excellent survey of a key issue, good bibliographies; F. Bridge and R. Bullen, *The Great Powers and the European States System, 1815–1914* (London, 1980) – the best brief introduction; W. Langer, *European Alliances and Alignments, 1871–1890* (New York, 1956) (edn with updated bibliographies) – absolutely indispensable although uncritical of Bismarck; A. Sked (ed.), *Europe's Balance of Power, 1815–1848* (London, 1979) – a fine collection of essays; A. Taylor, *The Struggle for Mastery in Europe, 1848–1918* (Oxford, 1954) – a mine of information and clever comment.

THEORETICAL WORKS
L. Dehio, *The Precarious Balance: the Politics of Power in Europe, 1494–1945* (London, 1963) – magisterial overall account of ideas governing foreign policy; F. Hinsley, *Power and the Pursuit of Peace: Theory and Practice in the History of Relations between States* (Cambridge, 1963) and *Nationalism and International System* (London, 1973) – two thoughtful essays.

SPECIAL WORKS
R. Bullen, *Palmerston, Guizot and the Collapse of the Entente Cordiale* (London, 1974) – surveys Anglo-French relations from 1830 to 1848; D. Johnson, *Guizot: Aspects of French History, 1787–1874* (London, 1963) – contains a good chapter on foreign policy.

W. Mosse, *The European Powers and the German Question, 1848–71,* with special reference to England and Russia (Cambridge, 1958) – excellent study with a good summary at the end; N. Rich, *Why the Crimean War? A Cautionary Tale* (London, 1985) – a competent recent treatment; P. Schroeder, *Austria, Great Britain and the Crimean War: the Destruction of the European Concert* (London, 1972) – a scholarly account.

W. Baumgart, *The Peace of Paris, 1856: Studies in War, Diplomacy and Peace-making* (Oxford, 1981) – authoritative handbook; D. Beales, *England and Italy, 1859–1860* (London, 1961) – clear and concise exposition of the English side of the question; D. Goldfrank, *The Origins of the Crimean War* (London, 1994); F. Coppa, *The Origins of the Italian Wars of Independence* (London, 1992); W. Carr, *The Origins of the Wars of German Unification* (London, 1991).

G. Kennan, *The Decline of Bismarck's European Order: Franco-Russian Relations, 1875–1890* (Princeton, NJ, 1979) – a fluent account; W. Medlicott, *The Congress of Berlin and After* (London, 1963) (2nd edn with new introduction) – the only detailed work on the Congress; E. Pottinger, *Napoleon III and the German Crisis, 1865–1966* (Cambridge, MA, 1968) – deals with a crucial issue; L. Steefel, *Bismarck, the Hohenzollern Candidacy and the Origins of the Franco-German War of 1870* (Cambridge, MA, 1963) – well-written but uncritical of Bismarck; B. Waller, *Bismarck at the Crossroads: the Re-orientation of German Foreign Policy after the Congress of Berlin* (London, 1974) – on the background of the dual alliance, critical of Bismarck.

B. Jelavich, *A History of the Balkans: Eighteenth and Nineteenth Centuries* (Cambridge, 1983) – one of two competent surveys on this subject by the same author.

INDIVIDUAL COUNTRIES

F. Bridge, *From Sadowa to Sarajevo: the Foreign Policy of Austria-Hungary* (London, 1972) – intelligent and vigorous account; I. Geiss, *German Foreign Policy, 1871–1914* (London, 1976) – good survey from the 'Fischer' (neo-Marxist) point of view; B. Jelavich, *A Century of Russian Foreign Policy, 1814–1914* (New York, 1964) – covers the ground, and *The Habsburg Empire in European Affairs, 1814–1918* (Chicago, IL, 1969) – lucid, concise, well-organized; P. Kennedy, *The Rise of Anglo-German Antagonism, 1860–1914* (London, 1980) – full treatment; C. Lowe and F. Marzari, *Italian Foreign Policy, 1870–1940* (London, 1975) – useful survey.

11

Europe and the wider world

BRUCE WALLER

The power struggle inside Europe was not confined to that continent. The battlefield had extended across the globe in the sixteenth century. Ever since, European eruptions reverberated along political fault lines selectively devastating even the remotest corners. These domestic struggles fought in exotic lands, and the relations of European states with the wider world, were fundamentally different from the relations between princes and states at home. What little mutual respect existed there was virtually absent in dealings with other continents. Whenever Europeans had a clear advantage in sophistication and technology, and the incentive to use it, firm control was established. Vast colonial empires were created. The force behind them, imperialism, is as old as man's history. But in modern times it assumed special prominence and affected in one way or another European relations with the rest of the world.

What is imperialism? Is it the search for, and attempt to retain, complete control over foreign peoples and territory? Or does partial or indirect control count as well? Let us look at the second possibility first. In his *Diplomacy of Imperialism*, W. L. Langer defines it this way: 'The rule or control, political or economic, direct or indirect, of one state, nation or people over other similar groups, or perhaps one might better say the disposition, urge or striving to establish such rule or control' (1935, p. 67). It should be perfectly obvious that this carefully worded definition is an attempt to accommodate various kinds of imperialism as well as a range of objections to more straightforward and narrow definitions. It resulted from half a century of debate on modern

imperialism. While it leaves nothing out, it also includes a myriad
of phenomena which sensible people would not regard as
imperialism. The phrase 'direct political or economic rule' is fairly
concrete. But what does control mean? Or what about the urge of
a people to establish indirect control over another similar group?
If this is imperialism, then the word is nearly synonymous with
'ambition' and thus meaningless. It is futile to attempt a definition
to cover all variations of a complex social process because it will
include too much which is irrelevant. The classic wide definition
is useless. At the other extreme, D. K. Fieldhouse seems to regard
imperialism as direct political control of foreign areas. This
definition is as narrow as Langer's is wide, yet it is very much closer
to the reality of nineteenth-century empires.

Prior to the Declaration of Independence by thirteen North
American colonies on 4 July 1776 economic control over depend-
encies was tight, but direct political dominion was the precondition for it. In contrast to the nineteenth-century empires, the
overwhelming mass of the early empires, established from the
sixteenth to the eighteenth century, comprised settlement areas.
Most of them followed the lead of the North American colonies,
and eventually broke away from their motherland when Europe
was weakened through years of strife inaugurated by the French
Revolution. In the decade and a half following Waterloo almost all
of South America became free from Spanish and Portuguese rule,
and within Europe itself Serbia and Greece had begun to break
away from Turkey. The process of decolonization was well
underway and many Europeans felt that it would continue. Yet
the recovery of Europe brought a tightening grip over the
remaining possessions and the gradual spread of rule to other
areas. But economic restrictions were more relaxed than in the past
or in the years following 1890. The exclusion of competitors from
the colonies, so typical of the earlier empires, was almost totally
abandoned, and tariff regulations dwindled. The colonies were
political entities. European economic control of areas other than
outright colonies strengthened, and in some areas, such as
Turkey, Egypt and Tunis, it greatly annoyed the local leaders. But
Turkey retained a good deal of independence throughout. And
Egypt and Tunis were not conquered for economic gain but rather
for obvious reasons of power politics and strategy. The former
South American colonies needed British capital, ingenuity and

trade, but avoided indirect colonization. Fieldhouse's definition is probably too narrow for the period after 1890, but for the earlier period it is workable.

Imperialism was the salient feature of relations with the outside world. The imperial spirit was ubiquitous. Whether it met with brief success as in strife-torn Mexico (which was under French sway for a couple of years in the mid-1860s), partial success as in China (which, starting with 1842, turned over Hong Kong to the British and relinquished sovereignty over various other ports), or near failure as in Japan (where only the ports were opened to foreigners in 1854), the conduct of European powers was broadly similar. Imperialism was clearly not universally efficacious; reasonably strong states could resist.

The imperious attitude had an ancient and venerable tradition going back to the crusades, when knights could gain remission for sin by spiking a heathen. It is hard to believe that the British would have tried to force opium on Italians; but they did exactly this on the Chinese without apparently worrying much whether it squared with the contemporaneous and sustained campaign against the slave trade. (Indeed, slavery as such was not obnoxious to the British, only its harsher manifestations.)

There were two distinct phases of imperialism within our period. First there was the imperialism of free trade, the steady forward creep after 1830, this year being the great divide in nineteenth-century colonial history. From 1776 to about 1830 the empires had been collapsing in an ever increasing tempo. We may take the French advance into Algeria in 1830 as a clear sign that the lowest ebb had been reached and that the tide of empire would swell again. The conquest of Algeria, an area of great economic potential, was pursued not for the purpose of national enrichment but to regain dwindled self-confidence and to augment state power in a way still acceptable to France's neighbours. The Algerian adventure stood at the beginning of a trend; its motives were also characteristic for many if not most of the subsequent imperial gains.

For decades the acquisition of colonies proceeded at a leisurely pace. It was more of a tidying-up operation than planned or even purposeful expansion. Small strategically placed bases or coaling stations, such as Aden and Obok, were snapped up, the first by Britain in 1839 and the second by France in 1862. The operating radius of West and Equatorial African factors was extended. The only African area with any appreciable hinterland was the Cape Colony, which extended a good way from the coast. It was also the only African colony with a large number of European settlers. Algeria came a poor second. In the Pacific, apart from New Zealand, taken under British sovereignty in 1840, the new island possessions were unimportant. The vastest acquisitions were made by Russia in central and far eastern Asia and Sakhalin. Next in size came the British annexations throughout India in the two decades after 1830 followed by the extension of indirect mastery and the relentless march in the north-west to the borders of Afghanistan, and in the north-east into southern Burma. Control in Malaya was also expanded. Then there was the French advance into Indo-China radiating inland from Saigon. Finally we have a new element in what was otherwise a British, French and Russian show: the initiative of the Belgian king in the Congo Basin in the 1870s. By the end of that decade India was thoroughly under British sway, Russia had nearly completed her central Asian expansion, and France had perhaps a third of her subsequent Indo-Chinese empire. Apart from the major acquisition of Algeria and the expansion from the southern Cape, the map of Africa had not been radically changed.

This represented an impressive, but not breath-taking advance in European holdings abroad and went some way to make up for the more considerable losses in the half-century before 1830. There was little European opposition to the French advance into Algeria. But there was a series of disputes on non-European issues which were especially dangerous in the 1830s when the fate of Egypt was at stake, and also later when Mediterranean issues arose. Afterwards the cabinets jealously watched and contested any threatened change in the Mediterranean balance. By 1870 it was evident that easy acquisitions could not be made near Europe. The quarrels even spilled over into ostensibly unimportant disputes in the Pacific. For example, in the mid-1840s the fate of a few missionaries in Tahiti kindled fires of emotion amongst the informed citizenry of Paris and London. The French and British governments had to work overtime to find a solution. A lack of congruity between the triviality of the dispute and the stir it caused was particularly evident here, but not entirely uncharacteristic for the period.

By 1873 the situation obtaining since the onset of the Algerian campaign in 1830 had changed. It did not cause, but it clearly facilitated the subsequent headlong rush for colonies. Altered politics, evolving economic and cultural attitudes, and technological advance in critical areas occurred simultaneously. First of all, the unification of Italy and Germany had been concluded and the Austrians had found a seemingly workable compromise which strengthened not just the state but also the opposing national movements. National feelings had been fulfilled from Palermo to Königsberg and were encouraged elsewhere in south-eastern Europe. They had been liberal in orientation, but they gradually became aggressively illiberal. Further victories could not be won with patient persistence, only with the kind of determined toughness which would leave liberal compromises discounted. Then, there were changes in the economy. The fragile and poorly integrated European economy of the 1830s and 1840s had grown vigorously over the next two decades. Integration had progressed to such a degree that there was a strong European and even worldwide boom which ended abruptly in 1873, precipitated significantly by an American bank crash. The drive towards free trade was quickly reversed. As it gradually emerged that the depression was more than merely transient, statesmen each tried various means to protect their own country's well-being. To a new spirit of aggressive national and therefore popular political competitiveness was added an economic dimension. Finally, mid-century optimism and idealism were wearing thin. A more self-centred and disillusioned realism began to displace it.

The hitherto unparalleled scramble for colonies, especially in Africa, which we call the 'new imperialism', was a logical reaction to this altered political, economic and cultural environment, and it was greatly facilitated by medical and technological advances, which will be dealt with at the end of this chapter. Although the search for the precipitating incident is a popular party game with no answer acceptable to all, it might be said that just as the French move into Algeria initiated the era of free-trade expansion after a period of rapid contraction, so the French occupation of Tunis in 1881 precipitated the new imperialism. Important shifts in the Mediterranean balance of power were especially unwelcome because of the intrinsic value of the area and its proximity to Europe. France already had Algeria, directly to the south; thus

Tunis to the east of it was of enormous strategic importance. That is why the Italians were hoping to take it. Indeed most Europeans in Tunis were Italian. Of course, from a French point of view it would be a painful blow if Italy controlled both sides of the narrows which divide the Mediterranean approximately in the middle. The French moved in 1881 to forestall the Italians. By this time they were the only European nation to have made a significant advance in the area. A battle over it, or at least a scramble for compensation, was as nearly inevitable as anything can be in history. That Europe was spared a war speaks for the statesmanship of its leaders. Whether the Africans had to pay the price, or whether colonialism brought the torch of civilization, one cannot say with any authority. But it looks as if the occupation of Tunis fifty years after that of Algeria initiated the scramble for compensation. Or did it?

The Russo-Turkish War of 1877–8 was an even more disturbing event which brought conspicuous shifts in Europe itself and the Great Powers to the brink of war. The crisis was resolved in the 'June days' of Berlin in 1878 during the last of the great congresses before Paris in 1919. In Berlin the Balkan map was redrawn. Russia advocated a small gain for herself and large changes in favour of the Balkan Slavs. Austria and Britain successfully blocked some of these proposals and in a grand compromise paid themselves with Turkish territory; Austria took Bosnia-Herzegovina (part of present-day Yugoslavia) and Britain Cyprus. Germany had been marginally involved in the preceding crisis and so made only a small and temporarily secret gain attained in agreement with Austria. It gave her a better legal claim to Schleswig, which she already possessed. That left Italy and France with nothing. At the congress the French were given explicit but informal hints on Tunis; the Italians were offered rather more vague allusions to Tripoli, which was less valuable economically and strategically than their real object, Tunis. Thus the charged atmosphere created by the Russo-Turkish War and the Congress of Berlin enabled the occupation of Tunis in 1881 to precipitate the scramble. We can of course look further in the past, before 1878, and we will find signs pointing towards the 'new imperialism'. The machinations of Leopold, the Belgian king, in the Congo are often mentioned, but they were of negligible importance compared to that of events in the Balkans from 1875. And in 1878 the engine was finally set in motion. If we look to, say, the taking of Egypt in 1882 as the start of the scramble, we miss the significance of the earlier French coup and its connection with European power calculations.

One needs only to recall the possessions acquired during the 1880s to realize both the rapidity and smoothness of the advance and the change from unhurried, if also hotly contested, aggrandisement during the previous forty or fifty years.

In the three quarters of a century before the occupation of Tunis an area about four times the size of the Indian subcontinent was annexed to existing empires. In the following quarter-century at least this much was again added. By 1914 the only area still free from European rule and without a colonial history was a broad band of territory from Ethiopia to Japan with a branch southward into Siam. Never before had empires grown so vigorously. And until the Spanish-American war of 1898, they grew almost entirely on land not hitherto under European control.

During the Congress of Berlin in 1878 the British seizure of Cyprus was announced. Tunis went to France three years later and the next year, 1882, Britain took Egypt, thus re-establishing a rough and ready Mediterranean balance without war. This fact as much as any other probably stimulated the avarice and jealousy of others: the dash for colonies promised reward without danger.

Perhaps just as astonishing as the relatively peaceful outcome (from a European vantage point) of activity on the African shore of the Mediterranean was a shift in colonial initiative. The source was entirely new: the Belgian king and his 'philanthropic' association. The object was the geographic centre of Equatorial Africa, well away from the coast. Leopold II's preoccupation with the interior was untypical for the late 1870s and early 1880s. South African settlers were remorselessly pressing northwards and Rhodes obtained a concession for the land to be named after him in 1889, but, apart from this, attention in the 1880s was devoted to the coastline. During the 1890s the march from the sea and through the jungle and desert began.

At the beginning of the 1880s the coastal colonies of West Africa were many but small. In East Africa they were also far apart. By the end of the decade the coast had been almost completely divided between the French, British, Germans and Italians. In West Africa especially many of the colonies were expanded trading posts. In the east, however, most were entirely new initiatives.

In Asia the Russian advance was modest and had nearly run its course. The Indian north-western frontier was almost stabilized and not much changed in the 1880s. On the north-eastern frontier Upper Burma was taken. Working out from Saigon, France annexed the whole of Annam up to Hanoi. In the Pacific the pace of partition was more measured.

Everywhere except in the Dark Continent the speed of colonization was much what it had been in previous decades or slower. What was different about the 1880s was the 'scramble for Africa'. The explanation for this odd phenomenon should not be sought there but rather in the rationality and irrationality of Europeans.

What is the reason for imperialism in this period? The overriding point is that expansion abroad was a vast movement involving various powers and several hundred people in crucial positions. Such a large number of individuals from very different backgrounds could not possibly have thought on identical lines or acted on identical grounds.

Let us start with some basic considerations. J. A. Schumpeter argued eloquently that man's primitive combative instinct is a major element. The same could be said for much of man's thought and activity. The will to survive is strong, and since survival is always precarious, the desire to dominate other people and things is powerful because in this way security can be increased. Co-operation with others in the spirit of give and take works too, but augmenting one's own strength and reducing that of others offers more apparent security. This is a partly irrational element, always present. In times of uncertainty it is bound to figure prominently. This may be stating the obvious, but it does show that purely rational explanations for imperialism offer an incomplete answer.

Before looking more closely at the nineteenth century, something else should be remembered which helps us understand what was behind some pretty unpromising acquisitions. That is the mystically enhanced memory of Pizarro and Cortez. History exerts a powerful influence on us all; but first it has to be reduced to a few necessarily distorted elements. The exploits of these two greatest of the *conquistadores* bent through time's prism worked magically on men's minds. The hope was kindled that small groups could accomplish great deeds, gain wealth, earn prestige and serve humanity. So a natural pugnacious instinct was reinforced and transfigured by the memory of Pizarro and Cortez.

The aspirations of nineteenth- and sixteenth-century imperialists were quintessentially the same. They were motivated by gold, glory, power and gospel. These four things are historical 'elements' which cannot be reduced further, but are capable of numerous combinations.

Gold, or the economic motive, is what most people today think was the motor. And in the nineteenth century it figured very prominently in the propaganda of imperialism. Outright robbery of one kind or another was not uncommon in the sixteenth century, but in the nineteenth it was rare. There was little left to steal. Some of the modern adventurers were certainly looking for something to purloin. Diamonds, gold and other valuable products were indeed found, but they had to be prized loose with the pick rather than the musket; and natives were, of course, deprived of their land by sleights of hand and pressed into service, but the profit of this was not sufficiently large to constitute loot.

The search for new markets was an element, especially after 1870. The serious quest for raw materials came a little later. But the fact remains that most of the new colonies – those gained in the course of the nineteenth century – did not provide much trade with the mother country. British free-trade policy limited the benefit gained from colonial commerce since rival states traded extensively in the British Empire. The other regimes were more carefully protected, and after the onset of the great depression in 1873 tariffs were increased. But even for them colonial trade was disappointing. The belief that large-scale production, mainly of primary products, using cheap land and labour would yield handsome profit was also sadly disappointed in many cases.

It was hoped that the new colonies would absorb the excess or unsuitable home population. There were ambitious dreams of bronzed German or Italian peasants ploughing the African soil and purchasing familiar products from home. But they preferred to go to North and South America instead. Although expectation far outstripped reality, these aspects of the economic factor certainly were present as motives. Indeed the argument that there was little trade with, or emigration to, the colonies does not disprove the validity of these things as a motive force. It is also a mistake to believe that any kind of exact profit-loss calculation figured prominently in people's minds. Jules Ferry once said that the colonies were to be his generation's legacy to the future.

Everyone knew that the North American colonies were regarded as barren when they were first settled and that the Caribbean islands were thought better prizes. But a few generations had dramatically altered all this. Who could have read the future of Timbuktu and the Klondike?

One final theory remains. It is the myth cultivated by J. A. Hobson and by Lenin that the colonies were to serve as refuge for surplus European money and source of exorbitant profit from investments or loans at usurious rates. Seldom has an idea so obviously untrue and easily refutable been so influential amongst scholars as well as the general public. We can put aside Lenin's claim that imperialism represented the highest stage of capitalism with a reference to the expansionism of pre-capitalist and non-capitalist societies. Capitalism in its youth, the sixteenth century, was giddy with imperialism. As for the return on capital, that invested in the colonies probably did bring an extra 0.5 per cent annually over what could be earned at home. But funds put in independent countries could yield substantially more. Most foreign investments went to places such as the USA, the British settlement colonies, India or to other European countries. Much of the investment abroad, in the colonies and elsewhere, went to develop the infrastructure. Thus one could argue that the colonies and foreign countries received money on the cheap for expensive but needed projects which could not yield spectacular returns. Whether the capitalists exploited or were exploited is perhaps not as easy to decide as some of the economic determinists assert.

To summarize, the search for economic benefit was a powerful motive, even if it frequently ended in disappointment. But an examination of the circumstances leading to the acquisition of individual colonies shows that other considerations were frequently a good deal more important.

The second factor is glory. The desire for personal and national standing does mix with the zest for enrichment, but is essentially different. It is possible to seek the one even at the expense of the other. Indeed, many did seek glory, and some few were hugely rewarded. Others perished unknown abroad, and still others returned home ill or financially ruined. It is not good form to admit a craving for prestige, but it is a powerful drive nevertheless. We cannot either prove or disprove the existence of unavowed aims, but it is probably true to say that he who planted the Union Jack or the *tricolore* where others had not dared venture, or where they had tried and failed to reach, had an exhilarating experience. Bureaucrats and ministers in Paris or London might complain about extra responsibilities, but they accepted them with a feeling of pride. Many historians have underlined the lack of ambition in the great nerve centres of empire before the mid-1870s. It has even been argued that the British Empire was created in a 'fit of absence of mind'. This view is not entirely wrong, but the critical student will smell a whiff of hypocrisy. He will wonder how the steady and impressive advance during the 'free-trade period' was possible with such a negative approach.

Glory or prestige is reflected in attitudes. It might have no substantial roots. Frequently however it is an aspect of power which has its own reward; power also enhances the standing of an individual or country. So the desire for prestige is sometimes behind the power game; the instinct for self-preservation is also certainly there. Today power depends largely on economic clout, but this was much less so in the nineteenth century. Empire-building was probably more a political and military phenomenon than an economic one, but all three strains were there in varying mixtures. Once started, imperial policy generated its own momentum. No colony was sure unless the communication lanes were secure as well. Every frontier is by definition endangered and so needs protection. Competition with others naturally accelerated. Those countries entering the race late – such as Germany and Italy – were driven by the same motives. But as late comers they suffered much more from what has picturesquely been called the 'fear of the closing door', the fear of being left out in the cold and without 'a place in the sun'. As late as 1914, most people were still convinced that the twentieth century would be that of great empires. No one wanted to be confined within Europe, for that was the badge of defeat.

Some historians argue that colonial expansion was the response to power vacuums and trouble on the fringe of empire, or that masterful proconsuls forged ahead against the will of the centre. There is a good deal to be said for this since trouble in and near the colonies was ubiquitous and the proconsuls in distant places frequently took things into their own hands. But it was not only, or even mainly, this. Home governments were embarrassed by their over-mighty agents abroad because they were undiplomatic, but those in charge understood the power game that was being played. We have an illustration of this in Anglo-Russian relations. London never believed the protestations of annoyance in St Petersburg about repeated advances in central Asia against strict orders. The British colonies in India and elsewhere were developing with the same dynamism, and London knew full well that a conquest was not necessarily unwelcome because it was inopportune. So the Russian assurances that no central Asiatic territory was wanted were indeed lacking in candour. But the other powers behaved similarly.

Another popular view, especially amongst German historians, is 'social imperialism', that is, expansion as a manoeuvre by the élites to divert the attention of their own population from the need for social amelioration at home. Certainly no leading nineteenth-century imperialist believed that expansion would undermine the social structure, and many thought that possessions abroad would benefit the economic and social well-being of the home country. But it is a very big step from this truism to the statement that the main purpose of imperialism was the ossification of the social status quo. Few men said as much; and then there were those on the left (socialists and democrats in Britain and elsewhere) who firmly believed that imperialism encouraged social improvement. If one considers that all those in industry – workers as well as businessmen – were likely to gain from the growth and consolidation of empire, this process was surely more a force for change than a prop for the status quo.

In the years immediately following 1830 colonial acquisitions were prudent. Existing colonies expanded, some promising areas were added, critical strategic points were occupied and coaling stations established. In the 1880s, however, one has the feeling that pre-emptive strikes became perhaps the main reason for colonization. There was a clear trend from judicious to injudicious acquisition. This obvious power-political and prestige-oriented scramble for commercially unpromising territory shows that the economic motive ranges well below these other considerations.

Having discussed gold, glory and power as motives for imperialism, one element remains: gospel. In the nineteenth century we must include missionaries of civilization as well as of religion. In our cynical times it is easy to underestimate the significance of these people who more than anyone made effective colonial rule possible. Some of their work was tainted by co-operation with traders or soldiers in the bush, but religious people often have to make some compromises in order to continue their labour. The missionaries were present in large numbers and performed an important 'socializing' function with the natives. Their work left more permanent traces than those of the traders and soldiers. We must also not forget the thousands of bureaucrats at all levels. In 1830 they were in fact mostly well-meaning amateurs; by 1890 they were mainly industrious and fair men sincerely dedicated to the interests of the colonies and willing to defend them against outside interference and even occasionally against their own government. The common view that colonial officials spent more time filling their pockets than fulfilling their duties is quite wrong. The colonies were run almost as well as the home countries. They were of course ruled autocratically and strictly, but the harshness was not usually arbitrary.

The large number of missionaries and bureaucrats, who went to posts where many of them died, left their home not necessarily to gain wealth or fame, but to serve humanity as they saw it or to turn prose into poetry. Their attitude was condescending and their personal failings were many but their purpose was not exploitation. Indeed, they took with them into the colonies the rule of law accompanied with technological expertise intelligently applied. This gift corroded the foundation of colonial societies more effectively than did traders or soldiers; it also provided these societies with the means of ultimately freeing themselves. After independence few tried to revert to their pre-colonial culture or even to sever the links with their former masters.

In the azure humanitarian sky dark clouds began to appear towards the end of our period. There can be no 'mission to the inferior races', in the words of Jules Ferry, the main French expanionist in the 1880s, without a feeling of superiority which is rarely entirely beneficent. In some circles the amoral teachings of Darwin were used increasingly to justify the subjugation of others. So a self-centred policy of racial domination or national aggrandizement rivalled the more generous approach and clothed itself in a mantle of 'scientific' respectability. Inevitably, perhaps, in such a vast and multi-faceted movement there was also a band of adventurers, escapees, ruffians, cranks and 'Prospero' types, who sometimes found a slot into which they fitted, or rose to an exotic challenge though they had failed at home. More often they were a source of disruption. Being less numerous than is commonly assumed, they contributed disproportionately to the folklore of the frontier, but little to its reality.

The nineteenth-century empires could never have been built had an animating ideal not appealed to hundreds of thousands of people with different backgrounds and goals in life. It would be utterly wrong to believe that a small and selfish group of 'faceless men' could manipulate the rest in their own interest. A coterie may well precipitate a war, but it could not dominate a broad multi-national movement spanning the decades.

European technological sophistication, organizational ability and discipline counted for much. The sixteenth-century *conquistadores* relied heavily on these things and used their advantage with a good deal more flair than their nineteenth-century successors who had a far greater technological superiority. In his 1981 book Daniel Headrick quite properly underlined the significance of the 'tools of empire'. Expansion into much of the land colonized in the nineteenth century was simply not feasible in 1830. Tropical Africa is the best example. In 1830 European contact was minimal, and because of the danger of malaria, few were prepared to develop it. Many of those who were did not survive. The introduction of quinine as a preventive measure changed this dramatically. It was this, above all, which enabled European expansion to proceed in the tropics. The regular ingestion of quinine was fairly cheap and straightforward, but it broke an insurmountable barrier. Two other innovations of incomparably greater complexity facilitated conquest. One was the armed steamboat, a small, sturdy iron craft used first on the wide and shallow Chinese rivers. There, by navigating far upstream, it was possible to shell the natives at a distance without fear of much loss and so ensure the continuation of the lucrative opium trade. The gunboat, a movable castle, was immediately tried wherever the principles of navigation allowed. In Africa a beginning was made on the Niger. But it was used elsewhere, even on the Congo, where the boats had to be reassembled after having been taken apart and carried for days through the jungle and past the rapids separating the lower and upper reaches of the river. The second thing giving an enormous advantage over adversaries was sheer fire-power. Cannon and small arms became very much more reliable, accurate and rapid-firing. Even the best equipped and experienced foes using eighteenth-century technology had to make disproportionate sacrifice to defeat a gunboat. Traditionally battles had been fought at close quarters. The gunboat, armed with modern weapons, could kill accurately and massively at a distance. Its opponents had nothing comparable.

In the fifty years before 1870 a series of innovations turned the musket into a modern rapid-firing rifle, an entirely new weapon. Muskets were used widely in Africa and elsewhere. Many backward societies could either make or repair them. The modern rifle could only be made and serviced in technologically advanced countries. In Africa the advantage of a column of musketeers over native opponents lay mainly in discipline and tactics, not so much in technology. But any given number of riflemen had a techno-logical advantage enabling them frequently to defeat determined native forces ten times as strong. Riflemen did not have the defensive protection of the gunboat, but they had equally impressive fire-power, which could be taken almost anywhere.

Without quinine tropical Africa could not have been conquered; without the gunboat and modern rifle, it probably would not have been. China and parts of India and South-East Asia might also have escaped bullying.

In previous centuries vast empires had been acquired but could not be maintained because of difficulties in communication and administration. One should pause for a moment to consider that the answer to a letter written in London on Christmas Day in 1830 might well not arrive back from India much before Christmas 1831. Without improved transportation of men, material and messages, enduring dominion over inhospitable and distant places was not feasible. Mid-century saw vast improvements in this key area. In 1865 the telegraph reached India. Four years later the Suez Canal opened with a ceremony which was appropriately the most lavish of the century. So the greatest feat of nineteenth-century French civil engineering increased the viability of the British Empire. Simultaneous advances in steamship technology made the passage to India into a tolerable adventure. Once in India, Europeans had at their disposal a sizeable railway network. So by 1890 most parts were in relatively easy reach of London. The same could not be said for Africa. But it is undeniably true that from a commercial and administrative point of view the far-flung nineteenth-century empires were much more viable than their sixteenth-century predecessors. Without the 'tools of empire' – quinine, steam, iron, electricity – imperialists in Calcutta or London, or wherever else, would not have got very far, nor would they have wanted to. The 'tools of empire' were developed to serve, but the vision of empire grew together with their effectiveness.

Further reading

THEORY AND BACKGROUND

H. Gollwitzer, *Europe in the Age of Imperialism* (London, 1969) – superb on the wider issues; V. Kiernan, *European Empires from Conquest to Collapse, 1815–1960* (London, 1982) – a handy outline; R. Owen and R. Sutcliffe (eds), *Studies in the Theory of Imperialism* (London, 1972) – a valuable collection.

GENERAL WORKS

M. Chamberlain, *The Scramble for Africa* (London, 1974) – excellent short account with useful documents, and *The New Imperialism*, revised edn. (London, 1984) – good introduction; D. K. Fieldhouse, *The Colonial Empires*, 2nd edn. (London, 1982) – best and fairest descriptive account, *Colonialism, 1870–1945: an Introduction* (London, 1981) – brief and thoughtful, and *Economics and Empire, 1830–1914*, 2nd edn. (London, 1984) – argues for continuity of expansion and importance of the 'periphery' as motivating factor.

SPECIAL STUDIES

R. Robinson and J. Gallagher, *Africa and the Victorians: the Official Mind of Imperialism* (London, 1961) – essential study which started the contemporary discussion; W. Louis (ed.), *Imperialism: the Robinson and Gallagher Controversy* (New York, 1976) – good introduction and conclusion by Louis showing relationship of Fieldhouse to Robinson and Gallagher.

H. Feis, *Europe the World's Banker* (New York, 1930) – still useful on the transfer of money; D. Headrick, *The Tools of Empire: Technology and European Imperialism in the Nineteenth Century* (Oxford, 1981) – convincingly demonstrates the overriding significance of technological innovation.

R. von Albertini, *European Colonial Rule, 1880–1940: the Impact of the West on India, Southeast Asia and Africa* (Oxford, 1982) – deals with the effect of imperialism on the colonized world.

COMPARATIVE STUDIES AND INDIVIDUAL COUNTRIES

W. Baumgart, *Imperialism: the Idea and Reality of British and French Colonial Expansion, 1880–1914* (Oxford, 1982) – a successful comparison;

P. Gifford and W. Louis (eds), *Britain and Germany in Africa: Imperial Rivalry and Colonial Rule* (London, 1967), and *France and Britain in Africa: Imperial Rivalry and Colonial Rule* (London, 1971) – two essential collections of essays.

D. Gillard, *The Struggle for Asia, 1828–1914: a Study in British and Russian Imperialism* (London, 1977) – admirable brief and elegant discussion of the 'great game' in Central Asia.

H. Brunschwig, *French Colonialism, 1871–1914: Myths and Realities* (London, 1966) – solid account and spirited discussion of delicate issues; J. Cooke, *The New French Imperialism, 1880–1914* (Newton Abbot, 1973) – mainly about policy-making on Africa.

D. Geyer, *Russian Imperialism: the Interaction of Domestic and Foreign Policy, 1860–1914* (Leamington Spa, 1987) – applies modernization theory to Russia and shows the irony of Russian-German relations with their political rivalry and close economic ties; W. Smith, *The German Colonial Empire* (Chapel Hill, NC, 1978) – a recent survey of German colonial policy rather than the colonial empire; H. U. Wehler, 'Bismarck's imperialism, 1862–1890', in *Past and Present*, no. 48 (1970) – summarizes his influential views on 'social imperialism'.

Chronology

Politics

1830	February	London conference declares Greece independent
	June	William IV king in Britain (to 1837)
	5 July	Capture of Algiers (followed by conquest of Algeria by 1847)
	27–29 July	Revolution in Paris; Louis Philippe king to February 1848
	August	Rebellion in Brussels
	September	'Diamond Duke' Charles of Brunswick deposed
	4 October	Belgian independence declared
	November	Polish revolution (to September 1831)
1831		Rebellions in Modena, Parma and Papal states Egyptian–Turkish war (ends in Treaty of Unkiar Skelessi July 1833)
1832	June	First electoral reform act in Britain
1833		Guizot's primary education reform in France
1834	April	Quadruple Alliance between England, France, Spain, Portugal
1835	March	Austrian Emperor Francis dies; Ferdinand emperor (to 1848)
1837	June	Victoria Queen of England (to 1901); Hanover separated from Britain
1839	April	International recognition of Belgian neutrality Egyptian–Turkish war (to 1840) Opium war (to 1842); Britain takes Hong Kong
1840	June	Frederick William III of Prussia dies; succeeded by Frederick William IV (king to 1861)
	December	Re-burial of Napoleon in *Invalides*
1841	July	London Straits Treaty: Bosphorus and Dardanelles closed to war ships of all nations
1847	April–June	United Diet meets in Berlin
	November	*Sonderbund* war in Switzerland
1848	January	Rebellion in Palermo
	February	Constitution in Naples
	22–24 February	Revolution in Paris; republic inaugurated
	26 February	National Workshops established

March	Piedmontese constitution
13–15 March	Rising in Vienna
18–19	Rising in Berlin
18 March	Tobacco boycott and rebellion in Milan
20 March	Louis of Bavaria loses his crown by losing his head over Lola Montez
25 March	Piedmont invades Lombardy
10 April	Large Chartist demonstration in London
April	Hungary separated from Austria
	Elections for French national assembly
	Austrian constitution decreed
May	Prussia invades Denmark
	Frankfurt Assembly opened
17 June	Prague unprising crushed
21 June	National workshops closed
23–26 June	'June days' in Paris
25 July	Austrian victory over Piedmont at Custozza
26 August	Malmö armistice between Prussia and Denmark
September	Serfs freed in Austria
	Kossuth dictator in Hungary
November	Wrangel occupies Berlin: Prussian revolution defeated
	Republican constitution in France
	Flight of Pope to Gaeta
2 December	Abdication of Ferdinand; Francis Joseph Austrian emperor (to 1916)
10 December	Louis Napoleon president of France
1849 February	Proclamation of Roman republic
March	Centralist constitution decreed in Austria
23 March	Radetzky defeats Piedmontese at Novara; Charles Albert abdicates; Victor Emmanuel king (to 1878)
April	Hungary claims independence from Austria
May	Popular risings in Germany
	Garibaldi in Rome
	Introduction of three class electoral law in Prussia
June	German national assembly forcibly disbanded
1 July	French troops occupy Rome
13 August	Hungarians capitulate to Russia
22 August	Venice surrenders
1850 January	Prussian constitution decreed
April	Pope returns to Rome
	Clayton–Bulwer Treaty on construction of Panama Canal
July	Prussian–Danish war ended
November	Cavour prime minister of Piedmont (dies in office 6 June 1861)
29 November	Prussian diplomatic defeat at Olmütz

1851	May	German Confederation renewed
	2 December	Napoleon's *coup d'état*
	31 December	Abolition of Austrian centralist constitution
1852	May	London protocol regulates Danish affairs
	2 December	Napoleon becomes emperor
1853		Taiping revolt in China
	April	Russia demands protectorate over Turkish Christians
	July	Russian invasion of Danube principalities
	November	Turkish fleet destroyed at Sinope
1854	September	British and French troops land in Crimea
1855	January	Piedmont joins France and Britain in Crimean War
	2 March	Emperor Nicholas of Russia dies (ruled from December 1825); Alexander II emperor (to 1881)
	May	Dissolution of Piedmontese monasteries
	September	Sebastopol taken
1856	1 February	Congress of Paris (to 30 March)
1857	August	Founding of Italian national association
1858	January	Attempted assassination of Napoleon by Orsini
	July	Cavour and Napoleon meet in Plombières
	October	Prince William regent in Prussia; New Era in Prussia
	November	India transferred from East India Company to British Crown
1859	3 May	Franco–Austrian war begins
	4 and 24 June	Battles of Magenta and Solferino; November Peace Treaty of Zurich
	August	Liberal concessions begin in France leading finally to the 'Liberal Empire'
	September	Founding of German national association
	December	Moldavia and Wallachia form Romania
1860	April	First Italian Parliament in Turin
	May	Garibaldi goes to Sicily
1861	2 January	Frederick William IV dies; William I king (to 1888)
	February	Russian serfs freed
	March	Kingdom of Italy proclaimed
	April	American Civil War (to April 1865)
		French Expedition to Mexico (until 1867)
1862	September	Bismarck prime minister in Prussia (to March 1890)
1863	January	American slaves freed
		Polish rebellion
1864	February	Prussia and Austria attack Denmark; October Peace concluded in Vienna
1865	August	Gastein convention
	October	Death of Palmerston
1866	April	Prussian–Italian offensive and defensive alliance
	June–July	Austro–Prussian war; 3 July Königgrätz; Peace Treaty of Prague (23 August) and Vienna (3 October)

		North German Confederation set up and Venetia goes to Italy
1867	April–May	Luxemburg crisis
	June	Austro–Hungarian Compromise
		Maximilian shot in Mexico
	August	Second British electoral reform
1870	2 January	Liberal Empire under Ollivier in France
	13 July	Ems telegram; 19 July France declares war on Prussia
	2 September	Battle of Sedan, capture of Napoleon
	4 September	Parisian revolution establishes republic
	20 September	Italians enter Rome
1871	January–March	London Black Sea conference
	January	German empire proclaimed
	March–May	Paris commune
	10 May	Peace of Frankfurt
1872		Secret ballot introduced in Britain
1873		Three Emperors' League
1875		Constitutional laws legalize republic in France
1875		Balkan crisis (to 1878) started by rebellion in Bosnia–Herzegovina
1876		Queen Victoria becomes Empress of India
1877	April	Russo–Turkish war (to March 1878)
	May	MacMahon's *coup d'état*
	December	Plevna capitulates to Russia
1878	9 January	Victor Emmanuel dies; Humbert king (to 1900)
	7 February	Pope Pius IX dies; Leo XIII pope (to 1903)
	3 March	Treaty of San Stefano
	June–July	Congress of Berlin
1879		End of liberal era in Germany and Austria
	July	French government returns to Paris
	October	Austro–German alliance
1881	13 March	Assassination of Alexander II; succeeded by Alexander III (to 1894)
	May	French occupation of Tunis
	June	Renewal of Three Emperors' League
1882		Establishment of Czech university in Prague
	May	Triple Alliance between Germany, Austria, Italy
	July	Britain occupies Egypt
1884	February	Russia takes Merv
	November	Berlin Congo Conference (to February 1885)
1884		Third British parliamentary reform
1885		General Gordon dies in Khartoum
1886		Boulanger crisis between Germany and France (to 1889)
1887	June	Russo–German Reinsurance Treaty
	August	Crispi becomes Italian prime minister
1888		As last American state Brazil abolishes slavery

9 March	Emperor William I dies; Frederick III dies 99 days later; William II emperor (to 1918)
1890 March	Bismarck unwillingly retires
	Reinsurance Treaty lapses

Economy and Society

1830 Cholera epidemic to 1831
1830 Manchester–Liverpool Railway
1831 Faraday discovers magnetic electricity
1831 (and 1834) Risings of silk workers in Lyon
1833 Factory inspection in Britain; ending of slavery in British colonies
1834 German Customs Union
1835 First German railway
1836 Chartist movement (to 1848)
1837 Railway from Paris to St Germain
Morse invents telegraph
Anilin colours invented
1839 Prussian factory act regulates child labour
Daguerreotype invented
1840 Proudhon writes *Qu'est-ce que la Propriété?*
Penny post in Britain
1841 First French factory act
List, *The National System of Political Economy*
1842 Nasmyth invents steam hammer
1844 Rochdale Pioneers founded
Factory act regulates work of children and women in Britain
Weavers' rebellion in Silesia
1846 British corn laws repealed
Deepest point in Irish famine
1846 General European economic crisis (to 1850)
1848 Gold discovered in California
Louis Blanc insists on right to work in France
Communist Manifesto
1849 Prussian trade act re-introduces guilds
1851 Great Exhibition in London
Discovery of gold in Australia
First seabed cable from Dover to Calais
1852 *Bon Marché* founded in Paris
First large French banks founded
1853 First underground train in London
Prussia forbids employment of children under 12
1854 Japan opened up to trade
Semmering Railway first to pass through high mountains
1855 Paris Exhibition
Invention of bicycle
1856 Bessemer converter devised

1858   First cable from Britain to United States
1859   Construction of Suez Canal (to 1869)
1860   Cobden Treaty between France and Britain
1862   Construction of transcontinental American railway (to 1869)
1863   Lassalle founds first socialist party
1866   Siemens builds electric generator
       Condensed milk production started in Switzerland
       First Congress of 'International' in Geneva
1867   Brenner railway
       Nobel discovers dynamite
1871   Legal recognition of trade unions in Britain
       Purchase of British army commissions ended
1873   Stock market crash: end of mid-Victorian boom, depression until 1896
1874   French factory inspection
1875   German SPD founded
1876   Philadelphia World Exhibition
       Bell devised telephone
1878   World Postal Union
       Thomas-Gilchrist steel-making process developed (to 1880)
1879   Edison invents light bulb
       Lesseps founds the Panama Canal Company
       German Protective Tariff
1880   St Gotthard tunnel opened
1883   Beginning of German compulsory health insurance
1884   Labour unions legalized in France
       Fabian society founded in Britain
       Eleven hour day introduced in Austria
1885   Gold discovered in Transvaal
1888   Hamburg and Bremen finally join German customs union
       First petrol motor
1889   Factory inspection in Belgium
       London docker strike
       Eiffel Tower in Paris
       Second 'International' founded
1890   McKinley Tariff in USA
       First workers protection conference in Berlin

Culture

1830   Delacroix, 'Liberty leading the people'
       Stendhal, *Le Rouge et le Noir*
       Comte, *Course of Positive Philosophy* (to 1842)
1831   Pushkin, *Eugene Onegin*
       Hugo, *Notre Dame de Paris*
       Pfizer, *Correspondence of Two Germans*
1832   Goethe, *Faust* (second part)
       Mazzini, 'Young Italy'; 1834 'Young Europe'

1835 Büchner, *Danton's Death*
1835 Strauss, *Life of Christ*
1836 Dickens, *Pickwick Papers*
1837 Carlyle, *History of the French Revolution*
1839 Stendhal, *La Chartreuse de Parme*
1841 Fallersleben, 'Deutschland, Deutschland über alles'
1842 Sue, *Les Mystères de Paris*
      Gogol, *Dead Souls*
1843 Gioberti, *The Moral and Civil Primacy of the Italians*
1844 Heine, *Germany, a Winter Fairy Tale*
1845 Dumas, *The Count of Monte Christo*
      Wagner, 'Tannhäuser'
1847 Balzac, *Human Comedy* finished
1848 Pre-Raphaelite brotherhood founded
1849 Lamartine, *History of the Revolution of 1848*
1850 Dickens, *David Copperfield*
      Courbet, 'Stonebreakers'
1851 Verdi, 'Rigoletto'
1853 Gobineau, *Essay on the Inequality of the Human Races* (finished in 1855)
1854 Dogma of immaculate conception
1855 Courbet founds school of realistic painting
1856 Neanderthal skeleton found
1857 Flaubert, *Madame Bovary*
      Baudelaire, *Les Fleurs du Mal*
1859 Goncharov, *Oblomov*
      Darwin, *The Origin of Species*
      Mill, *On Liberty*
1860 Burckhardt, *The Culture of the Renaissance in Italy*
1862 Turgenev, *Fathers and Sons*
1863 Renan, *Life of Jesus*
1864 Red Cross founded
      Syllabus of errors
1865 Foundation of Salvation Army
1866 Dostoyevsky, *Crime and Punishment*
1867 Marx, *Das Kapital* (first part)
      Invention of typewriter
1869 Anglican church disestablished in Ireland
      Tolstoy *War and Peace*
      December–July 1870 Vatican Council
1870 Schliemann's excavation of Troy (to 1882)
      18 July Papal infallibility dogma
      Compulsory elementary schooling in Britain
1871 Zola, *Les Rougon-Macquart* (cycle completed 1893)
      Darwin, *The Descent of Man*
1872 Nietzsche, *The Birth of Tragedy*
      Verne, *Around the World in Eighty Days*

1874 Strauss, 'Die Fledermaus'
      First Impressionist paintings
1875 Menzel 'Iron foundry'
      Brahms' first symphony
1876 Opening of Bayreuth Opera House. The 'Ring' performed
      Tolstoy, *Anna Karenina*
1877 Ibsen, *Pillars of Society*
      Invention of phonograph by Edison
1880 Dostoyevsky, *Brothers Karamazov*
1881 Ibsen, *Ghosts*
1884 Nietzsche, *Thus Spake Zarathustra*
1884 Bruckner's 7th symphony
1885 Zola, *Germinal*
1886 Rodin, 'Burghers of Calais'
1887 Freud begins to use hypnotism
1888 Strindberg, *Miss Julie*
      Pasteur Institute opens in Paris
1889 Hauptmann, *Before Sunrise*
1890 First workers theatre founded in Berlin
      Wilde, *Picture of Dorian Gray*

Contributors

Edward Acton is Professor of Modern European History at the University of East Anglia. Among his major publications are *Alexander Herzen and the Role of the Intellectual Revolutionary* (1979), *Re-thinking the Russian Revolution* (1990) and *Russia: The Tsarist and Soviet Legacy* (1995).

Michael Biddiss is Professor of History at the University of Reading. His interest is in the history of ideas and publications include *Father of Racist Ideology* ((1970), *The Age of the Masses* (1977) and *Images of Race* (1979). This latest work is a student's guide to *The Nuremberg Trial and the Third Reich* (1992).

Bruce Haddock is Senior Lecturer in Politics at University College, Swansea. He has written *An Introduction to Historical Thought* (1980) and *Vico's Political Thought* (1986). He is currently working on nineteenth-century Italian political philosophy.

Roger Price is Professor of European History at the University of Wales, Aberystwyth. His publications include *An Economic History of Modern France, c. 1730–1914* (1981), *The Modernization of Rural France* (1983), *A Social History of Nineteenth-Century France* (1987), *The Revolutions of 1848* (1988) and *A Concise History of France* (1993). He is currently writing *The French Second Empire: State and Society*.

Alan Sked is Senior Lecturer in International History at the London School of Economics. His publications include *Britain's Decline* (1987) and on Austrian history, *The Survival of the Habsburg Empire: Radetzky, The Imperial Army and the Class War, 1848* (1979) and *The Decline and Fall of the Habsburg Empire, 1815–1918* (1989).

Bruce Waller is Senior Lecturer in History at University College, Swansea. He has written articles on German history and *Bismarck at the Crossroads* (1974) and *Bismarck* (1985).

Index